Planning Paradis

DATE DUE

BRODART, CO.   Cat. No. 23-221

Society, Environment, and Place

Series Editors: Andrew Kirby and Janice Monk

Planning Paradise

Politics and Visioning of Land Use in Oregon

Peter A. Walker
Patrick T. Hurley

The University of Arizona Press   Tucson

The University of Arizona Press
© 2011 The Arizona Board of Regents

www.uapress.arizona.edu

Financial support for the publication of this book was provided in part
by the University of Oregon Department of Geography through the
generosity of Jim and Shirley Rippey, and by the University of Oregon's
Graduate School and College of Arts and Sciences.

Library of Congress Cataloging-in-Publication Data
Walker, Peter A.
  Planning paradise : politics and visioning of land use in Oregon /
Peter A. Walker, Patrick T. Hurley.
    p. cm. — (Society, environment, and place)
  Includes bibliographical references and index.
  ISBN 978-0-8165-2883-7 (paperback : alk. paper)
    1. Land use—Oregon.   2. Land use—Planning.   3. Cities
and towns—Growth.   4. Sustainable development—Oregon.
I. Hurley, Patrick T.   II. Title.
  HD211.O7W35 2011
  333.73'1309795—dc22   2010049630

⊗

Manufactured in the United States of America on acid-free, archival-quality
paper containing a minimum of 30 percent post-consumer waste and
processed chlorine free.

15   14   13   12   11   10   6   5   4   3   2   1

To my children, Emily, Patrick, and Paul—Oregonians.
—Peter Walker

To my mom and dad, Patricia and Charles, who fostered my love of learning. For my brother, Chuck, who always believed this was possible. And to my wife, Sibel, who supported me along the way.
—Patrick Hurley

Contents

Preface   ix

Acknowledgments   xiii

1   Introduction   3

2   Planning for Growth   22

3   A Star Is Born   42

4   Falling Star   76

5   "What Were People *Thinking?*"   111

6   Metro Visions   156

7   Central Destinations   180

8   Southern Discomforts   204

9   Paradise Lost?   230

Notes   255

Bibliography   277

Index   283

Preface

The politics of land use planning is a subject of especially intense passions in Oregon. Not surprisingly, one of the questions we sometimes got when doing research for this book was, what point of view do we take? Whose perspectives do we represent? What do we want our book to "do"? Our informants wanted to know how we planned to tell the *story* of Oregon's land use planning. These questions are important and fair because, if told well, stories can influence how the future unfolds.

To answer these questions, we observe that the story about Oregon's land use planning that we tell in this book is only partial and incomplete. In the eyes of some—if not all—readers, the choice of which parts of the Oregon land use planning story we include or omit could be seen as reflecting a particular point of view. We would not disagree. We submit, however, that it would be impossible to do otherwise. All stories are simplified models of almost infinitely complex realities. Thus, choices about which facts to put into the story and which to cut away to give the story a readable length and narrative clarity are to some extent inherently matters of subjective choice. We submit there is no getting around this, and we should acknowledge it.

For example, consider your breakfast this morning. How would you describe it? You would necessarily have to make choices about which facts are important to tell and which are reasonable to leave out. Would it be necessary to describe where the ingredients in your breakfast came from? Or how far they traveled? Or under what conditions the food was produced? Or, perhaps, the molecular structure of your toast? Or the alignment of the stars at the moment you took your first sip of coffee? Such questions might seem ridiculous and irrelevant to many people—but not all. The point is, by necessity, your choice of which level of specificity to use and which facts are reasonable to leave out of the story would be, to some degree, a necessarily subjective choice.

This example might seem trivial, but consider how this perspective on storytelling might apply to the study of the history and politics of land use planning in Oregon. Compared to your breakfast, there are probably far more "ingredients," far more "players," and a much longer time span. How would you decide which facts are a necessary part of the Oregon land use planning story and which can be left out?

Those were the questions we faced—and rarely did there seem to be any easy, objective way to decide. One of the striking things about interviewing many individuals for this book is that we found no universal agreement about many important aspects of this story—even seemingly "factual" ones. For example, many people attribute the emergence of Oregon's land use planning system primarily to the political skills of former Oregon governor Tom McCall. Others believe McCall was an important player but served mostly to articulate the political mood and conditions of the time rather than shaping the underlying dynamics. There is no simple "right" perspective on his contribution. Other aspects of the Oregon land use planning story are more subjective, and "right" perspectives are even more elusive. We did what we could in a relatively brief book to represent the main points of view. But we would be kidding ourselves—and our readers—if we pretended it was even possible to tell all sides of the story, much less represent all sides "equally."

Thus, in the interests of full disclosure, we note that this book was no doubt shaped to a degree by the fact that we are both professors in university environmental studies programs; our friends and colleagues are mostly people who strongly support land use planning; and we personally regard protection against uncontrolled growth as a high priority.

At the same time, in our careers as scholars we have often been as critical of the planning community as we have been of its political opponents. For example, in some of our previous research and publications, as in this book, we have argued that advocates for strong planning too often fail to take seriously the social equity dimensions of their positions, at the long-term political peril of the very programs they promote. By the same token, we have observed that opponents of land use planning too often vilify those who promote strong planning, failing to even attempt to understand and respect the different but deeply held values of people who will likely be their neighbors in increasing numbers for a long time. All sides tend to reduce complex issues to the cartoonish dimensions of "good guys" against "bad guys." As scholars, we strived to do something more: we have sincerely attempted to understand and reflect upon the differing perspectives on Oregon's often emotionally and politically charged land use questions, including those that differ from our own.

Nevertheless, we do not pretend we can step entirely out of our own skins to tell all sides of the Oregon land use planning story in exactly the ways its respective proponents might wish it to be told. Ultimately, we do come from a particular position, and our book does have a specific goal—call it tough love for Oregon planning. We are admirers of much of what the Oregon land use planning system has achieved. Like many who came to Oregon from elsewhere (California and Maryland), we are deeply impressed by much of what Oregon's land use planning has achieved in protecting farmland, forests, rural communities, and natural areas. Oregon's landscapes have retained many desirable qualities that have been lost in other states that struggled to deal with population and economic growth in the late twentieth and early twenty-first centuries. Yet, as social scientists, we are also worried about what seems to us to be some very significant, underlying systemic problems in Oregon's approach to land use planning.

After reading the initial draft of the manuscript for this book, an anonymous peer reviewer asked whether our intent was to help "blow up" the Oregon planning system. To be very clear, it absolutely is *not*. However, we are convinced that Oregon's land use planning has deep systemic faults and is in danger of blowing *itself* up. As we describe in this book, twice in the first decade of this century Oregon's planning system had political near-death experiences, and the political compromise that brought the system back from the brink gave major legal and conceptual concessions to opponents. Our concern is that many in Oregon's planning community continue to attribute the rocky first decade of the 2000s mainly to clever political tactics by opponents (and some tactical errors of their own), while failing to consider possible deeper, underlying sources of political vulnerability.

In highlighting these weaknesses, our hope is not to blow up Oregon's land use planning system but to encourage those who wish to protect Oregon's truly remarkable landscapes to think long and hard about what it might take to make this system, born in the early 1970s, adapt to the realities of the twenty-first century; to keep what is good about the system but also to face up to the possible need for adaptation, innovation, or even transformative changes if the system is to remain viable for decades to come. We believe such introspection can have much value for understanding the past and considering the future—in Oregon and beyond.

Acknowledgments

Carl Abbott, Sy Adler, Rick Allen, Ward Armstrong, Governor Vic Atiyeh, Richard Benner, David Bragdon, Michael Cavallaro, Jon Chandler, Shawn Cleave, Pat Daggett, Walt Daggett, Paul Dewey, Jennifer Donnelly, Ron Eber, John Echeverria, Bob Emmons, Nancie Fadeley, Hannah Gosnell, Harold Haugen, Greg Holmes, Dave Hunnicutt, Kate Jackson, Jon Jinings, Irina Just, Jim Just, Erik Kancler, Jeff LaLande, Robert Liberty, Nena Lovinger, Shane Lundgren, Greg Macpherson, Hector Macpherson, Kitty Macpherson, Sarah Marvin, Innisfree McKinnon, Janet McLennan, Bill Moshovsky, Mia Nelson, Darren Nichols, Adam Novick, Dan Phegley, Floyd Prozanski, John Renz, Henry Richmond, William Robbins, Lane Shetterly, Tom Skaar, Bob Stacey, Mike Thorne, John VanLandingham, Fred VanNatta, Dennis White, Richard Whitman, Ray Wilkeson, Anita Yap, Rob Zako, five additional anonymous interviewees, and two excellent anonymous peer reviewers are the real authors of this book. We just put some of their words on paper. We hope we did justice to their insights.

Cover photo: The Villebois planned "urban village" in Wilsonville, a Portland suburb. In the foreground the photo shows the new Graham Oaks Nature Park, an oak woodland habitat "re-created literally from the ground up," according to its creator, Portland Metro. The subdivision and re-created habitat sit at the Portland Metro urban growth boundary, under majestic Mount Hood. This is a place one might call a planned paradise. (P. Walker 2010)

Planning Paradise

1   Introduction

On May 18, 2008, then-presidential candidate Barack Obama stood before 75,000 wildly cheering, dancing, and waving Oregonians at Portland's
Tom McCall Waterfront Park and declared the overwhelming sentiment
of the largest rally of the campaign to that date: "Wow! Wow! Wow!"
said Obama. Defying regional climatic stereotypes, it was a brilliantly
sunny, shirtsleeve-warm day. Some supporters had waited for hours in
kayaks on the nearby Willamette River. The president-to-be, weary from
a historically long and difficult primary campaign, was visibly reener-
gized and uplifted by the enormous, impassioned welcome. On the banks
of Oregon's second largest river, looking toward majestic Mount Hood in
the distance, Obama went on to observe, "I think it is fair to say that this
is the most spectacular setting for the most spectacular crowd we have
had in this entire campaign—this is unbelievable!"[1]

The candidate may have been genuinely surprised, but to Oregonians,
Obama's praise for this "spectacular crowd" and the "spectacular setting" in which they live was merely to be expected. Being special and different is part of Oregon's political culture and history, very much a part of
the state's sense of identity. Whether or not Obama fully appreciated the
significance of making such an observation to this particular crowd while
standing in Tom McCall Waterfront Park (named after Oregon's iconic
pro-environmental former governor), his observance of their unique political culture and its ties to the natural environment was enthusiastically
greeted by the crowd as an affirmation of how things are and should be
in Oregon.

Indeed, for 200 years Oregon has held a special, almost mythic place
in the American imagination—a place not uncommonly described as
"paradise." As *Portland Oregonian* newspaper columnist Brian Meehan
has stated, "Before Oregon was a territory or even a destination on a long

trail, it was an idea. And the idea—an Eden where people prospected not for gold but for a better life—became the lifeblood that nurtured the . . . state to the beginning of the 21st century" (quoted in Arrieta-Walden, Rasmussen, and Harrah 2000: 9). Lest this sound overstated, consider Oregon through the eyes of early Euro-American migrants. After struggling westward over unimaginably high mountains and through what to them seemed shockingly desolate, dry, hostile terrain in the intermountain West (so unlike the green, moist eastern states and Europe from which most had come), arriving in cool, wet, green, and fertile western Oregon must indeed have seemed much like finding paradise (Robbins 1997: 124–125). Lewis and Clark (despite spending a soggy and miserable winter in what is today the coastal city of Astoria, Oregon) returned in 1806 with news that inspired an empire. Ideas of manifest destiny, the westward course of empire (Figure 1), and the pioneer spirit of the nation were directly tied to a place called the Oregon Country.[2] To get there, pioneers followed the Oregon Trail—the only practical route to many western states, including California, Washington, Idaho, Nevada, and Utah. Though the transcontinental railroad largely displaced the functional role of the Oregon Trail in 1869, Oregon remained the literal, geographical place tied to the symbolism of the new bicoastal American empire. The word "Oregon" was linked to ideas of boldness, difference, even greatness.

The voyage of discovery leading to Oregon and the Pacific Northwest has repeated several times in American history, with the theme of discovering "paradise" repeated as well. The Great Depression and the ecological and human catastrophe of the 1930s Dust Bowl spurred the largest concentrated internal migration in American history, with 2.5 million people fleeing Oklahoma, Texas, Kansas, and surrounding plains states. Most came to the Pacific coast. The majority of Dust Bowl refugees came to California, and the history of "Okie" migration to California is well known. Less well known are the migrants who came to Oregon and Washington—some of whom first went to California, only to find few opportunities (not the last time erstwhile Californians would head north in large numbers). What they found astonished many of them. Possibly the most famous "Okie" of all, songwriter Woody Guthrie, came to

Figure 1 Oregon capitol, Salem—the inscription reads:
"Westward the star of empire takes its way" (P. Walker 2009)

Oregon in 1941. On seeing the verdant, moist, and fertile Pacific Northwest for the first time, the rain-starved Dust Bowl poet declared, "I couldn't believe it, it's a paradise" (Cray 2004: 209). Guthrie stayed only a short time in the Pacific Northwest, but the region inspired some of his (and the nation's) greatest folk songs, including *Roll on Columbia, Grand Coulee Dam,* and *Oregon Trail.*

Guthrie saw the resources of the Pacific Northwest, and the power of the Columbia River in particular, as a rich resource to better the lives of ordinary people. The Bonneville Power Administration, which had commissioned Guthrie, saw other purposes. Some have argued that in World War II hydroelectric power from Pacific Northwest dams such as Bonneville and Grand Coulee enabled the United States to build Liberty ships and warplanes faster than Germany and Japan, giving the Allies a critical advantage (Reisner 1993). In the course of helping to win the war, an estimated 194,000 people moved to Oregon[3]—an 18 percent increase over the state's population in 1940. Overall, in the decade of the 1940s the state's population grew 40 percent. However, this rate of growth would not seem wildly uncharacteristic in Oregon in the coming decades, and questions began to emerge about how long "paradise" could survive.

It was not until the next major wave of in-migration to the state, however, that the battle for paradise would take its unique modern form. In the 1950s and 1960s, the state population grew rapidly, at 16 percent and 18 percent per decade, respectively. In the 1970s, the state's population grew by a stunning 26 percent—less than the 40 percent increase in the 1940s but a far greater total number of new Oregonians. In the 1970s alone, 541,623 additional people called Oregon home.[4] Since the 1970s, natural population increase (births minus deaths) has accounted for only about one-third of population growth, with the other two-thirds resulting from net in-migration.[5] Unlike nineteenth-century migrants seeking mainly economic betterment in an expanding empire, modern migrants to Oregon often seek refuge from, in their eyes, the ruinous modernity of the American nation. Modern immigrants arrive from shockingly desolate, dry, and hostile terrain of crassly commercialized, overdeveloped American landscapes. Southern California, in particular, became the model of bland placelessness that new Oregonians did *not* wish emulate. These migrants—many of whom saw the rural landscapes of their homes transformed into urban sprawl—have been among the most ardent protectors of Oregon's special qualities.

By the 1960s and 1970s, Oregon's landscapes, as most Oregonians had known them, *needed* defenders. Paradoxically, the sheer numbers of in-migrants coming to Oregon seeking refuge from the overcrowding, pollution, commercialization, and loss of community they experienced in other states threatened to bring the very same problems to Oregon. Problems with air and water quality, traffic congestion, litter, ocean beach development, and the disappearance of forest and agricultural land (particularly in the highly productive but densely populated lands of the Willamette Valley on the west side of the state) began to take on the earmarks of uncontrolled, poorly planned, commercialized, and polluted urban America. Worst of all, to many Oregonians, some parts of Oregon were beginning to look frighteningly like *Southern California*.

Without dispute, the single most articulate and effective voice in opposition to uncontrolled growth and the loss of quality of life in Oregon in the 1960s and 1970s was that of Tom McCall, governor of Oregon from 1967 to 1975. A native of Massachusetts, McCall spent part of his childhood growing up on his father's ranch near Prineville, a sparsely populated and ruggedly beautiful part of Oregon to the east of the magnificent Cascades Mountains. McCall began his career as a journalist and made environmental issues a signature subject of his reporting—including a televised exposé on industrial pollution of the Willamette River that made him well known to Oregonians. As a maverick Republican governor, McCall promoted landmark legislation that would cause Oregon, in the eyes of much of the country (and even internationally), to be seen as a leading innovator in foresighted environmental policies. McCall pushed for nationally unrivaled protection of ocean beaches in 1967, the Scenic Waterways Act of 1970, Oregon's famous Bottle Bill in 1971, and the nation's first-of-its-kind Forest Practices Act, also in 1971.

This book focuses on probably the most famous and, in the long term, controversial of all of Oregon's environmental and land use legislation of the era: the 1973 Oregon Land Conservation and Development Act, more commonly known by its legislative title, Senate Bill 100 (SB 100). This bill established the country's first and only comprehensive, statewide land use planning system (in chapter 2 we describe in some detail the planning structure created under SB 100). Tom McCall was not the nuts-and-bolts legislative craftsman for SB 100 or other landmark land use and environmental laws passed during his governorship as much as a voice of his time and place. McCall is often credited (or blamed) for making Oregon's unique environmental policies possible through his rhetorical gifts. But McCall was an insecure person who often sought public affection through populist policies (Walth 1994). He can be seen as, in many respects, a conduit for the expression of the broader environmental and development anxieties of the 1960s and 1970s.

Still, McCall's talent for giving voice to public concerns was profound. In advocating for comprehensive land use planning under SB 100, McCall railed against selfish developers whom he described as "grasping wastrels of the land."[6] The "wastrels," according to McCall, posed a "shameless threat to our environment and to the whole quality of our life and that is the unfettered despoiling of our land. Coastal condomania, sagebrush subdivisions and the ravenous rampage of suburbia, here in the Willamette Valley, all threaten to mock Oregon's status as the environmental model of this nation."[7] Perhaps most (in)famously, in a 1971 nationally televised interview on the *CBS Evening News*, McCall told the rest of the nation: "Come visit [Oregon] again and again. . . . But for heaven's sake, don't come here to live."

One of the authors of this book (Walker) was a child in California at the time and clearly remembers these words (which were widely and rightly interpreted as being directed largely at Californians) but did not know who had spoken them. McCall's words had transcended his own person. His "visit but don't stay" interview became the unofficial state motto (Walth 1994: 313–314), and McCall's voice merged with the mystique of Oregon as "the unofficial capital of the environmental movement" (Kunstler 1993: 204). Arguably, Oregon retained its status as a kind of nationally and internationally recognized "ecotopia" (Callenbach 1975) for more than a quarter century after the creation of its landmark environmental policies of the 1960s and 1970s.

By the beginning of the twenty-first century, however, the state that in the eyes of many represented the pinnacle of foresighted environmental policies was knocked hard from its once-lofty perch. During the decades since the creation of the state's much-celebrated statewide land use planning system under SB 100 in 1973, opponents attempted to tear down the state-level planning system three times (in 1976, 1978, and 1982) through statewide ballot measures that directly challenged the legal power of the planning system. Each time these attempts failed. However, in 1982, when polls showed the attempt to repeal the statewide planning system to be headed to victory, it was the impassioned pleas of still-popular ex-governor Tom McCall that turned aside the initiative. At the time, McCall was dying of advanced prostate cancer, which he openly used to garner sympathy for the cause, stating, "If the legacy we helped give Oregon and which made it twinkle from afar—if it goes, then I guess I wouldn't want to live in Oregon anyhow."[8] McCall won one last victory, and died in 1983. The political legacy that McCall forged remains a potent force to the present day, not least in the still powerful and active land use watchdog group 1000 Friends of Oregon that McCall helped to establish.

But over time the political terrain shifted. The first attack on Oregon's land use planning system that truly challenged the long-term viability of the state's land use planning system came in 2000. The property rights activist organization Oregonians in Action promoted statewide Ballot Measure 7 to amend the state constitution to require state and local governments to compensate owners if property values were reduced by land use regulations. The measure was passed by voters but was overturned by the state supreme court on procedural grounds in 2002. Oregonians in Action sharpened their legal skills on the next draft, Ballot Measure 37. Measure 37 did not amend the state constitution, but it was passed by a remarkable 61 percent of voters in November 2004 and was determined valid by the state supreme court in March 2006. By fall 2007, 6,857 claims for compensation were filed with the state[9] for more than $19.8 billion[10]—more than the state's general fund for the 2007–2009 biennium.

Measure 37 allowed state and local governments to waive land use regulations in lieu of compensation. As a poor state that already faced chronic budget crises, Oregon had few other options—state and county governments were forced to waive the state's much-celebrated land use regulations. Farms, forests, and open spaces that had been protected for three decades were suddenly open for development. The first major gaps had been blown open in the once-impenetrable wall of land use protection that was erected by SB 100 in 1973.

Advocates of land use planning responded in 2007 with Ballot Measure 49, which sharply limited the scale of new development allowable under Measure 37 but retained the core principle that government could be required to compensate or waive regulations that reduced private property values if the regulations were imposed after the owner bought the property. Thus, new regulation of private land in Oregon is now, at least in theory, difficult or impossible because the financial cost of compensating owners is prohibitive. Oregon's vaunted land use regulation system appears frozen. How, exactly, the compensation requirements of Measure 37 (which were retained in Measure 49) will play out over time remains to be seen. But without question, for the first time the Oregon model of land use regulation experienced a tectonic shift.

Property rights activists across the nation were elated. In a state that had become the "poster child" for land use planning, the country's strongest laws against unrestricted development were buckling (Harden 2005). Property rights activists in states around the West (including Alaska, Arizona, California, Colorado, Idaho, and Washington) quickly followed with "copycat" ballot measures (most failed). Planning advocates in Oregon and the nation shook their heads in disbelief. Without question, Tom McCall was spitting fire in his grave. One of us (Walker) was in Colorado in the summer of 2005 interviewing the director of a county land trust on an unrelated subject. The director stopped the interview in the middle of responding to an unrelated question, and asked, "You're from Oregon, so tell me about this Measure 37. What were people *thinking*?" The other author of this book (Hurley, a University of Oregon PhD alumnus) received similar questions as far away as South Carolina.

The question of *why* Measure 37 became law in Oregon (even in its later modified form under Measure 49) is of national importance, particularly in the fast-growing western states. For decades, Oregon was seen among planners across the country as the state that "got it right." Books have been written about the example that Oregon held up to the country (e.g., Judd and Beach 2003). The State of Oregon's own review of the scientific evidence regarding the effectiveness of the state's land use planning system showed that the system had been successful in meeting the core goals of encouraging citizen participation in land use planning while effectively preserving farm and forest land, managing growth, and protecting estuarine areas.[11] While noting difficulties in measurement, this overall conclusion is supported by an independent review by Gosnell and others (2010).[12] By most accounts, Oregon's land use planning system had been a model of success—until 61 percent of Oregon voters seemed to turn their backs on this system in November 2004.

There is disagreement about whether voters did so knowingly. Some advocates for the state's planning system claim the language of Measure 37 was deceptive and that many voters did not understand what they were voting for. Strong evidence supporting this claim can be seen in thousands of letters received by the state's land use management agencies from irate neighbors of Measure 37 claimants. Many neighbors did not know that Measure 37 would allow for new residential, commercial, and industrial development and resource extraction activities immediately next to their own homes and properties, including in protected wilderness areas.[13]

The question, however, remains: after achieving national celebrity, gaining strong evidence of its success in meeting its goals, and turning back decades of previous political attacks, why did the state's vaunted land use planning system succumb in 2004? Did the successes of Measure 7 and Measure 37 indicate that something more fundamental had "gone wrong" than mere political trickery, as many planning advocates argued? If so, what had changed? What did these changes suggest about the post–Measure 37 political landscape in Oregon, and about the future of the statewide planning system as a whole? What lessons might a close examination of the tumultuous land use politics in Oregon in the first decade of the 2000s hold for Oregon, and for other western states that aspire to protect valued landscapes in a more populous future?

These are some of the key questions we examine in this book. We find no reliable indication that Oregonians as a whole are less concerned with protecting the state's strikingly beautiful landscapes from runaway development now than in the 1970s. Politically speaking, the state is far more aligned with the Democratic Party today than in the 1970s. (Democrats strongly supported the original land use planning laws, in alliance with Republican Governor Tom McCall, against much of McCall's own party.) And property rights advocates have been active in Oregon at least since the 1980s. So, what *were* people thinking? These are questions of great importance for all who care about the effects of growth in transforming landscapes in Oregon and the American West. The celebrated planning system in Oregon has proven and, we argue, remains vulnerable. Blaming allegedly disengaged voters or political trickery by property rights activists does not go far in explaining the reversal of fortune for Oregon's land use planning system. As scholars whose interests lie in the politics, economics, and cultural aspects of land use planning, we suggest that we must look deeper.

Understanding the shifting terrain of land use planning in Oregon is important because it tells us much about the prospects for planning for future growth not only in Oregon but also in the many western states that will face similar challenges in maintaining the unique qualities that brought so many of us here to begin with. If Oregon is to remain a "paradise" in the future, it will not be a paradise found; by necessity, it will be a paradise *planned*. Fuller understanding of the political, economic, and cultural factors that made Oregon's much-celebrated system unstable may prove invaluable for improving such programs in Oregon and other fast-growing states.

The Politics of Planning: Oregon's Political Geography

To examine the political, economic, and cultural terrain of land use planning in Oregon, we return for a moment to the 2008 Obama-for-president rally at Tom McCall Waterfront Park in Portland. Obama specifically lauded Portland's environmental achievements: "It's time that the entire country learn from what's happening right here in Portland with mass transit and bicycle lanes *and funding alternative means of transportation*. That's the kind of solution we need for America." One blog commenter quipped, however, "I'd be more impressed if he used the 'learn from Portland' on a non-Portland audience."[14]

The comment referred to Oregon's highly divided political geography. To most Oregonians it would be no surprise that Obama's largest rally in the nation to that date occurred in Portland. Portland is the core of a "blue" (i.e., primarily Democratic, left-leaning) corridor that runs from the most northwestern corner of the state (bordering Washington State, along the Columbia River) to, roughly, the eastern suburbs of Portland,

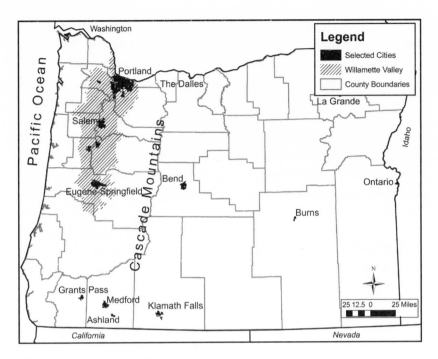

Figure 2   Oregon map (P. Hurley 2010)

and south to the city of Eugene in the Willamette Valley, with "purple"-ish (politically mixed) pockets in Jackson County and the city of Medford in the south, and Deschutes County and the city of Bend in central Oregon (Figure 2). Most of Oregon's eastern and southern counties are political landscapes painted solid red. Although some counties running eastward up the Columbia River Gorge have shown blue tendencies in recent elections, Oregon has long thought of its political geography in terms of a sharp east-west and rural-urban divide, with the populous and urbanized Willamette Valley (which includes Portland and is home to approximately 70 percent of the state's residents) comprising the core of left-leaning politics. The map of the 2008 presidential election results by county shows a strong concentration of Obama votes in the Willamette Valley and Portland. (In Multnomah County, where Portland is located, Obama won 64 percent of the vote, compared to Republican candidate John McCain's 36 percent.)

This was much the same pattern seen in the 2007 special election for Measure 49, which proponents framed as a referendum on controlling growth in general and hoped (correctly) would draw strong support from the Willamette Valley and Portland. (Interestingly, Measure 49 also drew considerable support from some central and northeastern counties—including those with large wind farms that can conflict with residential growth.) In a state that until recent years was considered a "battleground" or "swing" state in national elections, the seesaw victories of pro-growth Measure 37 in 2004 and slow-growth Measure 49 in 2007 might be perceived as a simple tug-of-war between the state's sharply divided political communities.

Such a view contains some truth but would obscure one of the state's most important political achievements in land use planning—the state's remarkable degree of genuine bipartisan support, at least historically, for land use planning. The state's main body of land use laws, enacted under SB 100 in 1973, not only was advocated by a Republican governor but also was strongly promoted by important Republicans in state government—most of all, Republican state senator Hector Macpherson Jr., a Willamette Valley dairy farmer. Decades later, at least some elements of a coalition remained: Measure 49, the 2007 effort to limit development under pro-property rights Measure 37, was endorsed by every major environmental organization *and* by the state's Farm Bureau—a traditionally politically conservative group.

However, even in 1973, by no means all Republicans agreed with McCall and Macpherson. Some bitterly opposed the land use planning system then—and now. At a 2008 town hall meeting organized by the Oregon Department of Land Conservation and Development in the far eastern city of Burns, a deep-"red" area politically, a participant angrily described McCall to us as a "traitor" who had "fucked us over."

Despite such sentiments, Oregon's land use planning system did *not* emerge from a "red" or "blue" political struggle along geographical lines. To meaningfully understand the politics of planning in Oregon, we must look deeper than simple, conventional left-right (west-east, etc.) politics. This is one of the tasks we take on in chapter 2. Before beginning that chapter, in the section below we very briefly outline the theoretical approach and structure of this book.

The Country and the City

We draw inspiration from the ideas of Welsh literary and social critic Raymond Williams (1921–1988). Williams's work strongly influenced a rich field of research on the relationships between cultural ideas of landscape and social relationships of power (e.g., Tuan 1977; Soja 1996; Duncan and Ley 1993). However, we draw largely from Williams's book *The Country and the City* (1973). It may be more than coincidental that *The Country and the City* was published in the very year that Oregon's unique land use planning system was instituted. Questions of rural spaces and environmental quality and the politics they engendered were very prominent in the early 1970s.

In his book, Williams argues that "country" and "city" are not mere geographical places but powerful cultural *visions* or ideals: "On the country has gathered the idea of a natural way of life; of peace, innocence, and simple virtue. On the city has gathered the idea of an achieved center: of learning, communication, light. Powerful hostile associations have also developed: on the city as a place of noise, worldliness and ambition; on the country as a place of backwardness, ignorance, limitation" (1973: 1). Williams argues that the country became imbued in British culture with Edenic qualities, much like romantic ideas of Oregon as a kind of "paradise." Most important, Williams stresses that the origins of visions of country and city are deeply intertwined.

As Nash (1982) has argued, cherishing nonurbanized landscapes emerged very much from the minds of *urban* people. It is urban people, overwhelmingly, who have valorized rural landscapes in the modern era. In the language of academic social science, urban people have "constructed" rural places in their minds as places of beauty, virtue, recreation, community. At the same time, many rural people in Oregon see urban landscapes as places of overcrowding, crime, pollution, loss of community, and immorality. Each has contributed to the valorization of rural landscapes, albeit in quite different ways that create much conflict. (As we will discuss, some rural people strongly resist the idea that rural landscapes should be repositories of aesthetic and ecological rather than economic values.) We, like Williams, argue that the ideas of rural landscapes produced in large part in the minds of urban people are highly *political*, in the sense that these ideas become justifications for policies of rural land use regulations that are strongly opposed by some rural people. Some people's seemingly benign romantic visions of the countryside are other people's real or perceived political oppression.

We also explore Williams's views on the political and economic roots of these visions of urban and rural landscapes. Writing of the English countryside of the eighteenth century, Williams argues that the idealized vision of the countryside was very much a response to the degradation of urban landscapes by the wealthy new capitalist elite classes of the Industrial Revolution who were most responsible for this urban degradation. Industrial Revolution–era English cities were often horrific places, familiar to any reader of Charles Dickens. According to Williams, however, while wealthy capitalists were happy to profit from the degrading effects of industrialization, they did not want to *see* the effects that their accumulation of wealth had on nature. With the Industrial Revolution, according to Williams, rural landscapes that had previously been the productive agricultural base of the economy became, instead, refuges for the rich, "organized for . . . the view, the ordered proprietary repose, the prospect . . . the facts of production had been banished" (1973: 124–125). The new industrialists went out of their way to not see any traces of the smog-choked, blackened cities that had produced the wealth that they now lavished on constructing highly controlled, quasi-natural, aesthetically pleasing rural landscapes. Any effects on the few remaining farmers and other nonwealthy rural folk of turning rural landscapes into nonproductive private parks apparently did not bother the new, wealthy ex-urban owners.

In Williams's Britain, visions of rural landscapes as, physically, places of peace and aesthetic quality and, socially, as places of backwardness helped pave the way for the new social, economic, and physical order: rural landscapes became, in effect, playgrounds for the rich. As we discuss in this book, this idea of rural landscapes becoming playgrounds for well-to-do urban or ex-urban people, while rural people become enlisted (often unhappily) into the service of a new postproductive economy, is a powerful current of political tension in Oregon. Oregon and Britain may have more in common than magnificent rocky coasts and a lot of soggy weather.

Outline of the Book

In chapter 2 we discuss Oregon's land use planning system within the historical context of U.S. land use planning theory and practice, provide a brief overview of the "nuts and bolts" of Oregon's planning system, and briefly map out the state's planning landscapes.

In chapter 3 we examine in some depth the social, cultural, political, and economic factors that contributed to the rise of Oregon's planning system as a national land use planning "celebrity" from the 1970s onward. We argue against certain popular perceptions and historical accounts that attribute the emergence of the state's remarkable planning system to the leadership of then-governor Tom McCall and the general environmental ethos of the time (e.g., Walth 1994). Scholarly research (e.g., Abbott and Howe 1993), including our own, shows conclusively that Oregon's pioneering planning system was created primarily by and for certain economic interests (mainly, commercial farmers in the Willamette Valley) who feared that sprawl would endanger their livelihoods. We argue it is imperative to have a clear understanding of the economic roots of Oregon's land use planning system because both the political vulnerability of the system and its potential solutions reside largely in the economic realm.

In chapter 4 we explore how Oregon lost much of the land use planning leadership that made the state a celebrity among planners across the country. We specifically examine the histories of Oregon statewide Ballot Measure 7 (2000), Ballot Measure 37 (2004), and Ballot Measure 49 (2007). We suggest that in the first decade of the 2000s these ballot initiatives collectively represented the first major political, legal, and institutional blows to the state's planning system, as created by SB 100 in 1973. By the end of that decade, the state's "land use wars" appeared to have calmed, but (as we argue in later chapters) probably mostly because the sagging economy at the time had taken nearly all development pressure out of the political system. The relative calm by the end of the first decade of the 2000s concealed the fact that the state's planning system had almost certainly been permanently weakened (or at least altered) and appeared vulnerable.

By closely examining the political battles that were the proximate causes of this alteration, we provide a basis for a closer examination, in chapter 5, of the underlying political, economic, and social forces that we argue provide a more meaningful understanding of Oregon's changing land use planning politics. We argue that in failing to understand, acknowledge, and address persistent questions of inflexibility and "unfairness" in the system, land use planners in Oregon allowed political opposition to land use planning to build to a boiling point. In addition, the demographic, political, economic, and social-cultural circumstances in Oregon at the beginning of the twenty-first century were quite unlike the conditions of the early 1970s, and planners and political leaders did not understand how significantly the terrain shifting under their feet had undermined the political foundation of the state's land use planning system. To be sure, deep-pocketed developers played an important role in passing Measure 7 and Measure 37, but they could not have passed these measures without significant popular support. We describe the changing circumstances that generated this political instability in a much-venerated planning system.

After examining the political genesis and tensions within Oregon's land use planning system as a whole, we turn to three case studies in different areas of the state to examine the ways these politics play out in differing social, cultural, economic, and geographic contexts.

In chapter 6, we start with a variant of Raymond Williams's ideas by examining the 2002 expansion of the Portland Metropolitan Area's urban growth boundary over a rural community called Damascus, a case in which we argue that the imaginings or visions of the urban power center quite literally re-created a rural place—or *attempted* to do so. In response to state planning requirements, the Portland Metro Council, in which the community of Damascus was not represented, chose to plan a new city in Damascus (with a population of as many as 150,000) to accommodate Portland's urban population growth. Quite literally, the country would *become* the city. As we describe, this unprecedented attempt by the council to create a wholly new city from mainly nonlocal planning visions led to some rather disastrous results. Portland has often been held up as "the prime symbol of the American anti-sprawl campaign" and is "widely considered to be the leader in the fight against sprawl" (Bruegmann 2005: 203, 207). Yet, we argue, Portland is also a harbinger of some less widely noted political tensions and fault lines.

The experience of the 2002 urban growth boundary expansion into the community of Damascus should teach important lessons for the Portland Metro area and beyond.

In chapter 7, we consider the ways that the state's planning system—designed largely in and for the densely populated Willamette Valley—play out on the less populous but rapidly growing eastern side of the Cascades Mountains, in the "New West" (Travis 2007) hotspot of Bend and surrounding Deschutes, Crook, and Jefferson counties. We focus specifically on the politics of "destination resorts"—communities that some say have become de facto rural subdivisions and a prime violation of the core principles of Oregon's planning system. In addition, in 2009, Central Oregon became ground zero for one of the most dramatic and contentious efforts to extend state-level control, overturning a county-level decision to approve two new destination resorts in a particularly politically and culturally significant area—the Metolius Basin. The political reverberations of the apparent strong-arm politics of state control over destination resorts in the Metolius Basin have yet to be fully felt but may undermine efforts to build good will and faith in the principle of *local* decision making within the context of statewide goal setting—a principle that many have long seen as a key political strength of the SB 100 model. The story of the Metolius Basin calls into serious question possible problems of social injustice and political volatility resulting from the exercise of strong state power over local land use decisions.

In chapter 8, we turn our attention to conservative southwestern Oregon, specifically the cities in the Bear Creek Valley in Jackson County. Like Bend and its surrounding area, Medford and the Jackson County area struggle to cope with rapid in-migration, especially from nearby California. But this is an area of Oregon characterized by particularly deep and continuing cultural and political tensions that fall partly along class, religious, ideological, and cultural lines. In 2000, a seemingly unlikely political phenomenon emerged: local government leaders proposed to work together in a "regional problem-solving" process that sought to give greater autonomy to local governments by working together in a 10-year process to develop their own long-term regional land use plan. Some have called this process a "land grab" by politically well-connected local power brokers; others have called it a model of successful local collaboration and decentralization of land use decision making (in a sense, almost the antithesis of the exercise of heavy state control in the Metolius Basin, described in chapter 7). The southern Oregon case study in chapter 8 reveals both the promise and potential shortcomings (for both the community and the state) of this kind of devolution of planning authority to the local level.

Finally, in chapter 9 we attempt to pull together some of the pieces of this complex history and politics of state-level land use planning in Oregon to offer some conclusions about the past and future of land use planning in Oregon—and, by extension, in other western states facing similar challenges of planning for a more populous future. In sum, while we find that Oregon's statewide planning system earned the praise it received for limiting the effects of growth (and nearly eliminating "sprawl"), we also find that the SB 100 model failed to provide ways to address two inexorable facts of history and society: change and social inequality. Without question, in 1973 SB 100 was a masterpiece of politically and technically savvy legislation—it successfully addressed the economic needs of key political constituencies including farmers and natural resource managers *at that time*, while also tapping into deeply rooted visions of quality of life and environmental values. The Oregon planning model did *not*, however, create mechanisms to adjust to demographic, economic, and ideological change. And the Oregon model more or less ignored questions of the unequal distribution of the costs and benefits of land use regulations—in particular, across the urban-rural divide. In the end, these gaps in Oregon's statewide land use model left the state's planning system weakened and vulnerable. Understandably, Oregon's planners have been reluctant to change a system that has worked so well in the past. But if they fail to adjust, the political experiences of the first decade of the 2000s suggest that Oregon's planners might suffer still greater political losses in the future, including possibly losing the system as a whole. Oregon's land use planners need to let go of some parts of the past and rediscover the boldness and innovative spirit that once made them the nation's planning leaders.

A key challenge is to undo some of the bureaucratization and institutional and ideological rigidity that have come to characterize planning in Oregon today. A greater degree of ideological and *political* sensitivity and innovation will be essential. Today's smart land use politics is our children's future and our environment's future. Better politics—a politics of openness, inclusion, and respect—can make the difference between an effective system that serves the interests of diverse human (and non-human) communities and a system that bogs down in political turmoil and conflict, with losses to all parties. If the social and political dimensions of planning choices are made explicit, we believe the process will be stronger than if these choices are shielded from view by notions that planning is merely rational, technical, and objective. By studying the political nature of planning, far from undermining the process, we can make planning stronger, more innovative, and better able to make transformative changes proportional to the challenges of our time and place. This is heady stuff. It is the stuff of *planning*. To paraphrase Wallace Stegner, by recognizing planning as much more than a technical task, we may achieve a planning system to match the magnificent challenges of the West.

2 Planning for Growth

Oregon is hands down the most visible and successful example of the comprehensive, regulatory approach to land protection and management.

—John Echeverria, Professor of Law, Vermont Law School, 2009[1]

Oregonians hate two things. They hate sprawl. And they hate density.

—Mike Burton, Portland Metro executive officer, 2001[2]

In this chapter, we begin by placing the Oregon land use planning system in the context of other planning systems and growth management efforts in the United States and the American West.[3] Our discussion touches on the system's relationship, first, to the emergence during the early 1970s of new land use controls and the political and economic forces that shaped debates about land use regulation at the time. By necessity, we provide only a thumbnail sketch of the development of land use controls in the United States.[4] Next, we discuss the relationship of the Oregon system to the wider landscape of land use regulatory approaches, and we discuss the overarching "goals" of the system, the way the system is structured, how it is supposed to function, and its key actors and decision-making mechanisms. We focus on key goals of the Oregon system that are most relevant to the book's subsequent chapters. These include an extended discussion of one of the Oregon system's key growth management tools, the urban growth boundary (UGB), and the general philosophy or logic behind the Oregon system and its approach to growth management.

Growth Management: A Comprehensive System

Oregon's approach to planning offers a comprehensive and systematic approach to limiting sprawl by regulating the land development process. To do so, the state establishes specific criteria and guidelines that oversee the creation, "acknowledgment" (i.e., approval), and updating of mandatory local comprehensive plans, including a process of administrative review by state planners and requiring zoning for the entire state (Knaap and Nelson 1992). In doing so, the approach brings together attention to particular elements (e.g., land use, natural resources, affordable housing) and enumeration of specific process elements (e.g., administrative review, approvals, updates). As a result, the Oregon system's program implementation has become "the model for state growth management" nationally (Randolph 2004: 185) and exemplifies many "best practices" in planning implementation theory (Calbick, Day, and Gunton 2003; Randolph 2004). Still, Oregon's approach is characterized by a top-down and interventionist philosophy of land use regulation, which places greater authority in the hands of the state than with officials in local communities (Popper 1981; Mason 2008). As such, Oregon stands out among those limited number of states in the United States, and particularly among states in the American West, that embrace statewide planning approaches (Knaap and Nelson 1992).

In the United States, urban sprawl—a distinct pattern of low-density suburban development—has long been a concern among planners, conservationists, environmentalists, and even a number of developers (Nelson and Duncan 1996; Hoch et al. 2000; Rome 2001; Randolph 2004). This type of growth is often seen as "wasteful of land and resources, costly to serve, damaging to the environment, and among other things, unsightly" (Nelson and Duncan 1996: 1–2; see also Rome 2001). In addition to urban sprawl, there is a growing pattern of, and concern about, a parallel form of sprawl in rural areas. In the American West, these transformations are at the heart of what some have called "a new settlement frontier" (Jackson and Kuhlken 2006), where new in-migrants seeking a better quality of life are occupying urban fringes and beyond, fueling a new resort geography, and gentrifying the range (Travis 2007). Exurbanization, or "rural sprawl," is said to share the same problems as its city cousin described above, with additional concern about the conversion of natural areas and productive farmland to residential or commercial uses (Knight, Wallace, and Riebsame 1995; Duane 1999; Furuseth and Lapping 1999; Brown et al. 2005) and ecological damages, including losses of biodiversity (Stein et al. 2000; Maestas, Knight, and Gilgert 2003; Brown et al. 2005).

Supposed efforts to control sprawl—or at the least to determine the appropriate siting of new land uses—is almost as old as this pattern of land development itself (Platt 2004). These efforts are most often attributed to the advent of zoning during the 1920s in Ohio and its subsequent conceptual embrace by a growing number of states through so-called state-enabling acts that authorized local communities to use zoning in dealing with growth and associated land use change. While zoning provides a way to protect existing land uses from the nuisances associated with potentially incompatible land uses (e.g., industrial sites within residential neighborhoods), it does not necessarily provide guidance on other key issues associated with urban expansion, such as timing and construction of critical infrastructure (e.g., sewer, water, roads) needed to support growing population centers. Confusion about the relationship of zoning to planning is rather common among the public at large, with some residents seeing the two as one and the same thing.

Although many observers trace the causes of sprawl, whether in its urban or rural forms, to American affluence, federal housing and investment policies, federal subsidies for transportation and infrastructure, land speculation, and a general widespread distaste for density, local land use regulation itself can also contribute to sprawl (Jackson 1985; Nelson and Duncan 1996; Hoch et al. 2000; Squires 2002). Restrictive land use regulations in urban areas (e.g., prohibiting small parcel sizes or zoning for single-family residential housing only) may help drive up land values and make development inside city boundaries costly and difficult in relation to development outside the city limits. At the same time, lower land prices in combination with low-density zoning in nonurban areas can force development that emanates from the city into a sprawling, land-intensive form. As a result, growth management in the United States often has been about counteracting existing uncoordinated land use public policies that can be a major cause of sprawl (Nelson and Duncan 1996).

In the process, as Bosselman and Callies (1972), Mason (2008), and others point out, growth management relies on wresting a great deal of power (in the form of control over land use decision making) from local governments. In doing so, effective growth management is said to rest on long-term planning that is comprehensive in both process and geographic scope (e.g., regions or states), directing urbanization—including capital

investment or land speculation—toward areas with appropriate infrastructure and away from rural lands with natural resource and ecological values, while involving the public in the process (Nelson and Duncan
1996; Hoch et al. 2000; Weitz 2000; Squires 2002; Randolph 2004).
Long before these became widely accepted ideas among planners nationwide, these were the principles that would guide Oregon Republican state
senator Hector Macpherson Jr., the architect of Oregon's planning system, in 1973 (see chapter 3). In Macpherson's words, the planning system
should identify the "wisest use for this and succeeding generations"; "the
public must be included in the land use decision-making process"; and
while both incentives and coercion are necessary for state-led planning,
"incentives are the preferred course of action."[5] In turn, Macpherson
derived much of his approach from Bosselman and Callies's (1972) landmark text on planning theory. Yet, Bosselman and Callies's theory had
never before come close to being actually or fully implemented in any
state prior to the creation of the Oregon system in 1973 (see chapter 3).
In this sense, Oregon was a true pioneer in American planning.

Even under this new framework, critical questions remained: What is
the correct balance between coercion and incentives? What is the correct
level of state versus local control? Are there trade-offs between efficiency
and decentralization of planning? These debates, recurring features of
planning in Oregon from the outset, have been and remain at the heart of
decisions about whether and how to establish planning systems elsewhere
in the United States.

While Oregon's system may be pioneering, it was not the first state
(nor is it the only state) to embrace the need for some type of state intervention. Indeed, Oregon's efforts in the early 1970s came at a time
characterized by tremendous interest in and momentum for implementing new models of planning (Popper 1981; Mason 2008; Bosselman and
Callies 1972).[6] Hawaii had already adopted statewide permitting in the
late 1960s (Mason 2008). In 1970, Vermont's Act 250 called for the establishment of a state land inventory, the creation of planning principles
to inform development, and review of some development proposals by
regional boards, while generally discouraging new construction on steep
slopes (Popper 1981). Florida's 1972 Environmental and Water Management Act established new rules for development in critical areas as well

as tools to evaluate regional impacts (Popper 1981). While the states of Hawaii, Florida, and Vermont were beginning to think comprehensively about where residential development should or should not occur within their borders, New York was busy creating the 1973 Adirondacks Private Land Use and Development Plan (Mason 2008), which allowed the state government to create a regional zoning plan that resulted in wholesale reductions of land development opportunities in the Adirondack Mountains (Terrie 2008; Mason 2008).

In addition to these and other state-level planning efforts, debates about the need for a *national* land use policy, in part to address the question of sprawl and resource protection, came to the forefront of national legislative discussions in the early 1970s (Plotkin 1987; Mason 2008). Efforts to pass the National Land Use Policy Act in 1973 came to naught, as constituencies aligned with local governments (read: local zoning control) and local developers/builders squared off against larger developers and environmentalists. (While environmentalists saw the possibility of addressing critical conservation needs, developers and building interests that operated in multiple jurisdictions sought the creation of standardized planning, zoning, and building rules.)

Within the United States today, a limited number of states undertake or require statewide planning that meet the base criteria for statewide growth management programs (Nelson and Duncan 1996; Randolph 2004), including "the establishment of statewide goals and policies, the creation of regional agencies charged with reviewing and coordinating local plans, and requirements that local governments prepare plans and implement their state goals" (Nelson and Duncan 1996: 20). Resulting plans often also address consistency and concurrency of action, protection of natural resources, efforts to establish compact forms of urban development, transit planning, economic development, and provisions to create affordable housing (Randolph 2004). When it comes to contemporary statewide programs, the American Planning Association has identified three different types or models that characterize the diverse programs: state-imposed planning, mandatory planning with a strong state role, and mandatory planning with a weak state role (Nelson and Duncan 1996). These categories reflect differences in the extent to which the state's system establishes an integrated vision of future development, dictates operational features, integrates goals and policies to guide planning activities, and creates measures that direct land use and development into particular places within a given state (see Weitz 2000). Thirteen states in the United States have some type of statewide planning program in place: Hawaii, Vermont, Oregon, Connecticut, Florida, New Hampshire, New Jersey, Rhode Island, Maine, Georgia, Washington, Maryland, and Delaware (Hoch et al. 2000; Randolph 2004). Of these thirteen states, six establish or designate some type of boundary to limit urban growth, while four others have processes for identifying priority areas where growth should occur.

How the goals for growth management are accomplished varies from program to program. For example, Maryland's highly celebrated "smart growth" approach relies on a combination of economic incentives and priority funding areas, which direct funds to urbanizing areas within designated growth areas and resource conservation areas outside these designated areas. Maryland's approach shares important similarities with the Oregon approach but is significantly different in its reliance on nonregulatory tools. These states may differ in the extent to which the state government takes the lead in planning, but unlike most states in the country, they have some level of statewide planning directives.

Statewide approaches to planning stand in stark contrast to most states in the United States, where planning is not widespread and zoning may or may not be practiced (Hoch et al. 2000). For example, in Pennsylvania, which has more than 1,500 individual townships and boroughs, local jurisdictions may or may not engage in any type of planning, even though they may have some limited forms of land use control. Thus, it would be wrong to assume that states without statewide programs do not address large-scale planning issues. A number of states maintain special planning or land use control programs that target specific concerns, particularly when it comes to environmental resources (e.g., coastal areas and wetlands), or physiographic regions within their states (Randolph 2004; Mason 2008). As in those states with comprehensive programs, a key feature of these planning programs centers on the ways in which local land use decision making has been partially or completely controlled by a state agency or appointed board (Weitz 2000; Mason 2008). In these cases, however, the authority of the state to act is limited to very specific geographic areas and forms of interaction. For example, North Carolina adopted a coastal management act in the 1970s that allowed the state to identify and set specific standards for areas of environmental concern (Mason 2008) but that specifically instructs the resulting program to work collaboratively with local governments to develop strategies for coastal environmental management.[7] Among large-scale regional planning initiatives, New York's efforts in the Adirondacks mentioned above, as well as in the Catskills, represent efforts to address forest, wilderness, and water resources.

At the same time, some states are beginning to appreciate the importance of greater state involvement in the planning process and are undertaking new land use reforms that draw on elements of the Oregon model, but in ways that suggest lessons learned from other, nonregulatory approaches (Hoch et al. 2000; Randolph 2004). For example, Tennessee has begun requiring some cities to employ urban growth boundaries while also implementing aspects of the open space conservation and farmland protection approach pioneered as part of the "smart growth" program in Maryland (Randolph 2004).

In the American West, the number of states that undertake statewide planning is extremely limited, though this does not mean planning is not active in these other states. For example, while only Washington (in addition to Oregon) makes the list of states with comprehensive programs, California is also widely recognized for its robust planning. In 1990 Washington established a growth management program similar to that of Oregon's, as "a method for comprehensive land use planning involving citizens, communities, counties, cities, and the private sector that would prevent uncoordinated and unplanned growth."[8] The program has 14 planning goals (see below). In contrast to Oregon, Washington's planning goals include specific recognition of "property rights" and the importance of avoiding "arbitrary and discriminatory actions."[9] California's approach to planning largely focuses on process rather than outcomes, centering on the requirement for counties and municipalities to create comprehensive plans that address specific and substantive elements (e.g., land use, housing) (Fulton and Shigley 2005), but also includes the review of plans and development decisions for their environmental impacts (Fulton and Shigley 2005; Randolph 2004) and their consistency (e.g., do plans and ordinances agree?). In addition, California is noted for its regional Coastal Commission with decision-making authority over some dimensions of land use development and planning along the coast, regional strategic coordination in the Sierra Nevada Mountains through the newly established Sierra Nevada Conservancy (Fulton and Shigley 2005), regional efforts to protect endangered species through cooperation with the federal government to establish habitat conservation programs, and statewide efforts to use tax incentives (e.g., differential assessments) to place farmlands under conservation measures (Mason 2008; Fulton and Shigley 2005).[10]

By contrast, Colorado and Arizona are representative of Western states that take the more common approach, delegating planning powers to individual local governments that create comprehensive plans, designate zoning districts, and regulate subdivision.[11] In Colorado, for example, cities and counties may use "land use controls and plans" to "protect wildlife, control population density and growth, and protect the surrounding environment, among other things," but these controls must "comply with the federal and state constitutional rights and duties."[12] While Colorado encourages interjurisdictional cooperation, this is not required. Finally, some states in the American West only marginally engage in planning or zoning. This is the case in Montana, where, as of 2008, only one county in the state had implemented comprehensive zoning.[13] The nearly opposite, hands-off approach in Montana helps to illustrate just how remarkably comprehensive (and complex) Oregon's land use regulatory system is—as we describe below.

The Framework of the Oregon System

The Oregon system is built on a foundation of 19 Statewide Planning Goals, with each goal representing a specific policy and approach to particular planning, development, or land use issues. Of the 19 goals, many pertain to the entire state. For example, Goals 3, 4, and 5 deal with natural resources generally found throughout the state. At the same time, mirroring initiatives undertaken by other states during the 1970s, several goals address particular areas within the state. For example, Goal 15 specifically addresses the "Willamette River Greenway" of northwestern

Oregon, while Goal 17 applies specifically to the state's "coastal shore-lands." These place-specific goals are beyond the immediate scope of this book, although, as we show in chapter 7, the commitment to addressing special places through state intervention remains alive.

All counties and cities in Oregon with populations above 2,500 must complete comprehensive plans that comply with specific guidelines and procedures specified by the planning goals. All plans were initially re-viewed, through a process known as "acknowledgment," for compliance with the 19 statewide goals, and they are regularly reviewed for their continued compliance (see below). Thus, following the creation of the system, jurisdictions within Oregon were charged with developing their plans, having them reviewed by the Department of Land Conservation and Development (DLCD) and acknowledged by the Land Conservation and Development Commission (LCDC; discussed below).

In the remainder of this section, we briefly review the Oregon Statewide Planning Goals that are most important for understanding the story of Oregon's planning system that we tell in this book. Some of the goals are not included in our discussion: Goal 9 (economic development), Goals 12 and 13 (transportation and energy conservation), Goal 15 (the Willamette River Greenway), and Goals 16–19 (pertaining to coastal areas).[14]

Oregon's system places a premium on citizen involvement. Goal 1 [OAR 660-015-0000(1)][15] makes this clear, detailing the state's commit-ment to involving citizens in "all phases of the planning process," includ-ing provisions addressing the need for a committee of involved citizens; specific ways of facilitating communication; opportunities to participate in or influence decisions during data collection, plan preparation, devel-opment of plan content, or plan adoption; the translation of technical in-formation into accessible formats; requiring feedback from policymakers; and the adequate provision of budgetary funds to support these efforts.[16] Goal 1 specifically requires that jurisdictions charged with completing comprehensive plans develop specific programs for engaging citizens that include these elements. These efforts "shall provide for continuity of citi-zen participation and information" so that citizens are able "to identify and comprehend the issues."[17]

Second only to citizen participation, the state's commitment to "land use planning" is a centerpiece of the Oregon system. Goal 2 [OAR 660-015-

0000(2)] details the system's focus on a policy framework that relies on planning as the basis for all land use decisions. Although this framework relies on zoning to anchor policy in specific places, it is the statewide goals that follow, and the long-term growth management principles they represent, that demonstrate the commitment to *both* the orderly land conversion from resource-oriented to urban uses and the simultaneous conservation of a natural resource base. Decisions and actions must be based on "an adequate factual base."[18] That is, analysis of current and *future* conditions, including appropriate inventories, is a key feature of planning practice in Oregon. Goal 2 makes clear that planning in the state must apply to city, county, state, and federal lands, while also clarifying that all subsequent goals are not recommendations but rather requirements, indicating that "governmental units shall review the guidelines set forth for the goals and either utilize the guidelines or develop alternative means that will achieve the goals." Further, "land-use plans shall state how the guidelines or alternative means utilized achieve the goals."[19]

Goal 2 also recognizes the need for exceptions and sets out the procedure for claiming or creating areas that cannot meet the requirements set forth in other goals. Jurisdictions may claim exceptions to planning goals, particularly those pertaining to lands outside of urban growth boundaries (UGBs; see below), when land is, among others, "physically developed to the extent that it is no longer available for uses allowed by the applicable goal," land "is irrevocably committed to uses not allowed by the applicable goal because existing adjacent uses and other relevant factors make uses allowed by the applicable goal impracticable," or "proposed uses are compatible with other adjacent uses."[20] This provision of the system, when applied to the actual landscape, has a number of important consequences. For example, a number of rural areas in the state, which might have otherwise been recognized as agricultural or forested areas, had been already parcelized to the extent that forestry and agriculture were impractical. In many cases, these so-called exception areas are found in highly desirable rural parts of the state and have helped meet the demand for both rural and exurban residential development.

Among the most recognized features of the Oregon system is its commitment to protecting agriculture. Goal 3 [OAR 660-015-0000(3)] deals with "agricultural lands" and specifically sets forth the state's commitment to *preserving* and *maintaining* these areas in a way that is "consistent with existing and future needs for agricultural products, forest and open space."[21] The crux of the goal lies in the use of zoning to "limit uses which can have significant adverse effects on agricultural and forest land, farm and forest uses or accepted farming or forest practices." Thus, only nonfarm uses that will not interfere with farming are allowed in these zones; conflicting uses are prohibited. Agricultural areas are determined through the use of soil inventories that rely on the U.S. Soil Conservation Service's Soil Capability Classification System. This system has six separate classes that evaluate the quality and productivity of the soil for agricultural-related endeavors. Agricultural lands are described by classes I–IV in western Oregon and by classes I–VI in eastern Oregon—classes V and VI are generally recognized as those suitable for livestock ranching. Within areas zoned for agriculture, the goal establishes a default minimum parcel size of 80 acres in farmland zones and 160 acres in rangeland zones. Individual counties are free to establish smaller minimum lot sizes, but these minimums must be appropriate to "maintain the existing commercial agricultural enterprise within the area" and meet requirements set out within the state's statutes.

For the purposes of planning and zoning, lands that would otherwise be classified as agricultural based on soils but are within UGBs are no longer recognized as agricultural land. Once areas are designated for urban uses, their utility for agricultural production or other nonurban uses is severely downplayed and urban uses and development intensities are prioritized (although this perspective is changing within Oregon's planning institutions—see chapter 6). This system of prioritizing certain lands for agriculture, forestry, or other natural resource uses and other lands for urban development is intended to send a clear and certain economic signal about the future.

Along with agricultural lands, the state's forestland or timberland base receives considerable attention. Goal 4 of the system [OAR 660-015-0000(4)] addresses issues related to "maintain[ing] the forest land base and [protecting] the state's forest economy." A key goal of the policy is "economically efficient forests practices that assure the continuous growing and harvesting of forest tree species as the leading use on forest land consistent with sound management of soil, air, water, and fish and wildlife resources and to provide recreational opportunities and agriculture."[22] In 1938, Oregon became the largest timber-producing state, and it remains among the nation's most important timber production areas. Goal 4 states that only forestry-related uses will be allowed on forest-zoned land. Only dwellings and other structures specifically authorized by law are permitted, thus strictly limiting residential or commercial encroachment into the state's still economically vital timberlands.

Recognizing the importance of natural resources to the state's physical development, its quality of life, and the safety of human settlement, Goals 5–7 deal with "Natural Resources, Scenic and Historic Areas, and Open Spaces" [OAR 660-015-0000(5)],[23] "Air, Water, and Land Resource Quality" [OAR 660-015-0000(6)],[24] and "Areas Subject to Natural Hazards" [OAR 660-015-0000(7)],[25] respectively. Of these, Goal 5 plays a key role in balancing resource extraction and conservation. Resources for which cities and counties must prepare inventories include riparian corridors, wildlife habitat, wetlands, federal wild and scenic waterways, groundwater resources, recreation trails approved by the state, natural areas, wilderness areas, mineral and aggregate resources, energy sources, cultural areas, historic resources, open space, and scenic view sites. Unlike the previous two resource-focused goals, however, Goal 5 does not specifically require local jurisdictions to zone areas containing the particular resources spelled out in the language of the goal. Rather, jurisdictions are directed to "adopt programs that will protect natural resources and conserve scenic, historic, and open space resources for present and future generations."[26]

Although generally intended to "satisfy the recreational needs of the citizens of the state and visitors," Goal 8 [OAR 660-015-0000(8)] is better known for the role it plays "in [the] siting of recreational facilities, particularly destination resorts."[27] The goal defines "destination resorts" as "self-contained development providing visitor-oriented accommodations and developed recreational facilities in a setting with high natural amenities."[28] Specific provisions detail the process by which areas that are eligible and those not eligible for the siting of destination resorts are to be identified. Importantly, the goal establishes the number of allowable housing units, based on a ratio of residential housing units to overnight accommodation units. For each overnight unit, no more than 2.5 residential dwelling units may be constructed. In other words, if a county approves a destination resort with 100 overnight units, a maximum of 250 residential units would be allowed. In addition, there are a number of sequencing requirements relative to overnight accommodations, which are intended to ensure that resorts do not simply build residential units and become, in effect, rural subdivisions (we return to this issue in chapter 7).

Housing and Infrastructure provision are dealt with in Goals 10 and 11. Goal 10 of the Oregon system, "Housing" [OAR 660-015-0000(10)], is intended to "provide for the housing needs of citizens of the state."[29] The goal requires jurisdictions to maintain an inventory of buildable lands and factors affecting the affordability of housing. It also contains a "fair share" provision requiring all jurisdictions to provide housing for all income levels (Abbott 2002), including "affordable housing." A second major concern in the management of growth is the timing and provision of infrastructure to support development. Goal 11 [OAR 660-015-0000(11)] describes the "timely, orderly, and efficient arrangement of public facilities and services" for urban and rural development.[30] Public facilities of concern to Goal 11 are "sewer, water (piped water for human consumption) and transportation facilities" that "support the land uses designated" within an urban growth boundary (see below). Urban facilities and services include "police protection; sanitary facilities; storm drainage facilities; planning, zoning and subdivision control; health services; recreation facilities and services; energy and communication services; and community governmental services."

Goal 14 addresses "Urbanization" [OAR 660-015-0000(14)] and details what perhaps is the most widely recognized element of Oregon's planning system: the urban growth boundary (UGB). Officially, the purpose of the goal is "to provide for an orderly and efficient transition from rural to urban land use, to accommodate urban population and urban employment inside urban growth boundaries, to ensure efficient use of land, and to provide for livable communities."[31] Contrary to popular perception, UGBs generally and in Oregon specifically are not static or unchanging planning tools, but rather are intended to change with particular needs, including population growth and *necessary* urban expansion. In Oregon, UGBs must be large enough to "accommodate long range urban population, consistent with a 20-year population forecast" and a "demonstrated need for housing, employment opportunities, livability or uses such as public facilities, streets and roads, schools, parks or open space." Critically, local governments must "demonstrate that needs cannot reasonably be accommodated on land already inside the urban growth boundary" "prior to expanding an urban growth boundary."[32]

In locating UGBs, local jurisdictions are to consider compatibility "with nearby agricultural and forest activities" as well as "the orderly and economic provision of public facilities" and the "environmental, energy, economic, and social consequences" of the boundary's expansion.[33] Thus, when it comes to urbanization and matters of sprawl, "within the UGB, the burden of proof rests on opponents of land development," while outside the UGB "the burden rests on developers to show that their land is easily supplied with necessary services" and "has little worth as open space or farmland" (Abbott 2002: 213). Effectively, single-family residential dwellings may be approved outside of UGBs only on lands where exceptions to the provisions of Goal 3 have been approved. Moreover, when coupled with the provisions of Goal 10, the UGB prohibits jurisdictions from using large-lot zoning (the traditional tool of exclusionary zoning) to block the provision and construction of multifamily housing, such as apartment buildings.

Beyond these goals, a number of associated elements of the planning system have been developed. In general, these programs or processes are intended to either supplement elements of the 19 goals or facilitate their application in situations that were not originally anticipated. Two components are important to mention here (and we explore these further in chapters 6 and 8).

First, following the first attempts to expand Portland's UGB and the resulting land use battles, the state passed new legislation in the 1990s to allow for the creation of so-called urban and rural reserves that would provide longer-term stability for lands outside UGBs *and* lands adjacent to UGBs that might potentially be seen as part of future UGB expansions. While rural reserves are intended "to provide long-term protection for agriculture, forestry or important natural landscape features that limit urban development or help define appropriate natural boundaries of urbanization," urban reserves are "lands outside an urban growth boundary that [specifically] will provide for" "future expansion [of the UGB] over a long-term period" and "the cost effective provision of public facilities and services within the area when the[se] lands are included" in the UGB.[34] The creation of urban or rural reserves requires coordination and agreement among the local jurisdiction whose UGB growth would be served, the jurisdiction in which the reserve is designated, and the state's land use agency. In doing so, however, the jurisdictions provide clarity about what areas outside the UGB will remain in agriculture, forestry, or other resource uses as defined by the system, *as well as* those areas destined to be urbanized. Designation of urban and rural reserves is intended to provide certainty for farmers as well as developers and both urban and rural residents about what the future will hold.

Second, also in the 1990s, there was growing recognition that some areas of the state needed an alternative mechanism to plan in a more regionally coordinated fashion. While the Oregon system is comprehensive in its approach to planning, only the Portland area (see below) worked in a way that follows principles of *regional* planning. In the absence of regional coordination, cities in close proximity to one another and with separate UGBs might grow in ways that contribute to greater farmland and forestland loss, threaten individual community identities, miss opportunities for greater efficiency in building infrastructure and coordinating transportation, and so on. Thus, in 1996 the state legislature passed legislation that provided for the creation of "up to four pilot programs of [a] collaborative Regional Problem-Solving process" that would "offer an opportunity to participate with appropriate state agencies and all local governments within the region affected by the problems that are the subject of the problem-solving process."[35] While the legislation reinforced the role of the state in overseeing the process, it mandated that all affected or involved state agencies participate in and help facilitate the completion of these special processes.

Administrative Oversight

As is common with most of Oregon's state agencies, there are two components to the administration of the Oregon planning system: (1) a panel of appointed and unpaid citizen volunteers, known in the case of land use planning as the Land Conservation and Development Commission (LCDC), and (2) the professional administrative agency that implements the policies of the state and LCDC: the Department of Land Conservation and Development (DLCD). In the case of land use and planning, the seven-member LCDC oversees the DLCD agency and, according to state law (Oregon Revised Statutes 197.030), is charged with "adopt[ing] state land-use goals and implement[ing] rules, assur[ing] local plan compliance with the goals, coordinat[ing] state and local planning, and manag[ing] the coastal zone program."[36] LCDC functions in many ways like both a state-level planning commission *and* legislative body when it comes to land use decisions. The commission hears advice from professional planners on a wide array of issues (like a planning commission), but it also has the power to make specific decisions about policy through "administrative rules" that influence landowners across the state.

In practice, the DLCD is a technical and analytical agency that assists with the development of new policies (through recommendations on actions to LCDC) that address ongoing or emerging land use issues. According to the agency's mission statement, DLCD is charged with guiding "statewide land use policy in order to foster livable, sustainable development in urban and rural communities; conserv[ing] coastal resources; protect[ing] farm and forestlands and other natural resources; and improv[ing] the well-being and prosperity of citizens, businesses, and communities throughout Oregon."[37] The agency is funded by the state's general fund, through special programs of the federal government (particularly the Federal Emergency Management Agency and National Oceanic and Atmospheric Administration), and federal transportation funds from the U.S. Department of Transportation.

DLCD also provides ongoing oversight and technical assistance with plan updates. According to state law, DLCD must work cooperatively with individual jurisdictions—cities and parts of counties within UGBs—to complete a so-called periodic review. Periodic reviews are intended "to ensure that comprehensive plans and land use regulations remain in compliance with the statewide planning goals," "that adequate provision" is made "for needed housing, economic development, transportation, public facilities and services," and that "urbanization [is] coordinated." The timing of periodic review depends in part on the type of city in question, with reviews occurring between every 7–10 years, and according to a schedule set by DLCD.

In special circumstances, periodic review may occur as early as just five years after the previous review.[38] Likewise, jurisdictions may decide that there have been no significant changes to the conditions associated with housing, economic development, transportation, public facilities and services, and urbanization and that no review is warranted. Either way, an evaluation report that includes opportunities for public input, as determined by the jurisdiction's citizen involvement program, must be turned over to the DLCD for review and approval. In cases where review is warranted, a scope of work is determined using the report submitted by the local jurisdiction. Importantly, the provisions of periodic review give LCDC "exclusive jurisdiction" to review and approve both the process by which planning decisions are made and the associated outcomes for any planning decisions that change UGBs, including expansions of more than 50 acres for cities with a population greater than 2,500 and of more than 100 acres for metropolitan service districts. This provision also applies to the designation of urban reserve areas.

Acknowledging the controversial nature of land use decisions, the state legislature created a separate body to serve as the frontline for legal challenges to the system. The Land Use Board of Appeals (LUBA) was created in 1979 by the state legislature (ORS 197.800) and was intended to "simplify the appeal process, speed resolution of land use disputes and provide consistent interpretation of state and local land use laws." It has sole jurisdiction over review of government land use decisions when petitions are filed; this is true both for land use controls that are passed by elected bodies (legislative) and those decisions made by planners and other agency personnel (quasi judicial),[39] although its decisions are sometimes appealed to the state's appeals court. The board consists of three members, who must be members of the Oregon State Bar. They are appointed by the governor for four-year terms and must be confirmed by the state senate.[40]

Oregon's Planning Landscapes

Notwithstanding place-specific goals, the Oregon planning system was created, to a great extent, as a coherent approach to urbanization across a state whose geography, demography, and economy is anything but uniform. The state's varied landscapes play a key role in shaping the politics of land use planning in the state, both within particular regions and local jurisdictions and at the state level where battles over systemic change must be waged.

As described in chapter 1, the 2009 U.S. Census indicates that about two-thirds of the state's population lives in the Willamette Valley (the northwestern quadrant of Oregon), including portions of the Portland-Beaverton, Eugene-Springfield, Salem, and Corvallis metropolitan areas. The Willamette Valley is characterized by moderate amounts of rainfall from October through May and a predominantly flat topography punctuated by clusters of volcanic buttes and hills and is home to the state's most productive farmland. Significantly, the Willamette Valley includes the state's largest city: Portland.

Since the creation of the Oregon system, the Portland area has been among the fastest and most continuously growing centers of urban population. However, Portland is but one of 25 separate jurisdictions that make up the Portland metropolitan area. The region has its own elected regional government, which is responsible for planning. Formally known as Portland Metro ("Metro"), this entity was created as the Portland Metropolitan Service District in 1977 as part of developments associated with the wider statewide planning movement, taking responsibility for the creation of the region's first urban growth boundary in 1979. Today, the goal of Metro is "to provide region-wide planning and coordination to manage pressing growth, infrastructure, and development issues that cross jurisdictional boundaries."[41] Six elected Metro councilors and an elected Metro president represent more than 1.5 million residents, while the regional authority's planning and development department is responsible for ongoing growth management initiatives covering the region's 25 separate cities. Over the years, a number of issues have been at the center of land use politics in Portland. These include the extent to which the UGB has facilitated economically efficient urban expansion versus the creation of affordable housing; fights over appropriate densities within individual jurisdictions, particularly when increased densities have been tied to construction of affordable (or lower income) housing; ongoing infill development; and where, when, and how to expand Metro's UGB (see chapter 6).

The creation of the Portland Metro UGB took place within the context of the more common U.S. experience of fragmented land use decision making and a general tendency toward deconcentrated, lower density suburban development (sprawl). This early sprawl was characteristic of patterns resulting from decisions made by then separate and independent jurisdictions that today make up Portland Metro (Abbott, Howe, and Adler 1994). As a result, infill development has been a major feature of urbanization and population growth within Portland Metro. The fastest growing region of the state over the past decade actually has been in the central portion of the state, known as Central Oregon, which is home to the Bend-Redmond metropolitan and Prineville "micropolitan" areas.[42] Central Oregon is characterized by high desert and historically was a region of irrigated agriculture, livestock ranching, and timber management at higher elevations. In the terms of recent studies on rapid urbanization in the landscapes of natural resource extraction, this is the "New West" (Jackson and Kuhlken 2006; Travis 2007). With recent rapid growth, concerns over UGB expansion are moving onto the planning agenda in the City of Bend. But in the rural countryside of Central Oregon, it has been the explosion of destination resorts that has stoked the flames of land use politics and conflict in recent years (see chapter 7).

The eastern one-third of the state is characterized by several mountain ranges, low population densities, and wide-open rural spaces. There are just three areas in the region that even qualify for the U.S. Census bureau's micropolitan classification: Pendleton, LaGrande, and Ontario (covering the entirety of Malheur County). Today, economic development, particularly for the region's small towns, rural residents, and landowners, is the key planning issue. In eastern Oregon, the sort of problems associated with urban and rural sprawl in the Willamette Valley, Central Oregon, and parts of southern Oregon are nearly nonexistent, and for that reason we do not address eastern Oregon in depth in this book.

The southwestern corner of the state, commonly referred to (somewhat inaccurately, in geographic terms) simply as "southern Oregon," has been characterized by substantial urban growth and relatively rapid rural-residential development, mainly in the Rogue River Valley, where population is concentrated in the Medford metropolitan and Grants Pass micropolitan areas. Outside the Rogue Valley, southern Oregon is characterized by small towns, diverse and rugged mountains, and a climate that is similarly mild but somewhat drier and sunnier than the Willamette Valley to the north—key ingredients for in-migrants seeking natural amenities and outdoor opportunities. In the 1980s and early 1990s, the region was a flashpoint of land use conflict over logging and the spotted owl (Brown 1995). More recently, however, given the fragmented nature of residential growth (mostly spread across a number of rather small jurisdictions with UGBs), concerns about regional planning or problem solving have been a key feature of land use planning and politics in the region (see chapter 8).

As we describe in chapter 3, it could be said that, at the broadest level, environmental politics in Oregon began in the state's spectacular high desert and coastal areas, which attracted both rapid development and the development of a new breed of environmental politics beginning in the 1960s—the foremost example being former Governor Tom McCall's battle for the state's one-of-a-kind 1967 Beach Bill. Regrettably, time and space do not allow us to do justice to the state's coastal region. We do, however, return to the ongoing fight over development in the state's high desert of Central Oregon, with its echoes of Tom McCall's personal passion for protecting this spectacular region (chapter 7). First, however, we turn to the question of how Oregon came to be the nation's foremost exemplar—for good or ill—of landscape regulation.

3   A Star Is Born

The story in Oregon goes like this: One day in the late 1960s, Linn County dairy farmer Hector Macpherson Jr. drove past a neighbor's farm and noticed a Caterpillar tractor moving soil. Macpherson shouted, "What ya plannin' to grow here?" The tractor driver replied, "Houses" (Rusk 1999: 156). According to Oregon legend, Macpherson saw that the farming economy and a way of life were being paved over by rural sprawl, got himself elected to the state senate, and wrote a law that has been the cornerstone of Oregon's land use planning system ever since (as well as a model that has been highly studied and influential for land use planning nationwide).

Reflecting on the story in 2009, Macpherson confirmed that it is essentially true: "I saw the whole subdivision of the area was starting in, and there was one on White Oak Drive that was really the trigger. I could see that these kinds of things were coming. . . . I had all kinds of things as a dairy farmer: the flies, the noise, manure." Macpherson's wife Kitty interjected, "The cows getting out." "You expected that [cows get out]," Macpherson continued, "but people called to ask me to not spread manure. . . . The farm is next to the church. People called to ask me to not spread manure the week before they got married!" Macpherson laughed. "I saw I was going to need protection if I was going to maintain my dairy farm."[1] When he arrived in the Oregon Senate, Macpherson met with powerbrokers and plotted, as he describes it, "like revolutionaries" to create that protection.[2] But these revolutionaries had soil under their fingernails: when asked if Willamette Valley farmers like him spearheaded the creation of the state's land use planning system, the usually modest Macpherson replied, "Absolutely." Today, those present during the creation of Oregon's land use planning system in the early 1970s agree that it was commercial farmers, not environmentalists or left-leaning city folk, who led the charge for land use planning (see Abbott and Howe 1993).

Even though led by conservative (mostly Republican) farmers, it is no exaggeration to say that the system of state-level land use planning they created was indeed "revolutionary." Oregon historian William Robbins observes that Oregon's planning "is nationally one of a kind. There is no other state—Hawaii and the state of Maine have tried in different directions—but they have never been as comprehensive or have functioned for such a long period of time as Oregon's system."[3]

Chapter 2 describes Oregon's unique land use planning system and compares it to the efforts by other states to cope with rapid growth and development in recent decades. In this chapter and chapter 4, we consider the political *how* and *why* questions: How did Oregon's unique statewide comprehensive land use planning system emerge? Why did it emerge in *Oregon*? Why *1973*? How and why did it survive essentially intact for three decades? What conditions led to the weakening and, ultimately, the near-death experiences of Oregon's planning system in 2000 and 2004? (We explore this last question in chapter 5, and again in chapter 9.) In the following section we briefly describe the conception and birth of the program.

The Birth of Oregon's Planning System

This book is largely about the celebrated land use planning system that Hector Macpherson and his allies engineered (commonly referred to under its legislative title, Senate Bill 100 [SB 100]) and the complex political life of that system from its inception up to today. To begin, however, we note that Oregon's planning system was not created from whole cloth in 1973; rather, pressure to address growth through state-level policy had been building since the 1960s.

Up to 1969, growth in Oregon was haphazard and largely unregulated. Zoning and planning were voluntary, and most land use plans, if they existed, were merely advisory. Zoning was mainly limited to cities. Where rural zoning existed, it often allowed subdivision of farmland, forestland, and rangeland into five-acre lots—a recipe for sprawl and a major threat and concern for farmers by the early and middle 1960s. Neighboring California (especially Southern California, as discussed later in this chapter) provided a powerful reminder of how uncontrolled growth can transform landscapes and farm economies—and, to many Oregonians, . a model to be strictly avoided.

In 1967, a conference titled "The Willamette Valley—What Is Our Future in Land Use?" focused on the pressure of urban growth on farming, including conflicts between residential and agricultural land uses, and growth-driven property tax increases on farmers. A legislative interim committee responded in 1969 with SB 10, the first statewide mandatory planning legislation. With strong support from farmers and a very popular Governor McCall, as well as other key Republican leaders,[4] SB 10 became law—making Oregon the second state (after California in 1955) to require all cities and counties to have plan by a certain date.

SB 10 was far from an easy sell with the Oregon legislature, however, and the political compromises made to secure passage of the bill ultimately undermined the effectiveness of the resulting law. SB 10 required all counties and cities to have a plan that met 10 broad goals, including protecting prime farmland and open spaces, by December 31, 1971. But hesitant legislators, under political attack from critics who called the bill "Soviet-style" planning, provided no funding and no mechanism to enforce compliance with SB 10, apart from an impracticable threat that if counties and cities failed to establish plans, the governor would do it for them. In hindsight, the flaws in this approach were clear. Few counties or cities complied with the law, and the governor's office had no administrative capacity and no political will to write plans for noncomplying cities and counties. It quickly became clear that if state-led planning was to be achieved, an administrative apparatus enabling the state to oversee planning in 277 cities and counties was needed. Lacking such an apparatus, SB 10, was a toothless tiger.

However, SB 10 accomplished something that, in the history of land use planning in Oregon, arguably proved even more important than an effective administrative system: it proved that the Oregon public would vote for state-led planning. In 1970, property rights activists tried to overturn SB 10 through a statewide ballot initiative, Measure 11. The effort failed, and Oregon voters upheld the idea of statewide land use planning by a respectable 56 percent. Henry Richmond, founder and former executive director of the land use watchdog group 1000 Friends of Oregon, observed that the failure of the 1970 ballot initiative to overturn state-led planning created "political capital" that helped make it possible in 1973 to pass a far better-crafted planning law created by Macpherson: SB 100.[5]

The push for more effective planning legislation in the early 1970s came largely from the fast-growing Willamette Valley, where the state's richest farmlands (as well as some high-value private commercial forest land) crashed head-on into the state's largest and fastest-growing cities. By the late 1960s and early 1970s, it was clear that farmland and forestland in the Willamette Valley was losing out in this encounter. Between 1950 and 1974, total farmland in counties that make up the Willamette Valley decreased by 926,905 acres—a 34 percent decrease (Richmond and Houchen 2007: 3). However, apart from the sparsely populated eastern counties, rapid growth was affecting most parts of the state.

Despite the passage of SB 10 in 1969, rapid development in the Willamette Valley continued unabated in places such as the community of Charbonneau, reinforcing the concerns of those who feared California-style sprawl coming to Oregon. Others, especially Willamette Valley farmers, feared a future in which the state's traditional agricultural and natural resources economy could no longer maintain sufficient access to land to provide a viable economic base for farming and forestry livelihoods and community. SB 10 had emerged first and foremost from the commercial farming community, but it marked a new kind of land use politics in Oregon in which economically minded farmers and foresters, aesthetic quality-of-life preservationists, and ecologically minded environmentalists could find common ground.

SB 10 was not only unenforceable but also lacked a clear vision of how to reconcile growth, livelihoods, and environmental values. Dairy farmer Hector Macpherson, however, had such a vision. Macpherson had specific ideas of how to bring "Order Out of Chaos" (the title of a famously hard-hitting speech Macpherson delivered to a conference on rural and urban land use sponsored by the Willamette Valley Chambers of Commerce in 1967). Macpherson's father had been a professor of agriculture at the Oregon Agricultural College (now Oregon State University) and later became a state legislator. Though Hector Macpherson Jr. grew up on the dairy farm of his father, Hector Sr., he was no stranger to the worlds of academics and politics. As a self-described "farmer who could talk," Macpherson recounted later that he was naturally thrust into positions of leadership on matters that challenged the farming community, including the Linn County Planning Commission in 1964. (The planning commission was formed at the request of the conservative Linn County Chamber of Commerce with advice from Macpherson.) Building from such experiences, as a state senator Macpherson went on to make history by proposing the pioneering statewide planning system for Oregon that had been attempted by no other state.

Decades later, it may be impossible to ascertain precisely how many dairy farmers in Oregon in 1972 had read the landmark ecological planning manifesto *Design with Nature* by Scottish landscape architect Ian McHarg (1969). History may record, however, that it took only one such cerebral dairy farmer to read McHarg's book and change the history of a state. Macpherson observed in 2009 that he had "read extensively" on planning innovations in California, where dairy farms were given protective zoning, and decided that something similar was needed for Oregon farmland. But Macpherson was particularly inspired by the principles of ecologically informed land use planning in McHarg's book—to the extent that he personally bought 120 acres of ecologically low-value land on hills near his farm in Linn County with the intent of subdividing this land and steering residential development into this relatively low-productivity area, thereby saving the highly productive valley flatland below for farming. This concept of "design with nature," by concentrating residential development in certain areas while preserving high-value farm, forest, and natural areas, became the core vision of the planning system in Macpherson's SB 100 and remains the core of Oregon's land use planning system today.

While motivated by Macpherson's visions of economically and ecologically informed land use planning, however, the actual legislation that became SB 100 focused on creating a state-level agency to coordinate planning by *local* authorities rather than immediately establishing statewide land use goals. In an effort to draft a bill that a majority of legislators could support, Macpherson and those who helped him write SB 100 ultimately retained county governments (which are typically conservative and subject to development pressures) as the main plan-creating bodies, while establishing a state-level agency, the Land Conservation and Development Commission (LCDC), and its administrative branch, the Department of Land Conservation and Development (DLCD), to ensure that local plans conformed to statewide goals.

SB 100 delegated the creation of statewide planning goals to the *public*—making it the first task of the newly created DLCD to hold "town hall"–style meetings with ordinary Oregonians across the state to determine what the public wanted as statewide land use goals. Throughout 1974, the tiny staff of the new state planning agency was fully occupied with 76 public meetings and workshops, in which more than 10,000 ordinary Oregonians participated in drafting the state's first 14 planning goals—an often-forgotten but remarkable achievement for a state agency. In more recent decades, critics (and some supporters) of the state land use planning system have accused DLCD of becoming an overreaching, deaf, and bloated state agency—and there is evidence to support such claims. In concept (and, arguably, in practice during its early days), however, the new state agency offered a pioneering system for joining state-level coordinating authority with local, participatory, "grassroots" public goal setting.

When asked in 2009 how he arrived at this model, Macpherson explained that he used as his point of departure the Model Land Development Code developed by Frederick Bosselman and the American Law Institute[6] (see Bosselman and Callies 1972). In the end, McHarg's vision of "design with nature" took something of a backseat in SB 100 to Bosselman's process-centered model of state and local coordination of planning and public participation. Macpherson described Bosselman and Callies's 1972 book *The Quiet Revolution in Land Use Control* as "our Bible, when we were putting [SB 100] together" (Abbott and Howe 1993: 20). In following decades, Bosselman's model code would become the standard "liberal" position on land use planning, and probably could not be described as revolutionary today. In 1973, however, statewide planning authority was viewed with enormous suspicion. Macpherson recalls that in public hearings on SB 100, "We got the weirdos and the wackos saying that it was all a communist plot hatched by the Trilateral Commission." Even then-governor Tom McCall at first took little active interest—

describing such strong state-directed planning as "an idea whose time has not yet come."[7]

McCall was probably right to be doubtful: state intervention in land use planning was so controversial that most legislators ("wackos" or not) did not want to touch it (Abbott and Howe 1993: 34; Walth 1994: 353). Even with political capital and momentum from the 1970 statewide referendum supporting SB 10, passing such a (then) radical bill proved no small task. When he first joined the state legislature in January 1971, Macpherson found no other legislators working on land use issues, and he therefore proposed a joint resolution to study ideas for statewide planning. He was denied funds by the senate president, Democrat John Burns. Macpherson went to Governor Tom McCall's office, where he met with McCall's assistant for governmental relations, Bob Logan. Logan showed more immediate interest than McCall and became a key supporter of an independent task force formed by Macpherson to write a new statewide land use law. Logan provided logistical support and federal funds not controlled by the legislature for the Macpherson action group. The first meeting was held on January 7, 1972.

In the remainder of this chapter we examine some of the political currents that converged to enable the passage of SB 100 some 17 months later, as well as the somewhat fragile political alliance that supported the resulting land use program after the passage of the bill.

Why Oregon? Why 1973?

Oregon has a deserved reputation for innovation in environmental policy and for general environmental consciousness. As described in chapter 1, it is no coincidence that in May of 2008, then-presidential candidate Barack Obama's largest political rally to that date was held in Portland, or that Obama specifically referred to Portland (and, by extension, Oregon) as a model for the nation of enlightened planning, energy, and transportation policy. To take another example, each year the University of Oregon's large and vibrant environmental studies graduate program attracts some of the most talented and committed aspiring environmental leaders from across the nation, many of whom state that they came to Oregon because of its environmentalist reputation. To some extent, Oregon's national environmental reputation that was established in the early 1970s, and expressed in such fictional accounts as Ernest Callenbach's 1975 book *Ecotopia* (in which Oregon is the geographic center of an environmentalist utopia in the Pacific Northwest), both reflected and reinforced real-life social currents in the 1970s—and still does today.

However, popular views that Oregon's unique land use planning system was a product of a culture of environmentalism is at best an incomplete explanation and at worst perpetuates misperceptions about how and why the program emerged. Scholars have conclusively refuted this interpretation (e.g., Abbott and Howe 1993). Instead, as we will describe, Oregon's one-of-a-kind land use planning system was first created for more prosaic economic reasons. Certainly in recent decades environmentalists have played a key role in maintaining and expanding the program. But Oregon's land use system was *not* primarily a creation of the environmental movement. The main link between the creation of Oregon's land use system and the environmental movement lay in the somewhat belated political and public relations boost that the program received from the larger-than-life personality of Oregon's environmentalist-wordsmith governor Tom McCall. Environmentalists in Oregon have put McCall's appealing face and words on political brochures and other forms of public relations supporting the state's land use planning system for decades—much to their benefit. But the near-personality cult that still surrounds McCall contributed to an overemphasis on McCall's role (e.g., Walth 1994) and the role of environmentalism, to the detriment of a fuller understanding of the political genesis of Oregon's unique land use planning system. A more realistic accounting of the historical emergence of Oregon's planning system may go a long way toward understanding both the strengths and the weaknesses of the program (as we discuss more fully in chapter 5).

How, then, do we explain the emergence of Oregon's unique land use planning system in 1973? We posed this question to dozens of key "players" who were directly involved with Oregon's statewide planning program in its early days (fortunately for us, many were quite young at the time and are alive and well today). We quickly found that the short answer to this question is that there is no short answer to this question. However, we did find that there is general consensus on the importance of a number of convergent forces in the politics of Oregon in the early 1970s.

Willamette Valley agriculture

To the extent that there is any single factor that those who were directly involved in the politics of the time agree was a driving force in the passage of SB 100, it was concern about the conversion of agricultural land to nonfarm uses, mostly in western Oregon's moist, agriculturally rich Willamette Valley. As the example of Hector Macpherson (cited at the beginning of this chapter) illustrates, much of the concern centered on conflicts between farming practices and rural-residential land use, as well as increased property taxes on farmers—both viewed as threats to the continued social and economic viability of farming in the Willamette Valley. Partly as a result of this concern, farmers up and down the valley (and elsewhere) took up positions of leadership in local planning even before the creation of the statewide program and later became involved in the state-level politics, where they took on key roles owing to their experience in planning.

Leadership by farmers was critical but only part of the story. Protecting agriculture was of interest to groups other than just farmers, and farmers themselves were by no means of one mind on the subject of land use planning. The drive to protect Willamette Valley agriculture included many who were not farmers themselves. For example, legislator L.B. Day (a Teamster and cannery worker who later played a pivotal role in forging the political compromises needed to pass SB 100) represented Marion County, the state's most important farm county. Day had been head of the cannery workers union, which represented all the people who worked in the food processing plants in the State of Oregon. Day and his cannery union had an interest in farmland protection that was unrelated to being a farmer but was also economically based.

From a more ideological perspective, environmentalists (largely from urban areas) also came to the defense of farmers. At the beginning of this chapter we mentioned the symbolic importance that growth in Charbonneau (a planned golf community on former farmland, located along Interstate 5 just south of Portland) had in shocking many urbanites into the fight to prevent "sprawl." Many came to see protecting farmers and farmland as an environmentalist concern (in some cases, even more so than protecting or creating parkland). A similar alliance of environmentalists and some farmers was critical again decades later with the passage of Ballot Measure 49 in 2007 to restore parts of the planning program lost to a previous property rights ballot measure (see chapter 4).

While alliances of urban, labor, and farming interests have formed in support of Oregon's planning system at critical historical junctures, farmers themselves were far from unanimous in support of land use planning. As Hector Macpherson recalled in 2009, the Grange, which represents smaller farmers, had always opposed land use planning, whereas the Oregon Farm Bureau, which represents large commercial farmers, was initially conflicted but eventually supported preserving farmland through SB 100. "It divided between the people who were actually making a living on the farm and those that were not and wanted farming as a lifestyle type thing," recalled Macpherson. "The people that really wanted to go on as multigenerational farms saw the need [for planning]. But it was the people who couldn't make it in farming and wanted to sell their land for more money that were the opposition, and still are."[8] This division within the farming community continues today and became a weak link in the political alliance for planning in the face of property rights ballot measures in 2000 and 2004 (see chapter 4).

In 1973, Macpherson anticipated this weakness and made major efforts to secure the support of farmers by means that were more prosaic than his pioneering planning system: significant helpings of state largesse for farmers. SB 101, also written and sponsored by Macpherson in 1973, recognized that "farm use zoning . . . substantially limits alternatives to the use of rural land, [and] with the importance of rural lands to the public, justifies incentives and privileges offered to encourage owners of rural lands to hold such lands in exclusive farm use zones."[9] Under SB 101, county tax assessors are directed to give land meeting the definition of farm use a "special assessment." Namely, land in farm use is taxed at the value of the land for farming rather than the value of land for other uses such as residential development. In addition, SB 101 provided "right to farm"–type protections that prohibited local governments from restricting farming practices (due to farm-related noise, dust, odors, etc.). Mike Thorne, a member of the 1973 Senate Committee on Environment and Land Use and chair of the Senate Agriculture Committee, recalls that such "incentives and privileges" for keeping land in farming played a critical role in passage of SB 100:

> I can remember the long hours at the end. I can remember the lobbyists for the forest industry, the lobby interests from the farm community. There was no question that the pressures were building. Hector Macpherson was right. People were moving into the farm community and buying blocks of land. Farmland values were going up, and property taxes were paid on sales price—market value based on sales. That was causing a lot of farmers rightfully a lot of concerns. Suddenly their property tax bill was going up by multiples of double. It was a *big* concern. So, underneath everything was a concern for redefining the basis for how you assess taxes on farm and forest land. That was contained to a great extent in Senate Bill 101 . . . so, what you created was an incentive for those people who probably would not have voted for the bill—and I probably would have been one of those who you would put into that category—[to vote for it]. I don't think the bill would have cleared the committee, and I don't think the Legislature would have passed it had there not been some reason for the very powerful rural farm and forest interests at that time to get on board. So, [SB 101] dampened the pressure that was causing [farmers] to sell property because they couldn't afford to pay the property tax. I think that's as much as anything the reason it finally passed. Sure, Tom McCall would come to our committee and the TV cameras would be there and he would rail, "You've got to get this bill passed." And yes, McCall deserves a tremendous amount of credit because he kept the pressure on. But underneath it all there was a lot of effort to find a way to convince people that it's economically something they could sign up for.[10]

Those involved in the creation of SB 100 and SB 101 called the two bills "companion" legislation, and while historical accounts of the much-celebrated SB 100 have often ignored SB 101, Macpherson described them as being "of equal importance" (Macpherson 2010). As Macpherson later recounted bluntly, SB 101 provided "all the goodies I could think of"[11] to encourage farmers to keep their land in farm use.

As described in chapter 4, SB 101 would later become a crux of much debate about the fairness of Oregon's land use planning system. According to property rights advocates, rural landowners whose land had been zoned for farm use suffered a reduction of property value that merited compensation. According to planning advocates (including Macpherson), SB 101 already provided compensation for the lost option to sell the land for nonfarm uses by reducing owners' property taxes. In 1973, however, Macpherson, Thorne, and others mainly saw tax benefits and farming protections in SB 101 as part of a political "deal" to secure the passage of the planning system contained in SB 100. Without these specific guarantees to support farmers, it is likely that Oregon's planning system in its present form would not exist.

As we discuss later in this chapter, following the passage of SB 100 supporters of the planning system made deliberate, strategic choices to boost support for the planning program from other economic interests as well—including homebuilders, large commercial forestry, and industry. From its creation to its maturation as possibly the nation's most celebrated state planning system, those who engineered the program understood that under the hood, the planning program needed an engine of economic support. As we discuss in chapter 4, it is no coincidence that by 2000 and 2004, when the planning program nearly collapsed in the face of property rights activism, key elements of the economic alliance that once powered the planning program had fallen away, leaving the program politically exposed. This point bears emphasis because much has been made of the "visionary" environmental dimensions of the program, possibly placing too much emphasis on the fickle currents of charismatic political leadership.

Leadership

If supporters of Oregon's planning system later lost sight of the need to maintain support from key economic sectors, this may have ironically resulted partly from the ability to rely on the power of the truly extraordinary political leadership that characterized the program in its early years. As Oregon historian William Robbins observes, "The late 1960s and the early 1970s brought together in the Oregon Legislature a remarkable—*incredible*—cadre of talent, of far-sighted people, who were interested in protecting farm and forest land, to countering sprawl . . . people from both sides of the aisle, Republicans and Democrats."[12]

Whether or not excessive reliance on political charisma may have spelled trouble for Oregon's planning system in later years, to say that Oregon's planning system was created by colorful and larger-than-life personalities scarcely seems adequate. The near-mythic role of then-governor Tom McCall is well known in Oregon and beyond, but McCall was only the most prominent of a group of exceptional leaders—some shared aspects of McCall's dynamism and charisma, and others worked more quietly but displayed no less exceptional political leadership. In the latter category, we have already described the pivotal role of the cerebral and gentlemanly but ambitious and resourceful Republican senator and dairy farmer Hector Macpherson. While history has given McCall the lion's share of the credit, it was without question Macpherson's intellectual ambition and steadfast political resolve that made SB 100 the pioneering bill it was and successfully brought it to the floor of the legislature.

Macpherson's patient and meticulous legislative engineering was perfectly complemented by Tom McCall's passionate and poetic capacity to inspire the Oregon public. Over the decades since the passage of SB 100, an enormous amount has been written and said about McCall, and there is little more we can say about the talents of a man who warned Oregonians against a "buffalo-hunter mentality" inserting "cancerous cells of unmentionable ugliness into our rural landscape." When McCall made such statements, it probably helped his credibility that he himself was from conservative Central Oregon rather than liberal Portland or the Willamette Valley. The only other note we might append to the McCall legacy is to emphasize that he not only possessed enormous oratorical talents but also possessed the capacity to concentrate his skills and energy at critical moments. During the struggle to move SB 100 through the state legislature, McCall joined Project Foresight, a two-year planning and design task force carried out by the Willamette Valley Environmental Protection and Development Planning Council. The project hired famed California landscape architect Lawrence Halprin to develop planning scenarios that, when released in a fall 1972 report, gave McCall powerful rhetorical tools that he wielded masterfully to build public and legislative support for the 1973 legislative session (Robbins 2004: 289). As Macpherson describes McCall's role, "Tom was the publicity man for the whole movement." In McCall, "we had a fella who could make speeches—boy!—they were great. He wasn't a nuts-and-bolts man. That's what my job was. But McCall was the salesman; [for example] his 'grasping wastrels of the land'! He was a real poet."[13]

If success has many fathers, several other men in addition to Macpherson and McCall could rightly claim paternity to the successful SB 100. Macpherson was the architect of the bill, but as a Republican in a state senate dominated by Democrats (18 to 12 in the 1973 session) he could not chair the Senate Committee on Environment and Land Use. That job went to the liberal Portland Democrat Ted Hallock. "Brilliant," "frenetic," "domineering," "volcanic," and "profane" are only a few adjectives that have been used to describe Hallock. A heavily decorated World War II flyer, radio and newspaper journalist, art aficionado, talented jazz drummer, and a nonstop talker, Hallock earned a reputation during 20 years of service in the Oregon legislature as a formidable political force. Hallock poured his enormous energy into SB 100—according to Macpherson, with "every nerve aquiver" at each step in the legislative process. Describing his own role, Hallock observed, "Hector [Macpherson] was interested in only one thing, the actual nobility of the bill, and the language of the bill. I could give a shit about that. I was in it to *pass* the bill."[14] "Hector is the father of state land use planning in Oregon. He deserves the primary credit. But I was the obstetrician!"[15] As a later governor of Oregon, John Kitzhaber, wrote in Hallock's obituary in 2007, "Indeed he was [the obstetrician]. The bill drew fire from almost every quarter and the chances of success seemed most unlikely. But Hallock proved to be a master in the legislative process, using, in his words, 'powers to embarrass, shame or con or beat the ascendant power of the legislature for the positive good of the state.'" Kitzhaber concluded that SB 100 "would never have been enacted into law without the commitment and perseverance of Hallock."[16]

As Oregon historian William Robbins has observed, a remarkable cadre of individuals made the controversial SB 100 into law, and it would be impossible within the limited space of this book to do justice to all the significant contributors to the passage of SB 100. However, we must mention at least two others before concluding simply that the leadership displayed in 1973 was indeed exceptional. No story of SB 100 could be complete without mentioning the incomparable L.B. Day. In its darkest hour when the bill looked dead, Macpherson and Hallock turned the lobbying campaign for the bill over to Day—the tough-as-nails ex-Teamster and cannery worker-turned-conservationist Republican politician. As Home Builders Association lobbyist Fred VanNatta recalls, his friend Day was "a bully."[17] Macpherson appointed Day as head of an ad hoc committee to hammer the bill into language that could win passage. After being shut in a meeting room with the hulking ex-Teamster, VanNatta observed, "He was loud, aggressive, and belligerent, threatening . . . by the time he's done, you figured, 'Well, I better ask for the bare minimum.' And that's what we got" (cited in Walth 1994: 360). Specifically, what SB 100's skeptics "got" was retention of counties (rather than the originally proposed "Councils of Governments" that would have portended a regional approach) as the main planning bodies, and the removal of designation of "Areas of Critical State Concern" where state authority would supersede local decision making (we discuss the recent ongoing politics of areas of critical state concern in chapter 7). Yet, without Day's "bullying" in the ad hoc committee, SB 100 would not have survived in any form recognizable as Oregon's planning system today.

Last but far from least, if success has many fathers, we emphasize that SB 100 had at least one vitally important mother as well. Former representative Nancie Fadeley, a Democrat who represented Springfield, recalls that when she received SB 100 in the House Committee on Environment and Land Use that she chaired, senate cosponsor Ted Hallock implored Fadeley, "You can't change a comma. You have to get the house to pass that bill *exactly* the way we sent it to you."[18] Hallock feared that if the state house changed any language in the bill, opponents would have another chance in a conference committee to take the whole bill down. Fadeley was a veteran political player, and land use was close to her heart. She had asked to chair the Committee on Environment and changed its name to the Committee on Environment and Land Use specifically so she could handle land use legislation. Her decision to accept Hallock's unusual request represented a rare ceding of political turf for a shared goal and sealed its passage. Fadeley recalls it was not an easy decision, because it required something of a leap of faith. Unlike any other legislation she had handled, by giving goal-setting and plan-making powers to the public and the counties it was not clear what the bill would actually *do*. Fadeley recalls, "I was very aware of the political land mines that lay ahead. I was uneasy."[19] Yet Fadeley worked tirelessly to secure the house votes needed to pass the bill, and succeeded—with a larger majority than in Hallock and Macpherson's senate. Fadeley, a leader of the League of Women Voters, also noted with pride that although women legislators were a small minority in 1973, *all* women legislators—from both parties, in both houses of the legislature—supported the bill.

Those who directly participated in the passage of SB 100 hold differing views about how much emphasis to place on the role of leadership (vs., e.g., economics) in explaining the passage of the bill. To be clear, the matter of *whether* extraordinary leadership was present is not in question. Tom McCall is certainly proof: how many state-level politicians in relatively lightly populated states that are somewhat peripheral to the national economy have had entire books written and video documentaries produced celebrating their lives and the legislation that they helped to create (e.g., Walth 1994; Abbott, Howe, and Adler 1994)? Rather, the question is, how far does the presence of these extraordinary personalities go in explaining the success of a piece of legislation as controversial as SB 100 in relation to other factors such as the underlying economics or broader social and political factors? We contemplate this question further in the concluding chapter of this book. Next, however, we consider several other contributing social factors, including the newly emergent, nationwide environmental movement of the early 1970s.

Environmentalism

If the degree of influence of environmentalism on the passage of SB 100 is open to question, the fact that Oregon was at the cutting edge of a vibrant national environmental movement in the late 1960s and early 1970s is not. As former state representative Nancie Fadeley observed in 2009, "Those were wonderful years for the environment." Fadeley goes further, suggesting that this broad environmental movement of the time played a role in the creation of Oregon's land use planning: "I feel extremely lucky, extremely blessed, that I was in a position to be able to affect land use planning in Oregon *at that time*, in the 1970s. And in *Oregon*. I don't think we could do today what we did then."[20] When we asked other leaders in the creation of Oregon's land use planning laws whether the environmental movement influenced the creation of the state's land use planning system, the response was more mixed.

No one can doubt, however, that it was a remarkable time in the history of ideas about the environment. If one thinks of the passage of SB 10 in 1969 and SB 100 in 1973 as marking the birth of Oregon's statewide land use planning system, these dates will be meaningful to those familiar with the history of environmentalism in the nation, and in Oregon. The publication of Rachel Carson's book *Silent Spring* (1962) raised awareness of the hazards of pesticides and, more generally, called into question the technological optimism of the post–World War II era. Paul Ehrlich's book *The Population Bomb* (1968) raised concerns about population growth and resource scarcity. In 1969 the Cuyahoga River in Ohio burst into flames and an oil well off the coast of Santa Barbara, California, blew out, dumping 235,000 gallons of oil on 30 miles of beaches. The resulting national mood of environmental alarm spurred arguably the most important period of federal environmental legislation in American history. The National Environmental Protection Act passed in 1969. In 1970, the Clean Air Act passed, along with the creation of the U.S. Environmental Protection Agency (and the celebration of the first Earth Day). In 1972, Congress passed a veritable flood of water-related and other laws, including the Clean Water Act, the Coastal Zone Management Act, and the Marine Mammal Protection Act. In 1973, the passage of the Endangered Species Act topped the environmental agenda. And momentum was building in Congress for a national land use policy.

This flurry of federal environmental activity had subtle but significant influences on Oregon's planning politics. Representative Nancie Fadeley recalls that in 1971, "I was in Washington, DC, for the National Council of State Legislatures. Periodically somebody would come in and say, 'I'm from the president's office and we want you to know that we are supporting land use planning, and there will be money to help you in implementing or preparing for it.' That was *Nixon*!"[21] And in fact, federal support for planning did help make the drafting of SB 100 possible. As described earlier in this chapter, state senator Hector Macpherson had been denied state funds to study and draft land use legislation. Instead, he received small but critical amounts of federal money from then-governor Tom McCall's assistant, Bob Logan. Logan's support outside the state budget enabled Macpherson "to do whatever I wanted," "flying below the radar" of other legislators who very likely would have complicated the committee's work (Macpherson 2010). Macpherson's informal committee consisted of 18 knowledgeable persons he invited personally. Macpherson was the chair and the only legislator. On April 4, 1972, the *Statesman Journal* newspaper (the main newspaper in the state's capitol, Salem) observed that the committee did not require the "extensive education" that formal legislative committees typically required, and it lacked the usual political "grandstanding." Had federal money not been available to support the committee, Oregon's planning laws might have been quite different.

If the 1960s and early 1970s marked something of a high-water mark for national environmental legislation, Oregon had its own remarkable environmental momentum during this period. In 1962, Tom McCall (at the time a television reporter) produced and hosted a hard-hitting, award-winning television documentary called *Pollution in Paradise* about the Willamette River, galvanizing public opposition to industrial pollution. In 1968, Governor McCall signed into law regulations that produced dramatic improvements in water quality—an achievement that historian William Robbins observes earned Oregon "national stature" well before the federal Clean Water Act.[22] In 1967, the Oregon legislature proposed and Governor McCall (with much drama, of course) beat back strong opposition to pass a bill that to this day guarantees public access to the state's exquisite beaches. In 1971, the most prominent product of a legislative session dubbed the "ecology session" was the Oregon Deposit Law, better known as the Bottle Bill, which reduced litter by requiring beverage containers sold in Oregon to be returnable with a minimum refund value. The 1971 Oregon Bottle Bill was the first of its type in the nation and the model for similar laws in at least eight other states. It was conceived of and pushed through the state legislature by a single, persistent unelected citizen. Thus, as William Robbins stresses, "Senate Bill 100 doesn't stand alone," and "it's very critical to look at [the creation of Oregon's land use planning system] in a larger context."[23] As citizen activist and biologist Bob Bacon recalled in 2007, the time period in Oregon was significant: "There was a feeling that one could do things, and have a cause, and be effective in it."[24]

There is no question that an electrifying sense of possibility for environmentalists and other activists permeated the air in the late 1960s and early 1970s, but the links between this air of political vitality and the creation of the state's land use planning system are not necessarily easy to pin down. Most of the key political figures in the creation of the land use legislation were farmers and Republicans, not environmentalists. Tom McCall was possibly the only major figure in the passage of SB 100 who could rightly be described as an ideological environmentalist, and he became active in the battle for its passage only after the bill was well along in the legislative process. Today, some who were active in the creation and passage of SB 100 doubt that the broader environmental movement of the time played a major role.[25]

When we asked about the perception by some that Oregon's unique land use planning system was part of the state's environmental movement of the 1960s and 1970s, Hector Macpherson replied, "I try to disabuse them of that idea," because the motivation for the state's land use legislation originated from the farm community. However, Macpherson went on to observe that, "by that time there were quite a number of people who were environmentally interested in [the land use planning] process, so it was easy to pull people in." Macpherson contacted Maradel Gale, then-president of the Oregon Environmental Council, to ask for her support for SB 100—and got it. Macpherson recognized the value of support from the environmentalist community and used it to get land use planning passed into law.

Similarly, when we asked Mike Thorne, a member of the Senate Committee on Environment and Land Use during the passage of SB 100, whether the culture of environmentalism affected the legislation, he replied: "No, no. It was strongly economic. No question about that." On further reflection, however, Thorne described what he saw as a subtle but important influence:

> It wasn't that it was an overpowering kind of sudden movement to environmental values. But there clearly was [some influence]. This is where [Tom] McCall gets some credit. He, you know—cleaning up the Willamette River, pressure on the wood products industry, the paper and pulp people—it [environmentalism] was real. I made a brochure for my

campaign, and the front picture of me on the brochure—and this was my main political leave-behind handout—was a picture of me kneeling in one of my farm fields, and I've got some dirt in my hand and I'm sort of pouring it back down on the ground and I'm dressed in jeans and a Western hat. And there's a comment about, "We need to make sure that this [land] is available for my family in future generations," or something like that. So there was a subtle connection between land use planning and environmental issues and how we use our resources. It was on my brochure. I don't think I consciously tried to do that. I wasn't trying to make a powerful environmental statement. It was just a fact of life. Generations need to use this [land]. And we need to make sure we're taking care of it so they can. It was kind of a subtle message in my brochure. . . . So, [the link between environmentalism and land use planning] is a fair point.[26]

Another way to think about the role of the environmental movements (nationally and in the state) in fostering Oregon's key land use planning legislation of the late 1960s and early 1970s is to consider how land use planning legislation might have fared in a different political climate. As historian William Robbins points out, "The political mood swings from liberal to conservative in national politics, and Oregon pretty much reflects that. Certainly after the election of Ronald Reagan in 1980 and the emphasis on freeing up the market became popular, and of course that's the big enemy of any kind of coherent, cohesive land use planning for livability and quality of life that McCall talked about."[27] Indeed, prior to Ballot Measures 7 and 37 (in 2000 and 2004, respectively—the subject of chapter 4), it was in 1982, when Reagan's conservative ideological revolution was revving up, that Oregon's land use planning system had its closest brush with repeal—only to be rescued by the passionate oratory of the then-dying Tom McCall. Thus, while direct links between the environmental movements of the late 1960s and early 1970s and the creation of Oregon's land use planning system may be somewhat difficult to pin down, it may be safe to say that the special political culture of that time was more conducive to legislative efforts for land use protection than any period before, or possibly since.

Nonpartisanship and a "Different"
Kind of Republican

Another aspect of the politics of the late 1960s and early 1970s in Oregon that played a role in the passage of SB 100 (all key "players" of the time agree on this point) was the relative absence of partisan political division compared to today. In particular, there was a strong streak of liberalism in the Republican Party in Oregon (as in the Republican Party nationally) that is relatively rare today. Although today we often speak of aspiring to "bipartisanship," those who were involved in politics at the time of the passage of SB 100 describe the political climate in terms that may be more aptly described as *non*partisanship, in the sense that it was not unusual for alliances and coalitions to form not around party affiliation but around the ideas and principles behind proposed policies, aided by a political culture of personal collegiality that is all but missing today. In 2009, Walt Daggett, the former secretary of the senate and a key legislative aide to Senator Ted Hallock in 1973, recalled that during the era of the passage of SB 100, "When a potentially controversial issue came up, legislators [of both parties] got together first and talked. Individually, in pairs, whatever. And Chuck's Steakhouse! More legislation was done right there than any place else in Salem [the state capitol]. That's where the real work was done. It was done by people who couldn't care whether you were a Republican, or a Communist. If you were sitting there and you had a vote, we wanted to talk."[28]

Mike Thorne remembers the relatively collegial political culture of the time this way:

> There were coalitions of ideals and principles as opposed to coalitions of party. . . . To me that was the fun of being around the legislature during the years I was there. . . . We'd get together and say, "hey guys, this thing isn't working. Let's get it back on track." Maybe go down and have dinner and a glass of wine or a beer and talk it over. You don't see *any* of that today. *None* of that. I can remember going to the Hindquarter [restaurant] in Salem, and there's Tom McCall at the table with a bunch of folks. I mean it was just, after the day was done, you got together and you talked about it. That doesn't happen today . . . you've got people so polarized now that they think it's a sin if they

even talk to the other guys. Back then problems were approached from the perspective of ideals and philosophy and principles as opposed to which party you were a part of.

Detailed analysis of the reasons for the changed political culture today is beyond the scope of this book, but one aspect of the different political culture of the late 1960s and early 1970s that bears examination for understanding the success of SB 10 and SB 100 was the strong presence of a moderate wing of the Republican Party that many in Oregon say is nearly extinct today. Certainly hard-right ideological Republicans have always been a part of the political culture of the state, then and now. However, moderate and even "Green" Republicans such as Tom McCall, Hector Macpherson, and L.B. Day were a significant political force at the time. To be sure, McCall and Macpherson (and others such as Oregon governor Mark Hatfield and U.S. senator Bob Packwood) were not necessarily favored Republicans within their party even at the time—but they nevertheless were present and often held key positions of power. For example, Macpherson describes how in 1973 Democratic senator Ted Hallock, chair of the Senate Committee on Environment and Land Use, recognized that "I was a different kind of Republican" with whom even a Portland liberal such as Hallock could work productively. This kind of cross-party alliance was key to the passage of SB 100: three Republicans (Macpherson, George Wingard, and Victor Atiyeh—a later governor of Oregon) and three Democrats (Hallock, Thorne, and Jack Ripper) on the Senate Committee on Environment and Land Use voted to send SB 100 to the floor of the Senate. The lone "nay" vote was Democrat John Burns from Portland, who complained that the bill was too "watered down."[29] In the committee, support for SB 100 was more consistent among Republicans.

In the legislature as a whole, support among Republicans was also widespread. SB 100 was passed by a Democratic-controlled state house and senate and signed into law by a Republican governor. While the overall vote in the legislature in support of the bill was stronger among Democrats than among Republicans, *the majority of Republicans in both legislative chambers supported the bill*: 58 percent of senate Republicans voted for the bill, while 56 percent of house Republicans voted in favor. Support among Democrats was stronger, with 69 percent of senate Democrats and 76 percent of house Democrats voting in favor. The most outspoken opponents came from both sides of the aisle—for example (as described above), Democratic senator John Burns from Portland requested an entry in the *Senate Journal* noting his dissatisfaction with the "watered-down" bill, while Republican senator L.W. Newbry from conservative Jackson County requested that the *Journal* note his opposition to the transfer of "unwarranted legislative powers to an appointed board."[30] Nevertheless, in both chambers of the legislature and among both parties, support was strong. Notably, with these margins of support, SB 100 would have passed even had the legislature been controlled by Republicans (albeit with a narrower margin of victory).

Thus, unlike today, when support or opposition to environmental bills often falls along strict party lines, the environment in general and land use planning in particular simply were not the partisan issues they are today. That spirit of nonpartisanship on these issues did not, however, survive much past the 1970s, as we will see in chapter 4.

Californication

In July 1982, former governor Tom McCall and then-governor Victor Atiyeh stood by the interstate highway in the high, rugged Siskiyou Mountains at the border of Oregon and California. A media event had been organized by Atiyeh to undo what he saw as a rigid antigrowth image that Oregon acquired under McCall's leadership, most memorably summarized in McCall's famous 1971 "visit but don't stay" quip (see chapter 1). The assumption on both sides of the border had long been that McCall directed his comment mainly at Californians, who made up the largest group of migrants to the state. The sign marking entry to Oregon from California read, "Welcome to Oregon, Enjoy Your Visit." Atiyeh interpreted the phrase "Enjoy Your Visit" as an unsubtle hint that Californians were not welcome to stay. In front of TV cameras, Atiyeh covered the offending words. McCall, as former governor, had been invited as a matter of protocol, and Atiyeh offered McCall an opportunity to speak "at the funeral of his own prose" (Walth 1994: 7).

To the consternation of the mannerly Atiyeh, and the delight of reporters, McCall did not repent: "There's been a lot of bad-mouthing about 'visit but don't stay.' It served its purpose. We were saying visit but don't stay because Oregon, queen bee though she is, is not yet ready for the swarm. I think you'll all be just as sick as I am if you find [Oregon] is nothing but a hungry hussy throwing herself at every stinking smokestack that's offered." At that moment, it is possible that a few of the cars and trucks roaring by McCall and Atiyeh on the freeway bore tangible evidence that the crude analogy that McCall was making had occurred to the public as well. A popular bumper sticker of that era read: "Don't Californicate Oregon."[31]

Today the story is old and well known in Oregon: The disillusioned and disaffected Californian, typically from an upscale professional job in Southern California or Silicon Valley, flees the traffic, crime, drugs, and pollution of an overdeveloped urban California landscape for green and peaceful Oregon. With equity from their homes in the (at the time) overheated California real estate market, the Californian can afford relative luxury in Oregon. A 5-, 10-, or 40-acre rural "ranchette," a border collie, and a four-wheel drive vehicle are de rigueur. The paradox, of course, is that if all urban refugees in California (and elsewhere) had the same idea, soon the very quality of life that attracted the migrant in the first place would be lost. Traffic, pollution, crime, and so on, would follow. Oregon would be Californicated.

As described in chapter 1, this caricatured story has much historical and demographic validity. Development pressure from California refugees sparked a huge rally of support for stronger growth control in Oregon.[32] However, with respect to the passage of land use planning legislation in Oregon, the cultural "story" of California in-migration and the resulting perceived despoliation of virgin Oregon was possibly of greater importance politically than actual "facts" alone. By the early 1970s Oregonians developed a loathing for "California-style" growth that bordered on a cultural mania. This ongoing abhorrence of things Californian has been observed for decades and has been described as sometimes "zealot-like" and "vitriolic."[33] Stories of California in-migrants in the 1980s having to quickly change their license plates or risk physical harm were legion (e.g., see Brown 1995).

More significantly, the fear of California-style growth gave planning legislation political traction that it might otherwise have lacked. The growth leviathan to the south gave Oregonians, and their landscape, a kind of special difference that they cherished—and still do. For a state with a very diminutive identity relative to the economic and cultural giant next door, California became the "other" from which Oregon could form its own identity. Like Canadians who work hard at being "not" the United States, Oregonians found identity in being not California. Also like Canada, Oregon's economy is dwarfed by its southern neighbor, and its economic dependence on California drives Oregonians to defend a non-California identity all the more vigorously. Responding to anti-California stridency, a native Oregonian living in Southern California put it this way in a 1979 op-ed article in the *Los Angeles Times*: "Oregon suffers from an inferiority complex. . . . it is California, the flashy neighbor, that everyone wants to see and move to. It is very humiliating to live right next to California and be constantly ignored. In order to give itself an identity in the national imagination, Oregon has conceived a kind of reverse psychology, 'less is more' approach. By publicizing the fact that it has little development and consequently none of the problems that come with development, Oregon hopes to achieve national attention."[34] Such a perspective would surely make many Oregonians bristle, then and now. But it is far from the only interpretation of Oregon's distinctive cultural and political identity. In describing Oregon's emerging land use planning system in 1978, a Los Angeles–based reporter gave this more charitable account:

> Oregon, in its oddly modest way, has been ahead of us [Californians] in land use planning for more than half a century. Its beaches were called a public highway in 1913,[35] opening the whole coast for [public] access. Its state parks are greened and groomed like no others in all the United States. Its 1973 act to establish a Land Conservation and Development Commission was only following historic footsteps. . . .
>
>   The Director of California's Office of Planning and Research . . . admits Oregonians have a peculiar awareness of their place, an appreciation of land and land problems much stronger than Californians. Odd alliances of liberal Republicans and conservative Democrats emerge in Oregon to find grounds for agreement on policy toward development and conservation.[36]

Whatever the psychology—a sense of inferiority, superiority, or simply difference—there is no question that Oregon's strong sense of cultural and political identity has formed through a complex dance with its giant and sometimes overbearing neighbor to the south. As Tom McCall wrote describing the passage of SB 100, "Undoubtedly, the prospect of Oregon experiencing population growth like that which Southern California underwent in the 50's and 60's, with its attendant problems of sprawl, congestion, and burgeoning development, was the principal force in turning Oregonians' attention to the issue of growth" (McCall 1974: 4). By the early 1970s, legislation that could be said to respond to the challenges of growth from California and elsewhere, while surpassing California and other states in terms of innovative governance, fit the pioneering, if quirky, political identity that Oregon cultivated and cherished. SB 100 unquestionably fit the "Oregon" style. It certainly did not hurt Oregon's land use advocates to point out that their proposals would help Oregon be "not like" California.

1000 Friends and a Fragile Alliance

When Governor McCall signed SB 100 into law on May 29, 1973, arguably the hardest work for Oregon's land use planning advocates still lay ahead. The bill itself contained no specific land use goals, and the first task of the new Land Conservation and Development Commission (LCDC) was to solicit public input from across the state to establish the goals—an enormously ambitious task. Moreover, the widespread noncompliance with SB 10, passed into law four years earlier, showed that the passage of state-level planning requirements is no guarantee that local plans will be forthcoming, or that these plans will necessarily conform to statewide goals once established. Although SB 100, unlike SB 10, created LCDC for this purpose, there was still no model for how to use this new statewide planning apparatus to create effective local plans. As SB 100 architect Hector Macpherson noted in 2009, although he had used the American Law Institute's Model Code for land use planning as his point of departure, "nobody had ever tried it before. In fact I'm not sure it was even feasible the way it was [written]."[37] In short, there was no blueprint for how to translate the ambitious objectives of SB 100 into an effective, viable state-level land use planning system coordinating the plans of hundreds of city and county governments while establishing and enforcing statewide goals. McCall and others were immediately and justifiably concerned that the new law would drift, becoming meaningless ink on paper.

In 1974, two extraordinary things happened that would put these fears to rest, at least for a time. First, the Department of Land Conservation and Development (DLCD, the administrative arm of LCDC) initiated a remarkable participatory public process that adopted the state's first 14 land use planning goals on December 27 of that year. Under the director-ship of Arnold Cogan, the 10-person staff of DLCD climbed into two vans in late 1973 and spent the next 15 months holding public meetings across the state. "We sat around big tables and we would just ask people what they liked about this state," Cogan recalled. "People told us these meetings were unlike any public meeting they had ever attended. We got applause at the end of these meetings."[38] More than 10,000 people attended these meetings, and citizens flooded DLCD with thousands of letters and phone calls. Cogan and DLCD established 14 goals to guide local planners in creating comprehensive plans for counties, cities, and towns. As reported in the *High Country News*, Cogan and other early visionaries hoped to "create the ideal Oregon, a place where small towns could remain small, urban areas would hum with efficiency, and farms and forests would surround cities in great ribbons of green. Within the 14 original goals are obvious nods to interest groups. . . . Everyone got a piece of the pie."[39] Perhaps most important, this remarkable public engagement campaign gave ordinary Oregonians a sense of genuine ownership of the planning program, making citizens a full partner in the emerging alliance for planning. In chapter 5 we suggest that the state later failed to nurture this critical public partnership—with grave results.

Also in 1974, however, a unique organization that would play a key role in overseeing the implementation and enforcement of these goals began to take form. This organization had roots in a seemingly unlikely place: deeply conservative Klamath County, where rancher Allen Bateman got fed up with what he saw as confusion and ineptitude by local officials. "You couldn't find a lawyer who knew a damn thing about land use. Oh, he'd take your money all right, but then you'd have to tell him what book to go to," Bateman told the *Eugene (OR) Register-Guard* in 1978.

"After spending a lot of money and a lot of time, I decided we needed professional people who knew the law."[40] Bateman, himself a Californian who fled to Oregon in 1961, was concerned that other Californians were ruining his adopted state: "A lot of people who are trying to subdivide Oregon got their PhDs in San Diego and then kept moving north. They are pretty sophisticated people. They go to a tiny county or city government or even to Salem, and they are hard to resist. We need someone on the other side who can keep them in line."

In the early years of Oregon's planning system, that someone was essentially one person: Henry Richmond, a young lawyer born in Yakima, Washington, who earned a law degree from the University of Oregon. As a law student, Richmond had incorporated the Ralph Nader–inspired Oregon Student Public Interest Research Group and gained experience with land use issues. In 1974, Richmond traversed the state with Bateman organizing the group 1000 Friends of Oregon (so named as a fundraising promotion to collect $1,000 each from 1,000 donors). In August of that year, Richmond wrote to Governor McCall stating, "We are convinced that Oregon now needs a statewide, full-time, professionally staffed citizen organization whose sole purpose is to urge state and local bodies of government to make good land use planning decisions. The organization would also be capable of seeking judicial review of issues dealing with proper administration of land use laws."[41] McCall responded with characteristic enthusiasm, endorsing the creation of 1000 Friends of Oregon in January 1975 and joining its board of directors.

1000 Friends of Oregon became the only single-purpose public interest law firm in the country, monitoring and advocating solely for effective implementation of SB 100. Beginning in January 1975, immediately after LCDC adopted its first 14 statewide goals, the 1000 Friends of Oregon staff (which initially consisted of 31-year-old Richmond and one secretary) emerged as an effective legal partner and watchdog, ensuring that LCDC properly implemented the state's new land use law (and, as with Oregon's land use program itself, Oregon's 1000 Friends model inspired creation of similar programs across the country, including 1000 Friends of Florida, 1000 Friends of Maryland, 1000 Friends of Iowa, and 1000 Friends of Washington).[42] As 1000 Friends of Oregon grew in size and budget (by 1992 it had a 22-person staff and a budget of $2 million),[43] its lawyers and planners played key roles in shaping legal precedents and the implementation of the state's planning laws to ensure compliance with statewide land use goals. In the first years after the passage of SB 100 and the adoption of statewide goals in 1975, some of Oregon's cities and counties challenged the theory that Oregon could enforce a mandate for planning and compliance with statewide goals. LCDC went to court time after time and, with attorneys and planners from 1000 Friends of Oregon at its side, "invariably won."[44]

The image of 1000 Friends of Oregon as a near-invincible legal heavyweight became something of a political liability in later years. But the Friends were too savvy to rely solely on courtroom muscle: Richmond and his organization also deliberately cultivated a broad alliance spanning a range of economic and ideological interests that provided the state's planning system with an underlying political support structure that played a crucial role in maintaining Oregon's planning system intact for three decades. From its early days, Richmond emphasized that 1000 Friends could not be simply anti-development; the group had to find ways to meet the needs of people and the economy as well as the environment. This philosophy was reflected in the composition of the 1000 Friends board of directors, which since its early days has included Republicans and Democrats, developers, and representatives of utilities and industry — something the *Los Angeles Times* described in 1978 as "one of the Oregon ecumenical marvels."[45]

Richmond also set a distinctive political style for his organization. In addition to 1000 Friends' "hard" tactics in the courtroom, the group embraced "soft" political diplomacy to convert likely adversaries into allies. In 1992, Richmond stated that "arts of persuasion are much more important than arts of litigation"[46] and described his group's efforts to work creatively to meet the needs, for example, of homebuilders and developers within the guidelines set by the state's planning laws. The president of the Home Builders Association of metropolitan Portland described how Richmond broke down distrust among his group's members, producing a potent political alliance between 1000 Friends and home builders that made political leaders' "eyes get big."[47] With no effective, organized opposition until the late 1980s (as we discuss in chapter 4), this pincer movement of hard legal tactics combined with a "soft" political diplomacy made

1000 Friends of Oregon into a dominant political player—according to the *Portland Business Journal*, "a powerful statewide force functioning like a shadow government in the land-use arena."[48]

Before concluding this chapter, we briefly review some of the pillars of this "shadow government"—the multitiered alliance built deliberately by 1000 Friends (partly as described to us by Henry Richmond in 2009).[49] This structure held fast for several decades, but later shifts in underlying economic and social conditions in Oregon made the alliance spearheaded by 1000 Friends more fragile. As we discuss in chapter 5, the virtual crumbling of some of these pillars by the early 2000s helps to explain the significant weakening and vulnerability of the state's land use planning system in that decade.

Agriculture

As described earlier, commercial farmers (particularly in the rich Willamette Valley) provided the major initial impetus for the creation of statewide planning in Oregon. Farmers who wanted to continue making their living from the land remained a key part of the alliance that supported the newly created Land Conservation and Development Commission and 1000 Friends of Oregon in upholding the new statewide planning laws.[50] While Oregon is known nationally as a timber-producing state, it also has a strong agricultural sector, and in the 1970s many farmers were making good livelihoods that appeared threatened—with fully a third of Willamette Valley farmland lost to development between 1950 and 1974.[51] After the creation of Oregon's land use planning system, the loss was nearly stopped, with a reduction of less than 5 percent of farmland in the population-dense Willamette Valley between 1974 and 2007.[52] In addition to significantly slowing development in farm areas and providing reduced farm-value tax assessment and right-to-farm protections, the new land use law gave farmers confidence about the future that allowed them to make capital investments in their farms and to purchase or lease new farmland at farm-value prices. As the state's land use planning system survived multiple repeal campaigns in the 1970s and 1980s, confidence in the state's farmland protection grew and the Oregon Farm Bureau (which had wavered before deciding to support SB 100 in

1973) and commercial farmers generally became among the strongest proponents of the land use program, taking some of the burden of advocacy for the state's land use planning system off the shoulders of urban and environmentalist supporters.

Forestry

Although some individual forest companies supported successful statewide ballot measures targeting Oregon's planning system in the early and mid-2000s, the state's large commercial forestry industry (since 1938, the largest in the country) has, as a whole, long supported the state's land use planning system. The forest industry was not central in the push to create the land use planning system in the early 1970s, but it became an important supporter (e.g., in opposing efforts to repeal the land use planning system in 1976, 1978, and 1982). Ward Armstrong, the chief Oregon lobbyist for timber giant Weyerhaeuser (and a member of the L.B. Day ad hoc task force for SB 100 in 1973) recalled in 2009 that the reason much of the timber industry supported the planning system was simple: it helped the industry grow trees.[53] Oregon west of the Cascades has some of the best timberland in the world, and in the 1970s and the next several decades the large timber companies had one goal: to produce lumber and plywood. Most industrial forest land is in remote areas where opportunities for land development are limited. To the extent such development occurs, nontimber land use generally creates more costs than benefits: even a handful of residential parcels can create conflicts with commercial timber practices (noise, aesthetic issues, spraying, logging vehicles on public roads, etc.). Because Oregon's planning system kept timber areas and residential areas separate, most of the forestry industry viewed it as a good thing. In addition, regulations that prevent smaller private forest owners from developing their land helps maintain a source of timber supply, as well as a buffer between large timber production and residential areas.[54] Moreover, much of the discussion leading to the creation of Oregon's land use planning system occurred in mid-1972 when the state's first-in-the-nation Forest Practices Act went into effect to protect the environment on private forestland, and at a time when the federal government was creating a veritable flood of environmental laws that frightened foresters. Weyerhaeuser's Armstrong recalls that supporting state land use planning while pressing, in exchange, for minimal state interventions in forest practices seemed simply "good strategy." The general position of large forest companies, as represented by the Oregon Forest Industries Council, remains much the same today.[55]

Industry

When the recession of the early 1980s kicked the legs out from under Oregon's once-dominant farm and timber economies, high-tech industry became a major player in Oregon (the so-called Silicon Forest). Even with the recovery of the mid-1980s, the forest industry began to relocate to Canada and southern U.S. states and came under environmental pressure (most famously, the spotted owl conflicts) by the late 1980s. The shining hope for Oregon was high-tech. These industries came because of lower costs and quality of life, but also because (as Governor McCall had predicted) the state's planning system gave industries clear rules and state-level assurance about the conditions on which they could locate in Oregon. Whereas industries in other states complained that they were subject to local in-fighting and petty coercion from local governments, Oregon's system provided clear rules and certainty.

For example, in 1982, James G. Law, the top plant locator for Hewlett Packard, which at the time had two plants in Oregon, traveled to Portland from the company's headquarters in Palo Alto, California, to urge Oregonians to vote against Ballot Measure 6, which would abolish the state planning system. The *Eugene Register-Guard* quoted Law as warning, "If you abandon it now . . . that means discouraging industry. . . . If you scrap LCDC, there is no firm alternative in place that I know of except to go back to the way things were. Since that provided less predictability, I would suggest refining the present system rather than abandoning it."[56] Law explained, for example, that at the time Hewlett Packard was bogged down in four-year courtroom battles to locate plants in California and Washington—whereas Oregon's system gave approval for a plant in about three months. Oregon's other high-tech (and lower-tech) industries quickly learned that the planning system provided major advantages and became key political supporters.

Home builders

Sitting in his small Salem office festooned with Republican Party memen-
tos, former home builders lobbyist Fred VanNatta recalled in 2009 that
his father, a small-town lawyer and rancher from Rainier, Oregon, told
him as a teenager: "Zoning is for them what ain't got a friend on the planning commission."[57] The younger VanNatta may have had little idea that
he would spend three and a half decades of his professional life lobbying
for "them what ain't got a friend" in local governments. VanNatta emphasized that, contrary to much conventional wisdom, the home building
industry—despite its politically conservative orientation—backed Oregon's planning system for pragmatic reasons from nearly the beginning of
the program. As a key lobbyist member of the ad hoc committee on land
use headed by L.B. Day that hammered SB 100 into a politically viable
form in 1973, VanNatta was in a position to know. He observes that the
final version of SB 100 had "heavy fingerprints" from home builders (as
well the forestry industry and farmers) and generally served their needs.
VanNatta points out that the state planning system provided a level of
legal certainty absent in many states, protections from "NIMBY" (not-in-
my-backyard) neighbors and local governments eager to use discretionary
authority to "blackmail" builders for various "offsite" expenditures, and
provisions preventing local governments from zoning away profitable affordable housing construction (see chapter 2):

> If there's no [state] plan in place, the local government can do any
> damn thing they want. So you may buy land that you can build houses
> on, or you may buy land you can [only] look at. You have no levers.
> The planning process brings certainty to the development process. You
> know when you buy a piece of land what the comprehensive plan says
> and what the zoning says and what you can *do* with it. Rational home
> builders want a process that they can get through. The land use plan-
> ning process provides the certainty that allows you to buy a piece of
> vacant land and [build] on it. The thoughtful members of our associa-
> tion understood that and we supported the process. . . . The people who
> believe that home builders have always and forever opposed land use
> planning haven't talked to real builders. . . . With the land use planning
> system in place and functioning, when the NIMBY neighbors come in,

why, the NIMBY neighbors lose. They would not lose if it were not for the planning system. Every time the local government folds to the NIMBY neighbors, it goes to [the state Land Use Board of Appeals], and the NIMBY neighbors lose. The trade-off for not building in the rural areas is that you *are* allowed to build in the cities.[58]

VanNatta also concurs with 1000 Friends of Oregon founder Henry Richmond, who observed that before SB 100, "homebuilders were being zoned out of the middle and bottom of the market. The local governments who had the zoning power all wanted the expensive housing in their areas. If every suburb does that, pretty soon you've got a shortage of sites zoned for smaller single-family lots that people want and homebuilders want to build." The Oregon Land Conservation and Development Commission created Goal 10 of SB 100, to "constrain the unbridled discretion of local officials. . . . LCDC started upholding the appeals of builder groups challenging the local zoning on the grounds that the zoning violated Goal 10 [for affordable housing]."[59] VanNatta agreed, stating, "That's the reason home builders still aren't out trying to kill the land use system—there are things there that are very positive."[60]

VanNatta and his successors at the Oregon Home Builders Association are also quick to point out, however, that these "positives" must be weighed against significant "negatives." Shifts in this balance for home builders, foresters, industry, and even farmers explain much of the changing politics of land use planning in Oregon by the early 2000s. In chapter 4 we also consider how ideas of benefits and costs and the sense of enfranchisement in the state's land use planning system have shifted for the most important member of this alliance—the Oregon citizen. We now turn to an examination of the dramatic things that can happen when planners and legislators—even in a state with a "celebrity" planning system—become insufficiently attentive to the changing economics and politics of land use planning.

4 Falling Star

Three decades after Tom McCall helped to launch Oregon's unique land use planning system by memorably inveighing against "the grasping wastrels of the land," a very different person became, arguably, the best known and most effective voice since McCall on the subject of Oregon's land use planning system. That person was an unlikely 91-year-old widow named Dorothy English. But English's views on the state's land use system differed radically from McCall's. In 2004, the following radio commercial was one of many advertisements featuring English that appealed to Oregon voters to support Ballot Measure 37—a property rights ballot initiative that would profoundly affect Oregon's storied land use planning system:

> DOROTHY ENGLISH (*elderly voice, with music in background*): My name is Dorothy English. My husband and I bought 40 acres in Multnomah County in 1953.
>
> NARRATOR (*male voice*): They raised their children on their property and hoped that someday they could give them part of their land.
>
> DOROTHY ENGLISH: But Multnomah County took that away from me.
>
> NARRATOR: For the last 20 years, Multnomah County has passed regulation after regulation on her property.
>
> DOROTHY ENGLISH: And now I can't do *anything* with my property.
>
> NARRATOR: The legislature tried to help, and Governor Kulongoski asked Multnomah County to work with her to fix the problems they caused. But what has Multnomah County done?
>
> DOROTHY ENGLISH: Nothing! I'm 91 years old, my husband is dead, and I don't know how much longer I can fight.
>
> NARRATOR: Measure 37 will protect your family from being treated the way Multnomah County has treated Dorothy and her family.

DOROTHY ENGLISH: Please! Vote Yes on Measure 37.

NARRATOR: Paid for by the Family Farm Preservation PAC [political
action committee].

The diminutive, stooped, and gravelly voiced grandmother Dorothy English would hardly seem a likely historical counterpart to the six-foot-five
baritone wordsmith Governor Tom McCall. Yet, to the extent that the
history of land use planning in Oregon has been driven at least in part by
the influence of unique individual personalities, the comparison is fair.
In the introductory chapter of this book, we observed that after the passage of Oregon's Ballot Measure 37 in 2004 (which effectively jettisoned
much of Oregon's planning system—we examine this measure in detail
later in this chapter), both authors of this book independently received
questions from people around the country, such as, "What were voters in
Oregon *thinking*?" In voting 61 percent in favor of Measure 37, it is almost certain that many were thinking about Dorothy English, and others
like her. In this chapter we examine the landmark battles for the future
of planning in Oregon that occurred in the first decade of the twenty-first
century. To tell that broader story, there is probably no more appropriate
place to start than with "Grandma Dorothy."

Dorothy English purchased 40 acres in Multnomah County with her
husband, Nykee English, in 1953, when essentially no development restrictions existed. The English family sold 11 acres of the property in
1974 and another 9 acres in 1977. With 19.74 acres remaining in 2004,
the regulatory and economic landscape had changed greatly. English's
property is just outside the Portland urban growth boundary and a
20-minute drive from downtown—making it a potentially valuable site
for development. Located in one of the most highly regulated counties
in a state with arguably the strongest land use regulations in the nation,
however, subdividing and building on the property was nearly impossible.
English stated that her attorney counted 61 rules that blocked her ability
to further subdivide the property. English and her attorney claimed that
she should be compensated $1,150,000, on the theory that this amount
reflected the difference in value between her property with her single
house, and what it would be worth with eight lots.

Dorothy English's rise to the status of a media icon started several
years earlier, with the political campaign for another pro-property rights

initiative, Ballot Measure 7 (which we examine later in this chapter). In a quavering, high-pitched voice that seemed to evoke immediate sympathy from listeners, English stated that regulators had "stolen" her property. Her compelling case quickly made her a brilliantly effective "poster girl" for the property rights movement in Oregon,[1] and English's case became a cause célèbre among property rights activists nationally, as well.

Seeing the political writing on the wall, in 2003 English's state senator, a former president of the Oregon chapter of the Sierra Club, sponsored a bill to specifically help English subdivide her property. The bill passed the legislature, but Multnomah County and the land use planning advocacy group 1000 Friends of Oregon opposed the bill and put pressure on Governor Ted Kulongoski. Kulongoski stated that while he was "sympathetic" to English's case, "The legislative process should not be used . . . for the benefit of an individual landowner," and "approval of such legislation would set an unwise precedent."[2] In a move that, in hindsight, the environmentalist community might see as a tactical blunder, the Democratic governor vetoed the bill, giving Dorothy English nothing—and handing a political prize to property rights advocates.

With Multnomah County and the Oregon government seemingly indifferent to the modest wishes of an elderly widow "victimized" by land use regulations, property rights activists found in Dorothy English a political card to play that was virtually impossible to beat. Who could *not* see the state and county governments as heartless bullies against this widowed (and, it would turn out, forceful) elderly lady? In the 2004 campaign for pro-property rights Measure 37, the *Portland Oregonian* newspaper observed, "In the weeks leading to Tuesday's election, English's pleading voice could be heard in cars, offices and living rooms throughout Oregon."[3]

Property rights activists and planning advocates continue to debate the meaning of the Dorothy English case. Critics observed that English was not the "sweet lady"[4] that some conservative activists and Measure 37 campaign ads suggested. English herself made this point emphatically. English's writings in newspaper editorials and advertisements blistered with declarations that environmentalists had "picked a fight with the wrong little old lady," and that she would "get even with the bastards."

The *Portland Oregonian* newspaper described English as "alternately wry and profane."[5]

More important, English's response to victory was the subject of differing interpretations. When Multnomah County granted English her Measure 37 waiver of development restrictions, English complained that the county failed to remove building codes and procedural requirements that were not in place when she bought property. She sued, and in June 2010 the Oregon Supreme Court ordered Multnomah County to pay her heirs the $1,150,000 that English had requested originally. The appearance that English would not take "yes" for an answer supported critics' claims that English was really a "greedy granny" who was interested mainly in money, not rights. The fact that English herself died two years before the supreme court finally granted her compensation was interpreted by property rights advocates as evidence that pro-government "wackos" were intent on winning at any cost by intentionally stalling until after English died.[6]

The factual history may be less important than the symbolic stature English attained as a hero to the property rights community, while the pro-planning community learned a painful lesson that *human* stories such as English's have enormous political power—a fact planning advocates showed they had learned by 2007, when they adopted nearly identical but countervailing human-interest stories as a key tactic in the campaign for Ballot Measure 49 (the so-called fix to Measure 37). Yet, no one denies that the gray-haired, stooped, and raspy-voiced Dorothy English became a key figure in the cast of outsized personalities who have shaped the political history of Oregon's land use planning system. But this time, the power of charisma was on the side of those in opposition to state land use planning. It was not the only reversal of fortune that the state's planning program confronted in the first decade of the 2000s.

A Turbulent History

As noted in chapter 1, in a particularly poignant speech in 1982, a then-dying former governor Tom McCall observed that Oregon's planning system had made the state "twinkle from afar." Even as he faced imminent death from cancer, in this speech McCall was fighting Measure 6, an initiative on the November 1982 ballot that would have repealed the state's land use planning system. McCall's quote was telling in that Oregon's planning system had indeed, in the eyes of many, made the state "twinkle from afar." It was also telling, however, that even with his last breaths (almost literally) McCall had to fight to keep the Oregon planning system intact. He succeeded: his speech is widely credited with having turned the public against the ballot measure (McCall died two months later). But the fact that a repeal of the statewide planning system came close to passage shows that what twinkled from afar was in fact fiery and turbulent when seen up close. Oregon's planning system was born in controversy, and keeping it intact was always *hard*.

Yet, even in the recession year of 1982, when critics claimed (despite substantial evidence to the contrary) that Oregon's planning system had reduced the state's economic vitality, Oregon voted much as it had in the past, with a significant margin supporting state-led land use planning. The first test of the Oregon public's commitment to state-level land use planning took place in 1970 when Ballot Measure 11 sought to repeal the earlier, less effective planning system created by 1969 Senate Bill 10. Measure 11 failed, 44 to 56 percent. The next major tests of Oregon voters' commitment to land use planning came in 1976 and 1978, with two similar initiatives (both under the title of Ballot Measure 10) to repeal the planning system. The 1976 and 1978 initiatives failed with "yes" votes of 43 percent and 39 percent, respectively. Even in the recession year of 1982, the repeal effort (Measure 6) gained only a slightly stronger support — a 45 percent "yes" vote.[7]

In the 1990s, opponents of the state planning system opted for a legislative approach, attempting one-piece-at-a-time efforts in the state legislature to weaken the program, but were mostly thwarted by Democratic governors, who have held the state's top office continuously since 1987.[8] In short, the state's planning system has been under attack almost from its inception, but voters and state officials consistently fended off major weakening of the system for three decades. In the year 2000, however, that long winning streak came to an end.

Measure 7

In the election of November 2000, Oregon voters had much to think about. In addition to choosing between George W. Bush and Al Gore for president (Oregonians narrowly chose Gore), the state's voters had to make decisions on 26 separate ballot initiatives—more than any election since 1914. In addition to the heated presidential campaign, the election climate was fired up with hot-button ballot initiatives that included tax cuts and an anti–gay rights measure. Physically positioned third from the bottom on the list of 26 ballot measures was a relatively low-profile initiative with this title: "Measure 7: Amends Constitution: Requires payment to landowner if government regulation reduces property values."[9]

Measure 7 was placed on the ballot by Oregon's perennial antitax and conservative political activist Bill Sizemore. Sizemore placed six other initiatives on the ballot in the same year and, unable to juggle such a large number of campaigns, handed leadership of Measure 7 to the property rights group Oregonians in Action. Measure 7 was endorsed by the Oregon Cattlemen's Association, the Oregon Grange, the Libertarian Party, and Sizemore's group, Oregon Taxpayers United. A long list of opponents of the initiative included the Oregon League of Women Voters, the Oregon Business Association, former Republican governor Mark Hatfield, Oregon Police and Prosecutors, the Oregon Education Association, Intel Corporation, Portland General Electric, virtually every state and national environmental organization with operations in Oregon, mayors of nine Oregon cities, and the Association of Oregon Counties.

These numerous opponents of Measure 7 had good reasons to worry. Whereas failed initiatives in the 1970s and 1980s had been framed *against* the state's land use planning system, Measure 7 was framed *for* property rights. Proponents described the ballot measure as a matter of fairness and civil liberties: if property owners are denied use of their land through regulations not in place at the time they bought it, government has "taken" value that should be compensated. The moral clarity of this argument had strong, ready appeal to many voters. Moreover, if such regulations are imposed for the benefit of the public as a whole (e.g., to preserve scenic qualities or wildlife habitat in rural areas), then the public as a whole should pay for the benefits rather than imposing the costs on (typically rural) landowners alone. Larry George, the director of Oregonians in Action, argued, "If the cost of any regulation became too burdensome, state and local governments could quit enforcing the regulation."[10]

That was exactly what opponents of Measure 7 feared. Opponents agreed with Larry George that governments unable to compensate landowners for land use rules could legally quit enforcing them. Unsurprisingly, however, planning advocates did not share George's view that ceasing to enforce land use regulations would be acceptable. Opponents of Measure 7 quantified the likely scale of compensation claims, using official estimates from the Oregon Secretary of State and the State Treasurer that the measure would cost the state $5.4 billion annually in compensation to uphold its regulatory system, an amount approximately equal to the state's entire annualized general fund for the 1999–2001 biennium.

Opponents decried this cost as a radical elevation of individual economic interests over the good of the community and predicted wholesale decimation of the state's celebrated protection of farmlands, coastal areas, rivers, wildlife areas, and urban growth boundaries (to name a few), leading to a loss of the state's treasured quality of life—a loss of the state's *identity*. Planning advocates and editorial pages in newspapers such as the *Portland Oregonian* (which endorsed presidential candidate George W. Bush on the same page)[11] warned that Measure 7 would be a nightmarish disaster for Oregon's quality of life. Framed by stark moral absolutes and near-apocalyptic predictions, Measure 7 seemed destined to make history.

And it did. On November 7, 2000, for the first time since the establishment of Oregon's unique state-level land use planning system three decades earlier, voters passed an initiative that would fundamentally alter the state's planning system, with 53 percent voting in favor of Measure 7.

On November 8, 2000, Oregon faced a different future than in its previous three decades. No one knew exactly what that future would be like. While the rest of the nation was transfixed by the spectacle of televised micro-examination of hanging chads by election officials in Florida, in Oregon a near-panic ensued among city councils and county commissions trying to determine how to handle and fund compensation claims or waive regulations. Little agreement emerged, except that real estate lawyers and appraisers would be very busy. (One appraiser quipped, "The only thing they could have done better is to put my telephone number in the law.")[12] Major legal questions loomed, such as whether governments unable to pay compensation could be sued (e.g., by neighbors of Measure 7 claimants) for failing to enforce laws that Measure 7 claims required them to not enforce.

Above the legal and political fracas, a frail but determined voice publicly promised to be the first in line when officials were ready to receive compensation claims: up-and-coming property rights media star Dorothy English.[13]

Adding another layer of uncertainty to the post-Measure 7 confusion, on December 6, 2000 (one day before the law was to go into effect), Circuit Judge Paul Lipscomb in Salem responded to lawsuits by the League of Oregon Cities and Tom McCall's widow, Audrey, by ruling that Measure 7 appeared to violate a constitutional ban on putting multiple topics in one measure, and filed a temporary injunction against it taking effect. While Lipscomb reviewed the case, a new politics of land use planning emerged. "I'll get you under Measure 7" became a common declaration against government actions. The number of Measure 7 claims being readied was unclear, but officials noted a palpable "chilling" effect among state and local planning agencies, anticipating that new regulations would immediately trigger Measure 7 compensation claims.[14]

When Judge Lipscomb finalized his ruling against Measure 7 on February 22, 2001, and the legislature deadlocked while attempting to draft a compromise alternative, Measure 7 was fast-tracked up to the state supreme court, where the fate of Oregon's land use planning system took another abrupt turn. The flurry of legal and administrative activity to decide how to implement Measure 7 — not to speak of the broader political questions of whether the bill's effect would be mild or apocalyptic — became moot. On October 4, 2002, the Oregon Supreme Court ruled that Measure 7 did in fact violate constitutional prohibitions against placing separate changes on a single amendment. Specifically, the court found that Measure 7 exempted owners of pornography shops and nude bars from a right to compensation for regulations that restrict their operations, placing "a price tag"[15] of zero on the rights of this single type of property use. The court ruled that this amounted to a freedom of speech issue, which

was unrelated to the issue of compensation for land use regulation—
and could not be combined in a single ballot measure.

Measure 7 died before ever taking effect. As a political precedent, however, it had a profound influence. The state supreme court ruled Measure
7 in violation of constitutional procedure—it did not rule on the measure's merits. More important, the public vote for Measure 7 revealed
genuine uneasiness and concerns about the fairness of Oregon's land use
laws and regulations, even in the face of dire warnings about the impacts
on the state's planning system. As we describe in the next section, this
lesson was not lost on Oregon's property rights community.

It is worth noting first, however, that Measure 7 was the most ambitious
property rights initiative in the nation at the time, and its failure to become law was almost a fluke (Abbott, Adler, and Howe 2003). Although
the Oregon Supreme Court rejected Measure 7 because of its exemption
of owners of pornographic businesses from compensation requirements,
the choice by the measure's creators to exempt sex businesses was largely
tactical. The prospect of governments being forced to pay taxpayer dollars to compensate pornographers for restrictions against operating their
businesses near schools, churches, or family-oriented shopping areas had
been used effectively against property rights initiatives in other states.
Given the significant margin of victory of Measure 7, however, there is
no knowing whether the initiative might have passed even without the
exemption against pornographers. Had the creators of Measure 7 made a
slightly different tactical choice, a revolutionary requirement to compensate owners for virtually any regulation affecting property value might
have been in the Oregon constitution today.

Measure 37

San Francisco has a bridge. Paris has a tower. Prineville, Oregon (estimated
population in 2009: 10,370)[16] has rimrock. This familiar American West
geologic formation (at least to anyone raised on Old West Hollywood),
with its high, near-vertical walls capped by a flat-top, red rock rim, is central to the identity and tourist economy of Prineville. This starkly beautiful high desert area of Central Oregon is where a young Tom McCall
spent much of this childhood, and it inspired his future vision.[17] From

central Prineville today, one looks up to see rimrock meeting the nearly always blue sky. Between land and sky, there is *only* rimrock—there is no house, no motel, no restaurant. But in 2006, the possibility that such structures might soon perch atop Prineville's rimrock became startlingly real to the city, and to many across the state—revealing the dramatic impacts of the passage of Oregon's 2004 property rights initiative, Measure 37, which passed with 60.6 percent support statewide, and majorities in every county except one (Benton).

Grover and Edith Palin purchased their 15-acre parcel at the foot of the rimrock in 1963 to raise children and horses. Only later did the Palin family learn that their parcel actually scaled the nearly vertical cliffs and lapped over onto a two-acre portion of the rimrock's edge. In 1978, however, Crook County created a 200-foot setback, making it impossible to build on all but a tiny sliver of the Palins' property atop the rimrock. With the Oregon Supreme Court's approval of Measure 37, the Palin family filed a claim in 2006 with Crook County and the City of Prineville to waive the setback regulations, which did not exist when they bought the property. Their claim was approved, but the Prineville City Council decided that preserving the city's iconic vista merited monetary compensation rather than waiving land use regulations. For the reduced value of their property resulting from enforcement of the setback rule, the city offered the Palins $47,760, as calculated by the city appraiser. The Palins balked, stating that they wanted only to build a home, not money.

However, the Palins then reapplied for Measure 37 compensation, this time claiming they wanted to build a restaurant, motel, and luxury homes atop the rimrock, which, by their appraisal, should command millions of dollars in compensation from the city. The *Bend (OR) Bulletin* reported that Grover Palin explained this apparent change of heart this way: "Edith and I wanted a retirement home; we didn't get it, so now if we don't get that we might as well see how much money we can get. I'm looking at pretty close to $5 million."[18] The city and the Palins finally settled at $180,000. Today the rimrock still meets the sky without interruption, the Palins cashed their check, and for the city the matter was closed.

This story remains, however, emblematic of the unresolved tensions in Oregon's apparent strong support for both land use planning and prop-

erty rights. The battle over the house on the rimrock was in certain respects the exception that proves the rule: no other government in Oregon
paid compensation for successful Measure 37 claims. Lacking funds, virtually every other government waived their land use rules.

Yet this tale illustrates the political and ethical dimensions of Oregon's
2004 property rights law in unusually clear terms. Property rights advocates praised the outcome: for a public benefit (preserving the rimrock),
government imposed land use rules not in existence when private owners
bought the property, and thus it was entirely fair that the *public* should
pay the owners just compensation for the resulting reduction in property
values. If the representative body of the public was unable to pay owners
for the reduction of property value, it would be unfair to impose the cost
of a public good on private owners and entirely fitting to require government to waive rules not in place at the time the property was purchased.

To planning advocates, the moral of the story of the house on the rimrock appeared equally clear: *all* property ownership involves risks that the
"rules of the game" may change, yet Measure 37 gave certain individual
owners a right to evade legitimate rules made through democratic governance, or commit "blackmail"—absurdly forcing democratic governments to pay for the right to govern. As Prineville city councilor Bobbi
Young stated to the *Bend Bulletin*, "We voted for [Measure 37], but we
certainly didn't think that would mean that people would build on our
rimrock."[19] It was among the many learning opportunities that Measure
37 would afford Oregonians.

While the prospect of a flurry of development through Measure 37
waivers of past land use regulations captured most of the public's attention, "just compensation" requirements for (and, in most cases, waivers
of) *past* land use regulations was only half the law. Measure 37 also
required compensation for reduction of property value for any new state
or local land use regulations enacted in the *future*. In the next section,
we describe the potential "chilling" effect on land use regulations that
was carried over from Measure 37 into Measure 49—the so-called fix to
Measure 37. Such future effects are even more difficult to predict.

Yet, the symbolic importance of the passage of such a muscular property rights compensation requirement into law in *Oregon* is difficult to
overstate. Immediately after the ballot victory of Measure 37, the execu-

tive director of the land use planning advocacy group 1000 Friends of Oregon, Bob Stacey, stated, "It's a very strange situation for Oregon to go from a national leader in community planning to a place where only with the greatest of caution will anybody even talk about planning and zoning."[20] A letter to the editor of the *Portland Oregonian* stated, "In one day, voters of this state gutted a 30-year history of putting quality of life over speculative gain."[21] Property rights activists would no doubt object to the pejorative tone, but no one disputed the significance of that day.

The effects of Measure 37 should not, however, have been surprising to anyone who had followed Oregon's recent land use politics. Measure 37 essentially retained the core principle of Measure 7, passed in 2000: if a state, county, or city government enacts a regulation that reduces property value, the government must pay landowners an amount equal to the reduction in value.

In Measure 37, governments were expressly given the option to remove, modify, or not apply regulations in lieu of monetary compensation. Such regulations could be statutes, administrative rules, comprehensive plans, zoning, subdivision ordinances, or other land use rules. Compensation was not required under Measure 37 for regulations in place at the time the owner acquired the property, or for regulations prohibiting "commonly and historically recognized" public nuisances, regulations necessary to protect public health and safety, regulations required to meet federal law, or regulations restricting the use of a property for selling pornography or performing nude dancing. If governments did not award compensation or waive regulations within 180 days of an owner filing a valid Measure 37 claim, the owner could sue the government and would be entitled to attorney fees and other legal costs. Measure 37 required compensation or waiver of regulations enacted after the owner or a family member of the owner (as far back as grandparents) purchased the property, as well as any new regulations enacted in the future.[22] For existing regulations, owners could file claims up to two years after the enactment of Measure 37; for future regulations, owners could file claims up to two years after the enactment of the new regulation.

Local governments were required to begin accepting Measure 37 claims on December 2, 2004. Dorothy English filed the state's first claim, at 12:01 a.m. that day by fax. Measure 37 was replaced three years later by

Measure 49 (see below). During that period, more than 7,500 claims were filed with the state and local jurisdictions, involving more than 750,000 acres, most of them proposing to build single-family homes on farmland or forestland around high-growth areas such as the Portland suburbs, Hood River, and Medford. In one of the few systematic efforts to track Measure 37 claims, Sheila Martin and colleagues at Portland State University (Martin et al. 2007) calculated that almost 92 percent of Measure 37 claims were for 200 acres or less (a claim size that would be typical of small-scale, family landowners). The remaining 8 percent of claims larger than 200 acres, however, accounted for approximately 62 percent of the total acreage claimed for development under Measure 37. Almost 35 percent of the total acreage claimed under Measure 37 was on land holdings of 1,000 acres or more—typical of very large landowners preparing for potential large-scale, multi-unit development (sometimes hundreds of units). In short, according to Martin's analysis, the great majority of claimants were most likely small-scale owners, but almost two-thirds of the land that would have been potentially opened to development was owned by large-scale owners. In terms of financial cost, Measure 37 compensation claims ultimately totaled more than $19.8 billion.[23] But only the Palin family received money; all other approved claims produced waivers of regulations.

A particularly controversial minority of Measure 37 claims sought very large-scale development, such as large businesses and subdivisions, a casino, hotels, shopping malls, and gravel quarries. Probably the most criticized Measure 37 claimant was the Plum Creek Timber Company (formerly Georgia Pacific Corporation, and the largest private landowner in the United States), which sought rights to build houses on 32,000 acres of forestland on the cherished and politically symbolic Oregon coast. Another large owner, in central Oregon's Deschutes County, proposed a pumice mine, power plant, and subdivision at the Newberry National Volcanic Monument. A politically important learning process had begun: as Governor Ted Kulongoski observed, "Most of these claims are not what people thought was going to happen with Measure 37."[24]

Before and after the passage of Measure 37, advocates accused the measure's opponents of sky-is-falling rhetoric, while opponents accused the supporters of Measure 37 of deliberately downplaying the likely impacts. In fact, it is impossible to know with certainty what the long-term impacts of Measure 37 would have been, for several reasons. Proponents claimed that many Measure 37 claims were simply legal "placeholders," allowing landowners to establish options, whether or not they intended to use these options. Moreover, there were significant barriers to exercising rights even when a Measure 37 claim was approved.

In particular, a key ambiguity emerged regarding whether owners could transfer Measure 37 development rights to new owners (Oregon courts eventually said no). Many successful Measure 37 claimants were small-scale owners without the capital and experience needed to develop their properties without transferring ownership to professional developers. Many investors, banks, and insurance companies declined to engage Measure 37 developments with uncertain transferability rights. At the same time, an unknown proportion of proposed developments could have been blocked by local governments on the basis of health and safety restrictions. Finally, the market realism of some proposed Measure 37 developments (in remote areas, e.g.) was uncertain, particularly with the bursting of the housing bubble by 2007.

Thus, the precise amount of land that would have ultimately been developed under Measure 37 is impossible to know. Unsurprisingly, however, this inherent uncertainty did not stop political players on both sides from offering vastly differing predictions, typically with grave assuredness.

In the short term, however, the effect of Measure 37 resembled neither paradise nor Armageddon as much as it resembled chaos. The new law provided no guidance for how claims were to be handled and determined valid by the state and local governments, and a 180-day clock for governments to issue decisions began ticking immediately when the first claims were filed after the law went into effect on December 2, 2004. The mad scramble by governments to establish procedures to handle Measure 7 claims four years earlier resumed. Heated disputes erupted over claims processing fees by counties and cities: some required no fee, while others charged fees of as much as $2,000—leading property rights advocates to accuse some local governments of intentionally thwarting the law by charging excessive fees. Governments argued that fees were necessary to assess complex claims properly and avoid diverting staff time from other functions.

More substantive questions also emerged, including whether family corporations or widow(er)s whose names were not on the property deed could inherit a Measure 37 right. Other major questions emerged over whether an approved Measure 37 development could be transferred to another owner, and whether neighbors of Measure 37 claimants must be notified that a Measure 37 claim could affect them—*and* whether these neighbors could in turn sue landowners or governments if approval of a development approved under Measure 37 reduced *their* property value. In the meantime, governments faced pressure to proceed even with such major questions unresolved, because failure to issue a decision within 180 days from the date a claim was filed would enable claimants to sue governments, absorbing vastly *more* scarce staff hours and funds. In the last days of the law's two-year window, the number of claims doubled, creating an enormous pig-in-a-python bulge of claims moving through an already overburdened system.

Procedural chaos under Measure 37 was matched by seeming philosophical incoherence. The measure was conceived and promoted to the public as a property rights measure that would restore fairness to Oregon's land use planning system. In fact, the law promoted the rights of a fairly narrow set of property owners—mainly those who bought property prior to the creation of Oregon's main body of land use planning law in the 1970s. While restoring the rights that owners held at the time they bought property seemed intuitively fair, Measure 37 treated these rights as if they existed in a vacuum, unconnected to the rights of other members of society, including the property rights of neighbors of successful Measure 37 claimants. Many neighbors of Measure 37 claimants found that rights "restored" to their neighbors could result in developments (subdivisions, commercial construction, gravel mines, etc.) that would reduce *their* property values and quality of life.

Many neighbors of Measure 37 claimants complained, for example, that they purchased their property precisely because they knew certain land use restrictions applied in their area and these laws provided assurance that "sprawl" would not follow them. If the conceptual aim of Measure 37 was to protect property owners from changes in the "rules of the game" resulting in reduced property values, ironically it did so by restoring the rights of certain owners while changing the rules of the game for other owners, who *also* bought with a given set of expectations about how the law affected their property. Measure 37 offered no aid to restore property value or quality of life for owners whose property was adversely affected when Measure 37 allowed development that was prohibited when these other owners bought their property. To many Measure 37 neighbors, the philosophical justification for restoring the rights and property values of one class of property owners at the potential expense of another class of property owners seemed murky.

More simply, many owners who bought property under the rules established by the state's planning system and had those rights abrogated by Measure 37 were hopping mad. If the chaos surrounding the processing and legal meanings of Measure 37 claims had not driven home the lesson that what you see in an appealing ballot title is not always what you get, the matter of neighbors' rights under Measure 37 made that lesson plain to many surprised voters.

Scott Lay, a property owner in Clackamas County stated: "I did vote for Measure 37 back when it was on the ballot, but like a lot of people I was not voting for what it seems to have become. Back then it was property owners being able to put a family member's house on their property. They might have a son or daughter who wants to live on their great land, but they couldn't do it [due to land use restrictions]. So, my understanding of [Measure] 37 wasn't that you take a nice piece of property and subdivide it into 14 small half-acre lots without regard to what it does to the surrounding environment or the neighbors or things like that."[25] In Yamhill County, Maralynn Abrams filed a Measure 37 claim to convert 342 acres into residential and commercial development, despite active protests of neighbors about the impacts on water quality, traffic, and noise. Neighbor Jim Parker complained, "A lot of folks didn't have any idea Measure 37 would allow something like the Abrams' claim. It's opened up a Pandora's box."[26]

Following the passage of Measure 37, the authors of this book read a random selection of 100 letters sent to the Oregon Department of Land Conservation and Development by neighbors of Measure 37 claimants, 99 of which were similarly critical. One stated, "By granting Measure 37 our right to live in an area with open space will be violated as will that right be violated for my neighbors and every person already living in [this area]. . . . If you grant Measure 37 you will greatly decrease the value of our properties in the eyes of those who own them!!!!" Another neighbor quantified their loss of property valued due to Measure 37: "People don't want to buy with a Measure 37 claim pending [for a subdivision] next door. [Mr. Smith][27] has depreciated the value of our land. Our lawyer and real estate agent have valued the loss at about 40%."

Of the 100 letters we reviewed, 38 complained about additional service and infrastructure needs for new development; 36 complained about increased traffic; 33 complained of reduced rural quality; 32 complained of the effects on the environment; 28 complained about the possibility of residential and commercial uses harming farmers. Other complaints included loss of rural community and the perceived inevitability of increased taxes to pay for services for new developments. One letter supported Measure 37. To be clear, this was *not* a scientific survey of neighbor responses; it was, however, indicative of the fact that many Oregonians (including some who had voted for Measure 37) were genuinely surprised and frightened by the impacts it presented in practice.

These fears of uncontrolled development, questions about the fairness of restoring property rights for one class of owners at the potential expense of others, and concerns about constraints on the ability of governments to make law for the public good became the chief legal and political arguments that planning advocates would use to challenge and eventually undo Measure 37. The first path Measure 37's opponents pursued led through the state's courts. On January 14, 2005, ten weeks after the passage of Measure 37, opponents filed a lawsuit in Marion County Circuit Court (Marion County is the seat of the state government and receives cases pertaining to state law). Plaintiffs included farmers, county farm bureaus, a neighbor of a Measure 37 claimant, and 86-year-old Hector Macpherson—the former Republican state legislator and architect of the state's main planning law. The thrust of the lawsuit was that Measure 37 violated Oregon's constitutional protections against laws that grant special privileges or immunities to any class of people. Nine months later, on October 14, 2005, Judge Mary Mertens James ruled in favor of the plaintiffs. Whereas four years earlier Measure 7 had been ruled unconstitutional on procedural grounds, Judge James's decision struck at the substance of the Measure 37, ruling that the measure unfairly favored certain groups and restricted legitimate government powers. The ruling was immediately appealed, but James ordered all processing of Measure 37 claims to be frozen.[28]

Among members of land use advocacy groups such as 1000 Friends of Oregon, champagne corks popped and celebratory libations bubbled forth. Celebrants might have been wiser keeping the corks in. The Oregon Supreme Court began hearing appeals of the Marion County decision on January 10, 2006. Only six weeks later, the supreme court unanimously struck down Judge James's ruling, stating that Measure 37 did not violate the state or federal constitutions.

The supreme court did not rule that Measure 37 was fair, or that it was good policy; it ruled that if 61 percent of the voters wished to grant certain landowners particular rights and restrict government regulation, the people of Oregon had a constitutional right to do so. On the roller coaster of planning politics, thousands of Measure 37 claims were now back on track and moving ahead. But when the public voted for Measure 37, 61 percent of Oregon voters had not yet encountered the many "learning opportunities" that the implementation of Measure 37 created. Bob Stacey, executive director of the planning advocacy group 1000 Friends of Oregon, vowed that the people of Oregon would get another chance to decide whether the policy that the supreme court had determined constitutionally valid was good policy. Having lost the legal battle, opponents of Measure 37 turned to the legislature and, ironically, to the ballot initiative process.

Polls showed that Measure 37 itself had once again primed the political pump of growth anxiety that had propelled the creation of Oregon's land use planning system in the first place. In a poll commissioned immediately after the enactment of Measure 37 by the Oregon Business Association and Portland State University's Institute of Portland Metropolitan Studies, the public relations and research firm Conkling Fiskum & McCormick found that while 60 percent of respondents favored individual rights over responsibility to the community, more than two-thirds believed that growth management makes Oregon a better place to live. Among respondents, 32 percent considered the state's land use laws "too strict," while another 32 percent considered them "about right," and 21 percent considered the state's land use system "not strict enough."[29]

In short, while Oregonians hold property rights dear, even at the time when Measure 37 had just been approved by 61 percent of voters, the public had by no means rejected the importance of sound growth controls. By 2007, another poll (by the national opinion research firm Fairbank, Maslin, Maullin & Associates) showed this commitment to sound planning had begun to take a toll on the public's opinion of Measure 37 itself, with more than two-thirds wanting to modify what it viewed as significant flaws in the Measure 37, or repeal it altogether.[30]

Reviving a proud Oregon tradition, Measure 37 even reminded Oregonians of the merits of blaming Californians. It was not unnoted by the Oregon public that the chief petitioners for Measure 37 (along with Dorothy English) were a couple from Southern California named Barbara and Gene Prete, who bought a 20-acre "ranchette" in Central Oregon (near the town of Sisters) in the early 1990s to raise horses, only to discover that a rule created after their purchase prohibited building a residential structure on their land (a rule created specifically to limit the kind of ranchette-style rural residential development that the Prete family had in mind). On February 26, 2006, five days after the Oregon Supreme Court reversed a lower court ruling against Measure 37, the *Portland Oregonian* newspaper ran a front-page article with the title "Californians are riding a new wave to Oregon." A native Oregonian responded with this letter to the editor:

> For the most part [Californians] are welcome, until they start messing with our land-use laws. . . . Southern California is a prime example of lack of land-use laws. We do not need newcomers moving to our state who have no respect for our history of protecting the land. I shudder when I see prime Western Oregon farmland being turned into mass tracts of mini-mansions or shopping malls. I do not want to drive through vast vistas of our High Desert east of the Cascades only to find mini-ranchettes punctuating the view. Welcome to Oregon, but please do not try to foist other states' land-use values upon us.[31]

One could almost hear the echo of Tom McCall's legendary thundering 1970s speeches once again. Anti-California bumper stickers, once common, began to reappear (Figure 3)—a sign something was about to happen. And it did.

Figure 3   Anxieties about Measure 37 seemed to reawaken an old tradition in Oregon (P. Walker 2009)

Measure 49

Politics is a tradition in the Macpherson family. In his law office at the top of a downtown Portland skyscraper, Greg Macpherson, a member of the Oregon Land Conservation and Development Commission and a former state legislator, keeps a framed photograph of his father, Hector Macpherson Jr., standing with former Oregon governor Tom McCall. Each Macpherson generation has made a signature political contribution: Greg Macpherson's grandfather, Hector Sr., was a state legislator (and, like Hector Jr., a dairy farmer) who founded the Oregon Department of Education. Greg Macpherson's signature political contribution may be remembered as rescuing the statewide land use planning system his father, Hector Jr., had designed. Greg Macpherson was a Democratic state representative and chair of the House Judiciary Committee, where he played a leading role in creating the bill that would become Measure 49—the ballot initiative to "fix" Measure 37. As he recalled in 2009:

> Going into the 2007 legislative session [the first to convene after the reinstatement of Measure 37 by the Oregon Supreme Court in February 2006], there was widespread recognition that something needed to be done about Measure 37. And it was coming to a crisis, because Measure 37 had a 180-day timeline within which a public entity had to either compensate a property owner or waive land use restrictions. It was kind of a gun to the head to require fast action. A whole onslaught of [Measure 37] claims came by a particular date [December 2, 2006, after which the process for filing a Measure 37 claim became much more difficult]. After those landed, that started the running of a six-month clock from when they hit by which the state or local government had to act. If they didn't act to waive a land use restriction, then they were on the hook for compensation. That's what Measure 37 said. The exposure based on the claims that were submitted was into the many billions of dollars. So there was a sense of crisis going into the session.

Moreover, Macpherson explained, state and local governments had no good options because waiving regulations on Measure 37 claims would *also* create a potential legal and fiscal disaster: "Lane Shetterly [the then-director of the Department of Land Conservation and Development] was telling us [the DLCD] was swamped and they were trying to stay current to try to get some kind of reasonable attention to these claims, but they were faced with a prospect that they might have to issue summary waivers based on inadequate information, which could expose the state to claims from *other* property owners who would be adversely affected by an action to approve invalid claims. It was a very dicey situation for the state to be in."[32]

At the same time, the public had begun to have a clearer understanding of what Measure 37 might mean to them. When Oregonians voted in favor of Measure 37 in 2004, no one on either side could say with certainty how many claims might be filed, or how much area might be affected. As claims poured into local and state offices, the potential scale of new development shocked many. In 2007 the Oregon Department of

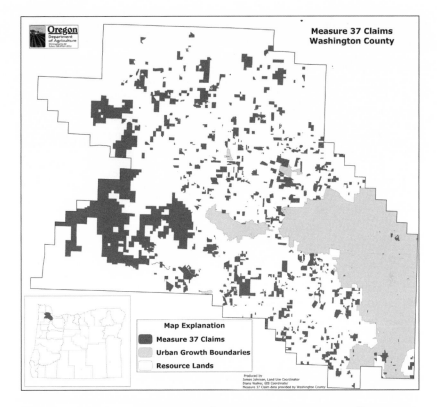

Figure 4 Measure 37 claims in Washington County (Diana Walker 2010, by permission)

Agriculture's Jim Johnson produced a highly influential series of county maps displaying the distribution of Measure 37 claims. Especially in rural areas of fast-growing counties such as the Portland Metro counties (Washington, Multnomah, and Clackamas), the distribution of Measure 37 claims (marked in reddish orange on the original maps) appeared like a severe case of acne spreading over the counties—with a similar level of public appeal (Figure 4). Many counties sent printed copies to all residents, raising public alarm. Some viewed the publication of these maps as the key point when the political tide turned against Measure 37.[33]

The president of the Oregon Senate, Democrat Peter Courtney, appointed a Senate Committee on Land Use Fairness. The senate and house leaderships then made a decision to turn the Senate Committee on Land

Use Fairness into the Special Joint Committee on Land Use Fairness, combining members of both chambers. Greg Macpherson had told the incoming speaker of the Oregon House of Representatives (Democrat Jeff Merkley, now a U.S. senator) that he wished to be on whatever house committee ended up handling the anticipated response to Measure 37. With the name "Macpherson," this seemed an obvious fit, and Merkley appointed Macpherson as the house cochair, serving with the senate house cochair, Democrat Floyd Prozanski (representing the City of Eugene and areas to the south). With the Measure 37 claims "clock" ticking, the committee began work quickly in late January 2007 to draft a legislative response to perceived flaws in Measure 37. Oregon's governor, Democrat Ted Kulongoski, strongly supported the legislature's efforts and assigned a top-level aid to help expedite a process the governor considered an urgent priority.

For years afterward, property rights and conservative activists would accuse the all-Democrat state leadership of shutting out opposing viewpoints from the drafting of the legislative response to Measure 37. In turn, the Democratic leadership, and even some Republicans, accused property rights advocates of shutting themselves out by proving themselves unwilling to make any significant compromises. Political history suggested that in 2007, conservatives and property rights advocates were unlikely to yield. In 2005, the legislature made concerted efforts to find "fixes" to the flaws seen by both advocates and opponents of Measure 37. Even supporters of Measure 37 had begun to see many flaws in the measure—especially the inability to transfer developments and development rights to new owners, but also the many other difficulties such as the inability of widows to inherit Measure 37 rights—and wanted solutions to these problems. Opponents feared the enormous potential scale of development if Measure 37 claims were actually approved and carried through to bricks-and-mortar edifices. Both sides had reasons to want to "fix" Measure 37 in 2005. Yet, as Lane Shetterly, a Republican and then-director of DLCD, recalled, pro-Measure 37 forces appeared unwilling to compromise:

> In the 2005 [legislative] session the governor's office was interested in facilitating a negotiated agreement between [property rights organization] Oregonians in Action and [planning advocates] 1000 Friends of

Oregon, as the surrogates for the larger forces at play in Measure 37. The idea was they could serve as a catalyst that we could then bring to the Legislature in bill form. I convened a meeting with Bob Stacey [executive director of 1000 Friends of Oregon] and Dave Hunnicutt [president of Oregonians in Action] at Carrows Restaurant. . . . They both came understanding that the subject of the meeting was, "Is there something we can agree on to work this out?" Bob came with his 20 points . . . Dave listened to Bob's presentation, and Dave said to Bob, "You could probably persuade me on most of the things you're asking for, but if I take it to my board and say this is what 1000 Friends is asking for, it's a nonstarter. I can't do it. And if I give you a list of things *we* would do that are acceptable to *us*, your board won't accept it." Dave looked at Bob's list, and said, "If you're going to do this, you're going to have to roll me." Dave was acknowledging that he wasn't in a position to really negotiate and agree to any fundamental changes in Measure 37, even though it wasn't going to deliver what had been promised, and I think Dave knew that. I think the organization [Oregonians in Action] had come to own Measure 37 so possessively that I don't think [Hunnicutt] could have gotten Oregonians in Action to agree [to any significant compromise].[34]

In fact, in mid-2005 the Oregon legislature had appeared close to a compromise that would have allowed transferability of Measure 37 rights in exchange for limits on the scale of Measure 37 developments (a compromise similar to Measure 49 in 2007), but the efforts failed when Dave Hunnicutt told the Republican-controlled House Committee on Land Use that the board of directors of Oregonians in Action felt uncomfortable with the compromise.[35] The legislative effort died.

In November 2006, a national wave of anger toward Republican president George W. Bush swept Democrats to power in the U.S. House of Representatives, and the ripple effects helped propel Democrats to power in the Oregon House of Representatives as well. With Democrats in control of both chambers of the Oregon legislature and the governor's office for the first time in many years, advocates of land use planning were in a position to "roll" (overpower) supporters of Measure 37. Many property rights proponents complain that is exactly what happened.

At the beginning of the new legislative session in January 2007, however, there were few signs that property rights advocates and conservatives were more ready to compromise on Measure 37 than they were in 2005. To the contrary, according to Greg Macpherson, some key property rights advocates were as rigid and uncompromising in defense of Measure 37 as ever, and seemed determined, as Macpherson recalled, to "run out the calendar" and force the state to implement Measure 37 in its original form. Thus, when asked in 2009 whether land use advocates "shut out" property rights advocates from the process of drafting the legislation that became Measure 49, Macpherson acknowledged they did, because they *had* to:

> More than any other issue I've worked on in my legislative career, [Measure 37 was] characterized by an inability of people at the ends of the spectrum to be able to engage each other in any meaningful way. It became apparent to us that the ends of the spectrum—particularly the conservative or right wing that thought Measure 37 was great, who were bent on dismantling Oregon's land use system—there was going to be no way to engage the real activists on that end of the spectrum. . . . So, to say that it was a process that didn't engage the far wing of the property rights movement I think would be fair to say, because it was demonstrated quite readily that these were not people who wanted to engage in a constructive, compromising process. They were just too fired up and too determined about preserving what they thought they'd won with Measure 37. We had to get engaged players who actually wanted to get to a compromise.[36]

As Macpherson's senate cochair on the Special Joint Committee on Land Use Fairness, Senator Floyd Prozanski, recalled in 2009: "I will admit that I made a decision as chair on the senate side to not have [conservative senator] Larry George [who was appointed by the senate leadership to the joint committee] involved, because he was a former president of Oregonians in Action. . . . We were supposed to be there with an open mind and an open heart."[37]

Open minds and hearts are scarce commodities in politics, but Macpherson and senate cochair Floyd Prozanski had an idea. Three and a half decades earlier, Macpherson's father, Hector Jr., formed an informal policy workgroup almost by accident when the Oregon Senate leadership denied him funds for a formal process, and he discovered that being freed of the requirements of a formal process allowed him to select a group of "open-minded," "engaged players" who crafted Senate Bill 100—the foundation of Oregon's statewide planning system. In helping to rescue his father's planning system, Greg Macpherson and Floyd Prozanski followed a similar model. In the process of taking many hours of public testimony, the Special Joint Committee on Land Use Fairness drew huge, passionate, polarized crowds. (The *Portland Oregonian* noted that "only in Oregon" would land-use planning meetings require a ticket line, overflow seating, and a live video feed.)[38] In a parallel process, Macpherson and four other legislators (Democratic senators Floyd Prozanski and Kurt Schrader, and Republican representatives Patti Smith and Bill Garrard) met privately as an unofficial workgroup to discuss pragmatically what could be done to resolve the problems of Measure 37. The two relatively moderate Republicans were invited in an effort to reach an agreement that could attract bipartisan support in the full legislature.

The five members of the land use workgroup, together with DLCD Director Lane Shetterly and then-Department of Justice attorney Richard Whitman, met twice a week in the evenings, focusing much of their discussion on a concept promoted by Governor Kulongoski that became known as the "express lane" that would allow landowners with a Measure 37 claim to apply for a limited number of additional homesites on a property faster and with less scrutiny than under existing procedures. The core idea was that all legitimate claimants would get *something* out of the process. A lengthy discussion ensued over what the number of "express lane" homesites should be—ranging from a single additional unit (supported by workgroup Democrats) to as many as 10 (supported by the group's two Republican members). The moment of compromise finally arrived when the workgroup agreed that the allowable number of units would be *both*: up to three additional homesites under the "express lane" option, and up to 10 additional homesites under a "conditional" claim subject to a higher level of state scrutiny of the pre–land use system rights of the claimant. This compromise became the core of the proposal that the workgroup offered as House Bill 3540, which was "referred" out to voters as Ballot Measure 49 in November 2007.

House Bill 3540 passed the 10-member Special Joint Committee on

Land Use Fairness on a 6–4 vote along party lines. The partisan split was a disappointment (but not a surprise) to Democrats on the committee who had hoped to present the full legislature with a strong bipartisan "fix" to Measure 37 that would provide cover from inevitable accusations by property rights advocates that Democratic legislators were going against the will of the people of Oregon who had voted in 2004 by 61 percent in favor of Measure 37. Lacking bipartisan support, Democratic leaders made a decision to "refer" the bill to a public vote (the vote to refer the bill to voters passed in the House 31–24—again, in a party-line vote). The argument Democratic leaders adopted was that in 2007, when voters had greater understanding of the effects of Measure 37, they would get a chance to say whether it was what they voted for. "We're giving the voters the opportunity to say, 'Yes, this is what we meant,' or 'No, it wasn't,'" stated Senator Prozanski.[39] It was a risky choice. With the overwhelming vote in favor of Measure 37 in 2004, no one knew precisely how much the public had changed its views. For legislators, however, it provided cover against accusations of arrogantly overriding the will of the people.

The campaign for Measure 49 was arguably a better gauge of Oregonians' views about the balance between the need to control growth and the importance of property rights than the vote for Measure 37 three years earlier. When Measure 7 and Measure 37 passed, Oregonians had come to know land use planning mainly through their experiences with local planning officials who often seemed inflexible and overreaching. Oregonians had three decades of experience with the "costs" of land use planning. By the mid-2000s, most Oregonians had either not lived in Oregon or had not yet been born in the heyday of Oregon's planning system, the time when Oregonians fought for the Beach Bill, the Bottle Bill, and Senate Bill 100. Relatively few Oregonians had any clear memory of the fight against sprawl and what the land use planning system was *for.*

With the passage of Measure 37 in November 2004, Oregonians discovered that land use planning is what keeps owners of neighboring property from doing things you do not like. Subdivisions, golf courses, pit mines, and strip malls planned under Measure 37 revived an Oregon tradition many Oregonians had forgotten or never known: the fight against runaway development. Oregonians relearned that "fairness" is a two-way street: an individual's property right to put in a convenience store may seem quite *un*fair to a neighbor who gains nothing but must bear the

Figure 5   A Measure 49 supporter celebrates victory on election night 2007 (P. Walker)

cost of additional noise, litter, loss of privacy, and so on. This provided planning advocates with evidence they could use to turn the Measure 37 "unfairness" argument on its head. In promoting small owners' rights to build a few houses while limiting big development, the pro-Measure 49 campaign in effect embraced a "Dorothy English" ethic. Looking back with us in 2009, Dave Hunnicutt chuckled, "They stole my campaign and ran it in reverse."[40]

However, no one knew exactly how *much* the attitude of the Oregon public had changed since the passage of Measure 37. On the evening of November 6, 2007, as election results came in, it quickly became apparent that Macpherson and Prozanski's gamble had paid off handsomely. Three years earlier, Measure 37 had passed with 60.6 percent of the vote. In 2007, Measure 49 passed with 62.1 percent of the vote—not only turning the 2004 vote around but exceeding the once daunting "61" percent vote that was widely heralded by Measure 37 supporters (by a tiny but symbolically important amount) (Figure 5). Greg Macpherson recalled that the unwillingness of Republicans to support a bipartisan plan, which forced Democrats to refer the bill to the voters, was a blessing in disguise: "As it turns out, it was a far, far better outcome to have gone to a public vote. Because the very strong vote in favor of Measure 49 really repudiated the strongest argument that the Measure 37 people had, which was that 61 percent of the people of Oregon had voted for their measure and, by golly, that ought to be enforced."[41] With an even larger margin (albeit not by much), the public vote in favor of Measure 49, "quashed that argument."

The most immediate effect of Measure 49 was not the initiative itself but the legislative effort leading up to Measure 49, which produced companion legislation (House Bill 3546) in May 2007 that gave state, county, and city governments an additional year to complete processing of Measure 37 claims. With a veritable avalanche of claims arriving just before the December 2, 2006 deadline, the 180-day clock would have expired later in May 2007. Greg Macpherson recalls that House Bill 3546 passed within "about two weeks of going off a cliff," when claims would either have had to be paid—at a cost of billions of dollars—or approved summarily, exposing government to massive litigation from aggrieved neighbors of Measure 37 claimants, who could sue government for approving Measure 37 claims without adequate review of the facts. Either would have been a fiscal and administrative disaster.

By extending the deadline to process claims, House Bill 3546 represented the beginning of the end for Measure 37. After receiving the deadline extension, the state and some local governments slowed their processing of Measure 37 claims (to "do it right"), while some localities put the processing of Measure 37 claims on hold, waiting to see whether Measure 49 would pass. When Measure 49 did pass, virtually all Measure 37 claims became null and void. Even claimants with an approved Measure 37 claim in hand lost all existing Measure 37 rights when Measure 49 went into effect. The only exceptions were the few approved Measure 37 claims that had enough physical construction in place to be approved as a "vested" right by a judge.

Measure 49 offered a *partial* restoration of the state's land use planning program. It eliminated claims for compensation or waivers for commercial and industrial uses. For residential claims, Measure 37 claimants received a form from the state asking applicants to choose from one of three options: claimants could select the "express lane" allowing them up to three homesites with relatively little review; in areas not designated as "high-value farmland" or "groundwater restricted," up to 10 homesites could be approved if owners could prove that land use regulations reduced the fair market value of their property by an amount at least equal to the value of the homesites to be created; or, claimants could proceed with their full development plan if they had done enough work on the project to win a ruling of a "vested" right under common law. Plans by ambitious developers to develop multihundred-unit subdivisions under Measure 37 were nixed. Measure 49 clarified issues such as transferability and inheritance rights: homes, parcels, and development rights established under Measure 49 *can* be sold to new owners, and widows (or widowers) who were not on the property deed *can* inherit Measure 49 rights.

Because the scale of development that would have actually occurred under Measure 37 is impossible to know with any precision, it is also not possible to know how much development Measure 49 prevented. What is clear is that the new law prohibited Measure 37 claims for commercial and industrial development altogether—though, again, the scale that would have occurred under Measure 37 is not possible to know. And Measure 49 drastically reduced the scale of many proposed large subdivisions that were proposed, even if only on paper. Several hundred of the approximately 7,500 former Measure 37 claimants who received letters from the Department of Land Conservation and Development requesting claimants elect from one of the three options available under Measure 49 never returned the form—thus losing their potential Measure 49 rights, and possibly suggesting that the relatively small-scale development allowed under Measure 49 was not what they wanted. However, just before Measure 49 was passed,[42] an estimated 42 percent of Measure 37 claims were for three or fewer homesites anyway, so Measure 49 would make little difference in the ultimate scale of development on many claims. When Measure 49 became law, more than 90 percent of former Measure 37 claimants who reapplied under Measure 49 opted for one to three homesites with the "express lane"[43]—suggesting that many Measure 37 claimants may indeed have fit the modest, "Dorothy English" model.

Others clearly did not fit this model, and the difference between a pro-spective post–Measure 37 landscape and a post–Measure 49 future was dramatic. In Washington County (near Portland), one of the few claim-by-claim studies conducted on the differing impacts of Measure 37 and Measure 49 showed that only 20 percent of Measure 37 claims asked for more than 10 homesites, but under the rules of Measure 49 the total number of homes authorized would drop by 84 percent.[44] State projections and private studies indicated that under Measure 37 more than 100,000 units would be built in rural areas; under Measure 49 the number would to fall to 13,000.[45]

Individual claims tell a similar story. In the city of Eugene, the Wild-ish Land Company received Measure 37 approval in December 2006 to develop 300 parcels on a 1,400-acre property near the city's cherished Mount Pisgah Arboretum and Buford Park, creating much local political turmoil. Measure 49 forced the Wildish Land Company to resubmit its claim, this time for a maximum of 10 units. (In September 2010, Wildish announced an agreement to sell 1,270 acres of the property to the Nature Conservancy, which would in turn transfer this spectacular land along the upper Willamette River to public ownership and add to the existing park acreage.) In fast-growing Hood River (a popular scenic and recre-ational destination for Portlanders, with some of the state's most pro-ductive pear-growing land), Bickford Orchards Inc. was approved under Measure 37 in December 2006 to develop 290 parcels on 77.09 acres for homes and a golf course. Along with many similar Measure 37 claims in the Hood River area, such developments raised alarm among farmers and planning advocates that the area's unique orchard economy would be lost forever through conflicts with new residential owners. In October 2009, Bickford received preliminary authorization from the state for a single new house on the property under Measure 49. In southern Oregon's Jack-son County, the Granger family won Measure 37 approval in February 2007 to divide 311 acres into 1-acre parcels with a house on each parcel. In September 2009, the Granger family was given preliminary Measure 49 authorization by the state to build up to three houses. Although dif-ficult to measure with precision, Measure 49 appeared to have created "Dorothy English"–style fairness *without* runaway development.

In 2009, the Oregon government mandated DLCD to finish process-ing existing Measure 49 claims by June 2010, at which point Measure 37 claims against past land use regulations became, administratively, part of history. However, the legacy of Measure 37 for *future* land use planning remains little discussed and difficult to predict. With political attention focused on "fixing" the immediate problem of existing Measure 37 claims, Measure 49 was written in a manner that maintained a core principle of Measure 37: the state must compensate owners or waive regulations if *new* regulations reduce property values. (Keeping this provision was necessary politically so that Measure 49 could not be described as a "repeal" of Measure 37.) For this reason, certain Oregon land use planning advocacy groups actually opposed Measure 49.[46]

At first glance, this provision might appear a death knell for future land use planning. Its actual future impact is far from clear, however—and is the subject of strikingly different opinions. It may be surprising to some planning advocates that Dave Hunnicutt, the president of the group that sponsored Measure 37, told us in 2009 that he and his group, Oregonians in Action, found much to like about Measure 49:

> Frankly, the thing that was most important for us about Measure 37 wasn't what it did for the people who were filing claims, but what it did going *forward*. Nobody ever talks about that. For us, Measure 37 drew a line in the sand and said, from now on if you adopt a new regulation and that lowers somebody's property values, you have to compensate them. If that means you adopt fewer regulations, that's fine. But you can't keep picking on a minority of property owners and saying, "you're going to pay for public benefits." Measure 49 had the exact same provisions. It was interesting, right after Measure 49 passed, [DLCD director] Richard Whitman came up to me and said, "Congratulations, you just won." And he meant it. . . . And in the campaign for Measure 49, you had [people] who had spent careers trying to stop stuff I was trying to do now advocating for a bill that said you can't pass new regulations in the future without compensating people. Ok! . . . For us, the most important part of Measure 37 was retained in Measure 49.[47]

This triumphal interpretation of the future implications of Measure 49 by Dave Hunnicutt and other property rights advocates is strongly disputed by many planning advocates, however. A typical view among pro–Measure 49 planning advocates was provided to us in 2009 by Richard

Benner, a former staff attorney for the planning group 1000 Friends of Oregon and director of the Department of Land Conservation and Development from 1991 to 2001:

> [Measure 49] isn't a disaster. . . . It's limited to [compensation for restrictions on] residential use, and the burdens of demonstrating that you actually lost money and that the regulation is responsible are substantial. After Measure 49 [passed], here [in Portland], people who had Measure 37 claims said, "ok, god damn it, now we're going to file a Measure 49 claim." They would submit something and we'd say, "Well, where's the appraisal?" They said, "Well, we're not going to do an appraisal." We said, "Well you have to. Measure 49 says you have to do an appraisal." They said, "Well shit, that's going to cost my client $10,000. Plus, I talked to an appraiser and they can't even measure this stuff [lost value due to new regulations]. It's impossible." We said, "Well, I'm sorry, that's what Measure 49 says." So, they didn't file. So, it's much less than a disaster. But, I wouldn't hazard a guess about the dampening effect of the adoption of new regulations, but I can tell you that all over the place people are thinking the days of heavy regulations are passed.[48]

On this latter point, in 2009 Bob Stacey, executive director of 1000 Friends of Oregon, explained that Oregon is in a unique position to accept curbs on new land use regulations in the future because its *existing* land use laws are already so strong:

> If I were in *any* other state I would have fought Measure 49 because it wouldn't be fair to a state that hasn't had a comprehensive land use planning system for 30 years. It wouldn't be fair to a state that hasn't had an opportunity to resolve fundamental tradeoffs between private rights and public interest. In Oregon, one can assume that the status quo, although not perfect . . . does resolve a lot of the tension between growth and development and management of natural resources. But we already have an urban growth boundary policy; we have an agricultural lands protection policy; we have a forest lands protection policy. And if the legislature decides in a particular case that the merits of a policy change justify it, they can change the rule of Measure 49. They can say, "In this instance compensation is not required." Measure 49 isn't a constitutional provision. It's a statutory provision.[49]

Nevertheless, Bob Stacey and others recognize that in the post–Measure 49 era, politically speaking, the burden of justifying legislation to navigate around the compensation requirements of Measure 49 would be greater than in the past. The director of DLCD, Richard Whitman, was a top attorney with the Oregon Department of Justice at the time that Measure 49 was created and was the main author of the law's actual text. Whitman offers a cautious view:

> Measure 49 has come up in various [land use policy] settings and essentially forced a discussion about whether there are ways to achieve a particular policy outcome without creating so much of an impact on a property owner. . . . I'll be very blunt. It does "chill" both legislation and regulation. I'll give you an example. There was legislation proposed in 2007 to prohibit development within a certain distance of the Oregon Trail. That legislation ended up not going anywhere in large part because of concerns about whether it would trigger Measure 49 claims. . . . There have been other instances. It does have a chilling effect. It is going to make it more difficult to regulate, and in some cases where it's really important to get something done, the legislature can decide to go forward, and authorize new regulation as exemptions to Measure 49, but they're going to have to make that conscious choice about whether this is important enough to exempt it from Measure 49. Does that mean it has a chilling effect? Yes. Does it mean we might not be able to be as responsive to some situations as we'd like to be? Yes. Is it worth it in terms of addressing equity issues? I don't know. But I don't view it as being the end of the world. I think at least right now it's a healthy development. I would say I do have some long-term concern about the chilling effect, and think that's just going to bear watching.[50]

Indeed it will, because for the immediate future one thing is certain: land use planning in the post–Measure 37 and post–Measure 49 era will be unlike land use planning in Oregon in the past. The state with arguably the most comprehensive and foresighted land use planning system in the country now *also* has one of the most aggressive pro–property rights "just compensation" requirements. For political reasons, that is unlikely to change soon. In an op-ed piece in the *Portland Oregonian* following the victory of Measure 49, property rights advocate Dave Hunnicutt wrote:

Measure 49 . . . puts Oregon on an irreversible path toward greater protection of individual property rights. Why? Because for the first time in Oregon's 34-year-old experiment with statewide centralized land-use planning, its most zealous advocates have acknowledged that there is a need to balance the rights of the individual property owner with the desires of the planning community, and that Oregon's system has done a poor job of balancing those competing interests. . . . They've worked hard to pass a measure that claims to provide protection to Oregon property owners if state or local governments adopt new land-use regulations in the future. . . . Measure 37 was a giant leap forward. Measure 49 is a small step backward. That's a win.[51]

Bob Stacey, executive director of 1000 Friends of Oregon, confirmed that Hunnicutt was essentially correct: when Measure 49 was being drafted (as House Bill 3540), Stacey was fully aware that the requirement to compensate landowners for the creation of new regulations in the future remained in the law: "I was told, 'you won't get rid of *that*,'" Stacey recalled.[52] Ballots count, and in the first decade of the 2000s Oregon voters decisively supported three statewide ballot measures (Measures 7, 37, and 49) each containing the "just compensation" provision. The dispute between property rights advocates and planning advocates about whether voters "knew" what they were voting for may be irrelevant as long as legislators remain unwilling to overturn a three-time statewide vote supporting this principle.

If a state government at the end of the first decade of the 2000s in which Democrats controlled both chambers of the legislature and the governor's office was unwilling to overturn the principle of just compensation, it appears unlikely any Oregon government will overturn that principle for the foreseeable future. If the future of land use policy in a state with the country's most comprehensive planning system *and* some of the nation's most aggressive property rights laws bears watching, how the state got into this rather odd position bears examination as well.

5 "What Were People *Thinking*?"

As mentioned in chapter 1, we wrote this book in part because of a particular event: in the summer of 2005, half a year after Oregon's Ballot Measure 37 passed, one of us (Walker) was in Colorado to interview the director of a land trust on an unrelated topic. The director changed subjects and posed a question about Oregon and Measure 37: "What were people *thinking*?" After beginning intensive fieldwork for this book in the summer of 2008, we think we are closer to being able to answer that question. We conclude, however, there is probably no *single* answer. What Oregon voters were "thinking" when they filled in their ballots in November 2004 had much to do with a number of economic, social, institutional, and political forces that had been shifting the ways Oregonians experience and think about land use planning in the decades since the program was created in 1973. The importance of understanding the shifting currents that shape Oregon's planning politics was illustrated well in 2002.

With the Oregon Supreme Court's invalidation of Ballot Measure 7 (which would have been a near-death blow to Oregon planning) in October of that year, supporters of Oregon's land use system were jubilant. Their enormous relief was mixed with a vague sense of affirmation that *of course* Measure 7 could not stand—this was *Oregon*. Their interests might have been better served by a stronger sense of humility and introspection about why Oregon voters approved Measure 7 at all, and what could be done to address these underlying problems. Portland Metro councilor Brian Newman later observed, "Measure 7 was a wake-up call. We just slept through it."[1] Bob Stacey, who took over as executive director of 1000 Friends of Oregon in the same month that the Oregon Supreme Court invalidated Measure 7, recalls how his organization was forced into a defensive stance and lost the initiative (literally and figuratively):

In October 2002 [when Measure 7 was ruled unconstitutional], I thought, "Well, that's finally behind us." That was probably the most short-sighted perspective I've ever had in this position, or any position. I thought, "Now we can get down to some progressive changes in land use policy" . . . but Oregonians in Action was working on revisions to the Measure 7 template. And in the early months of 2003 our staff started getting soaked up in time-consuming efforts to respond to draft ballot titles being submitted by Oregonians in Action. As I recall, at least a dozen or more . . . and ultimately one of them became Measure 37.[2]

One could say that 1000 Friends of Oregon—the pioneering, first land use watchdog group of its kind in the nation—was caught snoozing. The reincarnation of Measure 7 in the form of Measure 37 should have surprised no one. Following the state supreme court's invalidation of Measure 7 on technical grounds, property rights activists made no secret that they saw the court's decision as a temporary setback, and they publicly promised to return with more land use ballot initiatives.[3] Moreover, there was no reason to assume that the next property rights initiative would not pass. It did—and Measure 37 changed Oregon's history by enshrining the principle of "just compensation," probably permanently.

Yet, after Measure 7 was invalidated, when Oregon's land use advocates might have been working to take corrective action to avoid more such ballot initiatives, little changed. As Dave Hunnicutt, president of property-rights advocacy group Oregonians in Action, recalled to us in 2009, "What part of 'we need to make some changes' didn't the planning community understand? . . . [They] all figured, 'Well, Measure 7 is gone. So we don't need to worry about it.' What a stupid mistake! Ok, maybe the ballot measure is going to be invalidated, but the sentiment behind that ballot measure isn't going away."[4] Measure 37 proved Hunnicutt right. The passage of Ballot Measure 49 in 2007—*with compensation requirements for future regulation intact*—could be said to have proved him right again. Yet, by the end of the first decade of the 2000s, arguably the planning community *still* had not asked the hard questions about the possibility that "we need to make some changes"—a failure that is arguably equally "stupid" today.

To the extent that the pro-planning community in Oregon showed a capacity to think deeply about the growing political pressures against the state's land use regulations and push for reforms to resolve these, the community appeared able or willing to act mainly in response to crisis rather than acting proactively. For example, as described in depth by Abbott, Adler, and Howe (2003), after the passage of Measure 7 the 2001–2002 legislature formed the Special Joint Committee on Land Use Fairness, which attempted to craft legislation to replace Measure 7 by finding compromises to address the concerns of both property rights groups and land use planning advocates. However, the committee arguably never came close to resolving the most fundamental issues, and the legislative effort died. In the process, the planning community did engage in considerable introspection but did not appear to accept that the system had serious problems. Even after the passage of Measure 7, 78 percent of local planning directors in Oregon continued to see the state's system as basically sound (Abbott, Adler, and Howe 2003: 413). As soon as the looming crisis of Measure 7 was lifted by the state supreme court in October 2002, the momentum for reform largely dissipated, and business as usual resumed (including both sides preparing for new legal and political battles). Later, after the perceived victory for planners with Measure 49 in 2007, the collective sense that "well, that's behind us" resumed yet again. The idea that the land use program might have serious, systemic flaws that may guarantee future Measure 7– and Measure 37–type political attacks *still* did not seem clearly visible on the planning community's collective radar screen.

Instead, in both the post–Measure 7 and post–Measure 37 periods, the planning community overwhelmingly seemed content to blame their losses on mere clever political tactics by opponents. When we interviewed dozens of key "players" from Oregon's planning community and asked why they thought Measure 37 passed (and Measure 7 before that), we found virtual consensus. Most noted that the appealing ballot title essentially made the initiative a winner before the campaign even began. Virtually everyone we interviewed mentioned Dorothy English. And it is surely true that some of the tactics by property rights activists were brilliantly effective. As Dave Hunnicutt recalled to us, "We had a human face—here's what happens when you over-regulate and refuse to do anything about it. Here's what you get: Dorothy English. . . . The campaign was *easy*, and we just cleaned their clock."[5] Even today, some land use planning advocates still explain their Measure 37 loss with an assertion that the people of Oregon were mugged by a blue-haired nonagenarian con artist.

While such views may contain some truth, much more was at work. First, the Dorothy English story had to resonate with voters. When voters heard English tell her gravelly voiced story, they had to have reasons to trust her—to think, "yes, I believe that." As we describe in this chapter, over the decades that Oregon's statewide planning system matured and expanded, the general public had more and more reasons to find Dorothy English's story believable. This is a reality some planning advocates still ignore—at their grave peril, in our view. Even more important, clever politicking and a charismatic political symbol such as Dorothy English do not explain why the planning system had apparently become vulnerable. In 1970, 1976, 1978, and 1982, initiatives to repeal statewide planning were on the ballot, and each failed (the first of these, in 1970, was in response to the unsuccessful effort in 1969 to launch statewide planning with SB 10). This would seem to lead to the question, what was different about the early 2000s?

"Off the Reservation":
The Unraveling of a Fragile Alliance

In the view of some key players in Oregon's land use system, part of the answer lies in the unraveling of a fragile political alliance built decades earlier in support of the statewide planning program, which seemed to have at least partially broken down by the early 2000s. As described in chapter 3, the land use planning advocacy group 1000 Friends of Oregon cultivated an alliance of support for the statewide planning system.

Henry Richmond, the founder of 1000 Friends, recalls that the state planning system was born of remarkable leadership in the early 1970s, but "from 1976 on, it was the process of changing the system so that other interests benefited besides just environmentalists—that's what 1000 Friends of Oregon did by wooing homebuilders, wooing the forest products industry, and wooing the electronics industry and *helping* them.

[That's how] the program gained political strength." Over time, however, shifting economic and social currents undermined this carefully crafted alliance. By the early 2000s, Richmond recalled, some key industries that had supported the planning system for decades had drifted "off the reservation."[6] Apart from farmers (who remained mostly supportive but still divided internally as they had been since Senate Bill 100 was created),[7] when the state's planning system faced Measure 7 and Measure 37, 1000 Friends of Oregon stood nearly alone as the defender of Oregon's planning system. How did this happen?

Although home builders were not a key constituency in the formation of the state's planning system in the early 1970s (they supported an initial repeal effort in 1976), by the late 1970s home builders became important supporters of the planning program because it provided certainty for builders, protected them from NIMBY (not-in-my-back-yard) lawsuits, and prevented local governments from creating zoning restrictions that would constrain builders' choices (e.g., local zoning to allow construction only of high-end homes). According to home builder lobbyist Fred VanNatta, builders were especially relieved that state-level planning prevented local authorities from "blackmailing" builders by requiring local capital expenditures in return for building permits.[8] By the early 2000s, however, much of the initial appeal of the program had faded, and for some builders the "costs" of the planning program began to outweigh the "benefits." As Henry Richmond describes it,

> Once [the state Land Conservation and Development Commission] began upholding builders' appeals of local zoning on the grounds that these restrictions violated Goal 10 [the state's affordable housing goal], builders got behind the program. But, it's sort of like, "What have you done for me *lately*?" The builders now take for granted the higher densities and faster permitting times they got from the planning system, and they're more concerned about issues of expanding the urban growth boundary, or how to finance infrastructure for land brought into the urban growth boundary. Nobody's figured out an answer to that. So all of a sudden [builders] are an unhappy participant in the program.[9]

Another major ally that 1000 Friends of Oregon "wooed" early on was the forest products industry. The largest forest products companies in

Oregon remain mainly in the business of producing commercial timber, and most still support the state planning program because it helps these companies to avoid conflicts from residential use "sprawling" into the rural areas where fire from nearby houses might be a threat and the industry does its noisy, dangerous, and often toxic (in the form of pesticides) work. However, with the spotted owl controversy of the 1980s and 1990s and, later, heightened concerns about protection for salmon, along with the creation of more rigorous forest practices laws in neighboring California and Washington, Oregon's forest companies became more fearful that the state of Oregon might adopt similar policies. Thus, the anti-regulatory elements of Measure 7 and Measure 37 became attractive, and certain companies (but not the Oregon Forest Industries Council, which represents the industry) emerged as by far the largest financial supporters of these ballot initiatives[10]—providing for about three-quarters of the total financial contributions to the Yes-on-Measure 37 campaign in 2004.

This is not as surprising as one might first think, since, as Ward Armstrong (retired chief lobbyist for Weyerhaeuser Corporation) notes, the timber industry is changing fast. New owners located far away who get more of their supply from Canada or developing countries, or even represent unrelated industries (e.g., insurance companies), may see the "asset" differently and may want greater flexibility to break up and convert forestlands. With changes in federal tax law, more and more forestland is held by real estate investment trusts (including giant Plum Creek Timber) that profit by development. Armstrong calls such changes the "greatest threat to the forest industry in Oregon."[11] These changes could also become a major threat to Oregon's land use planning system. At the present, however, according to Oregon Forest Industries Council president Ray Wilkeson, large timber companies operating in Oregon mostly support the planning system as a way to avoid conflicts with residential land use, including increased risk of fire.[12] But the industry is far from monolithic or stable, and planning advocates can assume that at least certain timber companies will remain among their most powerful adversaries.

A third key source of political support for the planning system has been the high-tech electronics industry. In the 1980s, this industry was widely seen as the new economic hope for the state. Electronics companies found the relative certainty and efficiency of siting plants, as well as the availability of affordable housing provided by Oregon's planning system, very attractive (much as Governor Tom McCall had once argued). So, high-tech became a prominent supporter of the planning system. But, like what happened with the home builders, by the early 2000s much of this support had dropped away. By that time, some companies such as Hewlett Packard and Intel had begun laying off employees in Oregon for the first time, and most high-tech companies were not buying as much land as they had in the past (new sites were instead being located in other countries, e.g., China and India). There remained some expansion but relatively little compared to previous decades. Thus, these companies became less concerned and less active as political supporters of the planning system.

As described in chapter 3, although farmers have long been among the strongest supporters of Oregon's land use planning system, agriculture, too, is changing in ways that may ultimately undermine *or* possibly strengthen support for the program. Most farmland in Oregon is still owned and operated by relatively small owners. But like their counterparts nationwide, small farmers in Oregon operate in near-perpetual crisis. Future conditions that undermine the viability of small farming are likely to undermine the ability to maintain land in farm use, thus weakening support for the state's planning system and pushing farmers toward selling land to developers. But the future of Oregon farming is hard to predict. Relatively small, niche-market growers (e.g., organics, seed stock production) are expanding, as are so-called hobby farms (Gosnell et al. 2010). Some sectors, such as wine grapes and greenhouse plant nurseries, are thriving. The largest donor to the No-on-Measure 37 and the Yes-on-Measure 49 campaigns, for example, was Eric Lemelson, a Yamhill County vintner who gave more than $1 million to support Measure 49.

Even farmers of more modest means and conservative politics have found new reasons to support the state's planning program. For example, Measure 49 was approved by majorities of voters in conservative eastern Oregon's Umatilla and Union counties, where farmers are finding new profits by plugging their large landholdings into an expanding market for wind energy. How such new markets will play out in Oregon is anyone's guess, but land use advocates may be wise to recall that the fortunes of Oregon's farmers and the fortunes of Oregon's planning system have always gone together. Policies that help farmers to stay in business may be essential to maintaining political support for state's planning system.

The loss of support from one industry or the emergence of opposition from another does not, however, translate in a direct way into political vulnerability of the planning system. Certainly, the weakening, for example, of support from high-tech industries was a palpable political and financial blow. Yet, even with some of its key support fallen away, planning advocates routinely collect far more money in statewide political campaigns than their opponents. By mid-October 2007, for example, the (pro-planning) Yes-on-Measure 49 campaign reported raising $4.1 million, more than twice the amount raised by the No-on-49 campaign,[13] despite the weakened political alliance supporting the planning program. In 2004, the No-on-Measure 37 campaign raised almost four times the amount of campaign funds as the Yes-on-Measure 37 campaign—and *lost*. Moreover, with votes separated by only three years, Oregonians shifted 20 points from their support of Measure 37 in 2004 to their support of Measure 49 in 2007. The political and financial support of farmers, high-tech companies, foresters, and home builders did not shift by 20 percent in three years. Clearly, fuller explanation of the remarkable fall, and partial recovery, of Oregon's planning system is needed.

Bubble Trouble

One key explanation can be found in the price of land. If Oregon's land use politics in the first decade of the 2000s was on a roller coaster ride, it is probably no coincidence that the ups and downs closely tracked the rise and fall in the housing market. At the end of the 1990s, housing prices in Oregon (as in the rest of the country) began to pull sharply upward; by 2004, when voters approved Measure 37, housing prices were on a seemingly (at the time) unstoppable upward trajectory.[14] With heavy restrictions on the development of rural land and three decades of growth pressure built up inside the state's UGBs, the differential in prices between land inside and outside of Oregon's UGBs reached unprecedented levels, creating enormous economic opportunities and pressure to convert rural land to residential (or other) development—*if* regulations restricting rural development could be lifted. As observed by Mike Thorne, a legislator on the Oregon Senate Committee on Environment and Land Use that created the state's planning system in 1973, by the early 2000s,

> we were expanding out to where pressures were building around the growth boundaries and you look inside the growth boundary and a lot might cost $100,000, but you look outside the boundary, just across the fence on a piece of farmland, and that lot might be worth $10,000. . . . You got people who suddenly saw land that they could develop being worth a lot of money. They're saying, "Well, gee, this is my land." People wanted to get value from the property. They used the excuse that the system was overly restrictive. So it was a no-brainer from my perspective why Measure 37 passed. People were reacting to the fact that suddenly they saw they could sell their land for a lot of money. . . . People had not seen [property] values like that [in 2004] ever before.[15]

Conversely, the fall of Measure 37 closely tracked the fall of the housing market. Measure 49, which sharply restricted development options previously available under Measure 2004, passed in November 2007, when the bursting of the regional housing bubble had become unmistakable. The political urgency to undo restrictions on development quickly loses traction in a contracting housing economy. Dave Hunnicutt, president of Oregonians in Action, observed in 2009, "Land use planning is relatively harmless if there's no market. If there's no market for the use you want to make, then land use regulation has no economic impact on you. It's only when you wish to utilize your property in a way that there's a demand for, and can't because of a series of regulations, that you realize the impact of those regulations."[16]

By the end of the first decade of the 2000s, the housing market was more or less stagnant, very little new housing was being constructed, and the land use battles of that decade (Measures 7, 37, and 49) looked like a thing of the past. But in our research, we found that many of those most experienced with the history of the planning system in Oregon predict with confidence that when the economy picks up again, price pressure and development opportunities will put political pressure on the planning system again.

Mike Thorne, who served as chair of the Oregon Task Force on Land Use Planning (the "Big Look") from 2006 to 2009, predicted, "If you don't try to think about future pressures, and how urban growth boundaries are filling up and how developments are taking place, and try to figure out a way to adjust for that, we're going to have another round of [land use ballot battles] as soon as this economy gets going again."[17]

To be sure, the history of the land use planning program clearly shows that growth creates pressure on *both* sides of planning politics. It was no coincidence that Oregon's statewide planning system was created in the 1970s when the state experienced the fastest growth since World War II and public alarm about sprawl was widespread (Knaap and Nelson 1992). But in the early 1970s the planning community had the field largely to themselves—there were no significant, organized property rights groups to represent the interests of some property owners in cashing in on a high-growth economy. This was no longer the case in the mid-2000s housing bubble, and the planning community seemed caught somewhat off guard with respect to how politically effective the property rights community had become. At the beginning of the second decade of the 2000s, with growth nearly nonexistent and political interest in both pro- and anti-growth policies in near-hibernation, the planning community might be wise to think ahead about how to avoid being taken by surprise again by anti-regulatory pressure in the next upturn. When we asked 1000 Friends of Oregon founder Henry Richmond whether he expected new anti-planning ballot initiatives as the economy recovers, he responded, "I do. I *do*."[18]

Fairness

On September 23, 2008, the Oregon Task Force on Land Use Planning (the "Big Look") held a public "town hall" meeting in Klamath Falls, a famously conservative area that became known in the national property rights community for the 2001 "Klamath Bucket Brigade" that protested a federal decision to deny irrigation water to farmers in order to help endangered salmon. In public testimony at the Big Look meeting, one frustrated land owner offered this colorful complaint about the state's planning system: "The planning [department cited] me for $2,160 in fines for camping, and having an inoperable vehicle, and an outhouse [on my property]. I believe the Constitution states that I have God-given rights, and one of those God-given rights is the right to shelter and a place to crap." We were surprised to learn that the Constitution or God had opinions on these matters. However, in our experience attending most of the Big Look town hall meetings (and listening to audio recordings of the others), we found that nontrivial variations on this story—restrictions on residential use by rural landowners—were by far the most common complaint across the state. Planners in Oregon are familiar with similar emotions (including invocations of God and the Constitution) when owners call after learning they cannot have or modify a dwelling on land that is zoned under state rules for exclusive farm or forest use or restricted for other reasons. In our observations at the Big Look meetings, we saw that owners were not infrequently shocked and deeply angered by the idea that they could own a property and be blocked from building or modifying a home or using their property in other ways that to them seemed plainly reasonable.

Nor, however, is this kind of frustration limited to rural areas. For example, for those familiar with the culture of rural areas in the American West generally, it should hardly come as a surprise that rural areas in Oregon strongly supported pro-property rights Measure 37 by overwhelming margins. What is probably more surprising is that support for Measure 37 was both strong and widespread in many *urban* areas as well. Majorities of voters supported Measure 37 in all but one of Oregon's 36 counties (Benton—home of Oregon State University). For many familiar with Portland's famously liberal politics, it was somewhat shocking that Measure 37 won in all three of the Portland Metro counties, as well as *in the City of Portland itself* (by a small margin—see Mason 2008: 236). Observers attribute this result to the plethora of state and local regulations in Oregon's urban areas that limit individual development rights even at very small scales (grievous tales of homeowners denied a permit to build a deck abound). When voters in the Portland Metro area heard plaintive commercials featuring grandmother Dorothy English, who claimed to only want to build a few houses for her grandchildren on her 20-acre parcel just outside the Portland urban growth boundary (UGB), many Portland area voters could empathize.

John Renz, a planner and regional representative of the Oregon Department of Land Conservation and Development (DLCD) in southern Oregon, argues that this perception of excessive, nonsensical microregulation of individual property owners is the single greatest source of frustration he finds among the public, and the strongest motivation for the property rights backlash Oregon experienced with both Measure 7 and Measure 37: "After Lane Shetterly became director [of DLCD, in February 2004], he came down here [to southern Oregon] and spent three days with me. I said to him, 'Lane, we wouldn't need Measure 37, or Measure 7, or any of that, if we just allowed every legal parcel of land to have a residence, just as a right. That's what Americans expect. They don't imagine that you can have a piece of land but not have a home.' To me, that would have defused the whole thing [the property rights backlash]." Moreover, Renz argued, the perceived unfairness of the rules is compounded by the fact that some people with access to expertise in planning can circumvent these rules: "I worked on enough farm applications as a Josephine County planner that I could probably get a house on any farm parcel in the state. That's why people hire consultants to do it. The ordinary citizen is not going to know how to do it. [The ordinary citizen] is intimidated by those laws and rules because they are so complex. And the ordinary person is not going to know the case law and stuff—the system has become too complex for the ordinary citizen to use."[19]

The problem of unequal access to the planning system, resulting in sometimes gross violations of the principles of the state's planning program for the privileged (Figure 6) while those with fewer resources can be fined for an unpermitted outhouse, has contributed to making many in the state not only unsupportive of the planning program but deeply hostile toward it. In 1998, the *Portland Oregonian* newspaper ran a five-part series on the 25th anniversary of the state's land use planning system, with the title "Legacy on the Line."[20] The series emphasized the perceived ineffectiveness of the state's planning system in preventing development in wealthy areas and perceived subsidies to high-income "hobby farmers" through the state's property tax assessment system that was created to support "real" farmers. This perception of unfairness in favor of the wealthy is often mentioned in the same breath as complaints about these very individuals being the ones most likely to support further land use restrictions that will "shut the door behind them." In addition, there is a long-standing (and inconclusive) debate about the degree to which land

Figure 6   This 10,728-square-foot "farm house" sits on 20 acres of land zoned for exclusive farm use near Canby that seems to grow German luxury cars (P. Walker 2009)

use restrictions outside UGBs cause urban housing prices to rise, putting undue burdens on the poor.

Thus, whether accurate or not, the state's planning system is widely perceived as unfair in multiple ways. At a Big Look town hall meeting in Bend in 2008, staff circulated a questionnaire to audience members asking how the planning system could be improved. A participant quietly pushed a questionnaire across the table for us to see. In the blank space that invited suggestions to make the state's planning system better, the participant had written, "KILL THE LAWYERS!!!"

While professional planners in Oregon encounter such hostility on a daily basis, planning advocates acknowledge that they were slow to grasp the emotional (and, ultimately, political) potency of such complaints. 1000 Friends of Oregon founder Henry Richmond stated to us that in the period leading up to the property rights ballot initiative Measure 7 in 2000, "there was a perception that the [state planning] program got a little greedy in terms of its regulation of rural lands, and there was some tightening that troubled people." More specifically, Bob Stacey, the executive director of 1000 Friends at the time that Measure 37 was passed, noted that planning advocates such as he were slow to understand the significance of the right to build a home:

> I get upset about the idea that if you own a piece of ground in the country you automatically ought to be able to build a house on it. But I think that's where a lot of people start. It's a blind spot that betrays my technical background, I guess, and it wasn't apparent to me in 2003 that that was going to be a fundamental, core argument or that ultimately that would be the most efficacious way to resolve the Measure 37 problem in 2007 [with Measure 49]. But I've had folks from elsewhere tell me since, "You know, a core problem that the land use planning system in Oregon has is the effort to preserve agricultural land to the *exclusion* of a dwelling on farm acreage." That's something we're going to have wrestle with, because it's a fundamental part of the protection strategy for agricultural land. But it does beg the question of where regulations' effectiveness peters out and the desirability of land stewardship incentives for property ownership and property management and conservation easement acquisition starts to come in to make a "complete package." We've been doing a lot of thinking about that [at 1000 Friends] . . . but there's not a lot of appetite for raising money to undertake that kind of strategy.[21]

The question of the right of a land owner to build a house on land zoned for farm or forest use was solved by Measure 49 for some owners—those who purchased the land before current regulations existed—but potentially added still more "unfairness" from the perspective of those who purchased later. And the matter of residential use on rural land is far from the only policy for which the land use planning system had come to be seen by many Oregonians as onerous, arbitrary, and unfair. When we asked people all across the state why Measure 37 succeeded and they mentioned Dorothy English, they were proving that Dorothy English had become a symbol of a real problem in the view of many Oregonians. By the first decade of the 2000s, the *story* of Dorothy English, and a sense that the state's land use planning system had run amok, resonated strongly with many Oregonians. A system born of the glamorous vision of Governor Tom McCall had lost its sheen, becoming something closer to a garden-variety onerous, unfair bureaucracy.

Some proponents of the Oregon planning system have attempted to balance this perception of unfairness by pointing to certain equity benefits of the system, such as promotion of more affordable housing and tax benefits for rural property owners. Others have questioned the fairness of property owners simply expecting to profit from increased land values that they did nothing to earn (following George 1979). For example, in the wake of Measure 37, 1000 Friends founder Henry Richmond published an extensive economic analysis of the "fairness" that the state planning system provides to rural property owners in the form of reduced taxation (Richmond and Houchen 2007). Property rights advocates dispute the notion that tax relief has been commensurate with lost potential land value, and such arguments tend to bog down in a battle of numbers with technical calculations of losses and gains in taxes and property values. Whatever the merits of the pro-equity arguments in favor of the state planning system, proponents have been frustrated that these arguments tend to get relatively little political traction.

As for profits from unearned gains in the real estate market, property rights advocates respond that this is simply the way things are in a market economy. More important, the planning community should understand that whether or not an owner deserves sympathy for a lost opportunity to "cash in" on high property values may be an interesting philosophical question, but it misses the point, *politically* speaking: from the viewpoint of many individual property owners, the loss of an opportunity (real or perceived) for significant personal financial betterment is often felt as a stinging injustice. Collectively, the many property owners in Oregon who—right or wrong—share this perception of injustice inject enormous volatility into the politics of land use planning. Merely dismissing this sense of injustice (even outrage) on philosophical grounds (George 1979) will not make this emotional—and ultimately *political*—reality go away. In fact, in our observation the very dismissiveness among some planning advocates of the perhaps flawed but very human anger at being denied an opportunity for personal financial gain inflames the state's already volatile land use politics. More empathy on *all* sides could go a long way.

Bureaucratization

In the flurry of post–Measure 37 postmortems, a *Portland Oregonian* newspaper op-ed in 2004 opined, "there are too many policy wonks, too few visionaries."[22] As Bob Stacey explained,

> In 1973 [when the planning program was created] everything was new. . . . By 2004 [when Measure 37 passed], it was more than 30 years old . . . and the implementation of state land use planning law was no longer done on a big statewide stage, with big visionary struggles about competing views of the future. Instead, planning was carried out across a permit counter, in county court houses and city halls. So, by 2004, if people had interactions with the statewide planning system, they were likely interactions with a zoning code administrator, a permit technician, somebody whose job was to figure out whether there was some reason they had to say "no" — or, depending on your perspective, trying to *find* a way to say "no." And there were more regulations. What had started out as a broad policy statement . . . had turned into a series of regulations . . .
>
> When I was a kid fresh out of law school [in the mid-1970s], we were doing things that would make the future better. There was an excitement all across the board. The people on the Land Conservation and Development Commission, county planners, local officials, legislators, citizens who were involved in that process — they were changing the world. But today there's a defensiveness, and regret, and the feeling of indecision. You recognize that the movement is now associated with government bureaucracy. Something fundamental changed. There's a real need to reengage citizens at the policy-setting level.[23]

As the state planning program matured from the grand, almost utopian "visioning" politics of the Tom McCall era into the complex yet mundane, day-to-day bureaucratic tasks of actually administering such a large and ambitious program, there may have been something almost inevitable about the loss of public enthusiasm for — of even a kind of romance with — Oregon's planning system. This would appear consistent with Robert Michels, Eden Paul, and Cedar Paul's (1915) idea of the "iron law of oligarchy" — the idea that even bureaucracies born of revolutionary and idealistic movements tend over time to become dominated by narrow interests, while the governed community tends to become more passive and less involved—a recipe for conflict and alienation from state authority. Experiences in other states with ambitious planning goals and large bureaucracies, such as Washington State, suggest that some degree of bureaucratic sclerosis may indeed be inevitable.[24]

Specifically, as Oregon's land use system matured, a kind of tension inherent to any bureaucracy emerged between the need for flexibility and the problem of complexity. When we traveled the state observing ordinary Oregonians voicing their concerns about the planning system in the Big Look town hall meetings in 2008, the most commonly expressed problems were that the system applies a "one-size-fits-all" approach to planning and that the system is too complex and difficult for ordinary citizens to understand or navigate.

Yet, from the perspective of political and administrative leadership, these two complaints seemed almost contradictory, because complexity in the system had developed in part as a *response* to the perception of inflexible, "one-size-fits all" approaches. Oregon historian William Robbins reminded us that, "No legislative session after 1973 ever left land use planning untouched. It was always modified. There were always amendments to it."[25] Each time the program flexed to address specific problems or concerns, it also became more complicated. For administrators, this "have your cake and eat it too" problem was a paramount source of frustration. As former Republican legislator and DLCD director Lane Shetterly explained the problem to us,

> I heard a constant refrain when I was [director of DLCD] that people want two things: a land use system that provides predictability [i.e., simplicity], and flexibility. Well, those are almost opposite sides of the same coin. . . . As the legislature responded to pleas for flexibility and adjustments in the program to meet this circumstance that hadn't really been thought out or addressed or overlooked in the original iterations of Senate Bill 100, over the years the legislature . . . also created complexity.
>
> [For example,] if you want a farm dwelling in circumstances that would not have been allowed at all under Senate Bill 100, then under

what circumstances can you have that farm dwelling? You don't want everybody to have it just because they file an application—it's got to be on a farm. Well, then what is a "*farm*"? During the early years people would file farm plans along with the application to build a house out on a piece of rural land. People would say, "Oh, we're going to plant blueberries." So they get an approval, and maybe they plant blueberries, but they never tend them. They build the house, the blueberries go away, and what you've got left is a house on a ten-acre parcel out in the countryside. So that gave rise to, "ok we need to put some sideboards around what a farm is." So we got the $80,000 or 80-acre minimum test. Those became the surrogate ways of defining what is a farm. It provided certainty, it provided predictability, but you lost flexibility.

So there's this [inherent] tension. . . . As issues came forward [and the system adjusted], it created this complexity that became really difficult for people to implement and understand. After a while the purpose was lost, and all they could see was the complexity. People forgot why the complexity was there in the first place. It was to respond to a certain need. But you develop an exception . . . and it's just a matter of time before someone else comes along and says the rule doesn't quite fit their situation, so it's grossly unfair to them. . . . So now it's this evil program that's keeping people down. So what do you do? You go back and add more complexity to it to fix their problem! But of course their neighbor will be coming right behind them with some other problem. I don't know how to fix that. You could throw out the system and create a simple, straightforward, totally predictable system. But that would be absolutely unacceptable because it lacks any flexibility. . . . That's just a reality we're going to have to continue to deal with. . . . I don't know how you avoid it.[26]

While most would acknowledge that there can be an inherent tension between flexibility and complexity in any bureaucratic system, critics of Oregon's land use program (and even some supporters) suggest that some of the perceived rigidity in the state planning system is unnecessary and self-inflicted—the product of narrow, bureaucratic ways of thinking rather than an inevitable characteristic of a large administrative system. In other words, there can be inflexibility for good reasons, and in other situations there can be inflexibility for no good reason—other, perhaps, than a lack of creative thinking by administrators. John Renz, a DLCD regional representative in southern Oregon who works at the interface between state-level policy and local planning in his region, described to us an example of how, with appropriate leadership, his agency can be more flexible and responsive than many critics would assume:

It comes down to personnel and how different management personnel interpret the law. . . . For example, Shady Cove is the largest city in the state with no water system [population 2,820[27]]. The wells start drying up in Shady Cove in June, and they start having to haul water. They approached us [DLCD] about a deal that a developer wanted to make with them. The developer wanted to bring 100 acres into the UGB, and in exchange he would put together the nucleus of a water system that could be extended throughout the whole city. When I first heard about this, I said, "I can't see how you're going to show a need for more residential land. It's just not possible to do. You're sparsely developed now."

But we kept up the dialog. Eventually they pointed out that there are a lot of approved subdivisions [inside the UGB] but they aren't built because they don't have any water . . . so, it's not really buildable. It looks that way on paper, but it's not. So, I had [a specialist from DLCD headquarters in Salem] come down, and she's the kind of person who sees things in black and white and isn't very flexible. I said, "Look, we have an opportunity to move this city forward if we can find a way to make this work." She couldn't find a way to make it work. She just said, "You can't do it." That resulted in a conversation with Lane Shetterly [DLCD director] in which she sort of challenged him and said, "Are you going to obey the law or not?" He said, "Of course we're going to obey the law. But, we're going to make the law work for the situation." So [Shetterly] came and he and I met with the Shady Cove mayor. Pretty soon we came to a handshake agreement. . . . Basically [Shetterly] said, "We'll make it happen for you, but you've got to do some things for us," because we wanted Shady Cove to get rid of low-density zoning, to do a local street network plan, and do some things that were urban in nature, and act more like a city rather than a rural subdivision. And the mayor gave us his word and said, "We'll do it. You do your part, and we'll do our part." . . . and by God, it worked.

Now, what did we do to get flexible? We went back to talk to the consultant for the City of Shady Cove . . . and said, "Why don't we do this. We'll do a buildable lands inventory that says that all these previously approved subdivisions that haven't been built are unbuildable because there's no water, and we need to expand the UGB in order to get the water system"—which is what we did. If somebody had challenged it, we would have probably lost, and we'd have more rigid case law. But nobody did, and we lucked out. Shady Cove is happy. . . . And [the state] got a better city . . . I think it was the right thing.[28]

Renz suggested, however, that the ability of the state agency to enter into this arrangement depended on the management style of personnel operating in DLCD and its regional office at the time. Had other personnel been in place, there might have been a far more "rigid" interpretation of state land use laws, resulting in a missed opportunity. At the same time, said Renz, many local governments and private owners assume the worst about the state agency, and he sometimes has to remind the people he works with that the state is more flexible than they may think and that the state would not just blindly force local governments "into something that's stupid." But local people have to be willing to engage in dialog with the agency. In short, depending on management styles, there *can* be more flexibility than is often assumed, but to some degree, public attitudes about inflexible government can be a self-fulfilling prophecy. Relations of trust or mistrust build up over time and can either reinforce or break down problems of inflexibility.

This is true not only for the state land use agency but also for the advocacy groups that support it and the groups that oppose it. In Oregon the role of land use planning advocacy has become nearly synonymous with 1000 Friends of Oregon (but there are others, as we describe in chapter 7), which has frequently been accused of inflexibility. Moreover, 1000 Friends gained a reputation for being almost reflexively and ruthlessly litigious—a fact that many of our informants suggested may have ultimately hurt the very cause 1000 Friends was defending. In its first decades, 1000 Friends went to court time and time again to force the state

to uphold strict interpretations of planning law, and *almost always won.*
In some cases, this aggressive legal strategy by 1000 Friends prevented
DLCD from demonstrating flexibility even when the individual property
owners involved had legitimate causes for grievance that grabbed headlines and generated public antipathy not only toward 1000 Friends but
also toward DLCD and land use planning in general. Over time, more
and more Oregonians would agree with the moniker that the property
rights community slapped on the group: "1000 *Fiends* of Oregon." As
former LCDC chair Stafford Hansel has described, "We began to get
headlines. Every [law]suit that's brought, we get a bad headline out of
it. We're lucky if we only get a bad headline in the *Portland Oregonian.*
More than likely, we're going to get one at [the place of the dispute]. So
land use [planning] has almost become a bad word in areas [where] it
didn't used to be."[29]

But in Oregon's land use battles, it usually takes two to tango, and
Oregonians in Action, Oregon's leading property rights organization, has
also been accused of rigidity. Many say, for example, that the group's
unwillingness to compromise led to the failure of the 2005 legislature
to find agreeable solutions to resolve the many problems found in the
implementation of Measure 37. Oregonians in Action had won big with
Measure 37, and showed little interest in offering compromises even if
these compromises might avert further legal and political conflict. And,
like 1000 Friends, Oregonians in Action has often taken disputes into
court as a first resort.

Thus, during the political and administrative turmoil following the
passage of Measure 37, *Portland Oregonian* newspaper columnist Andy
Parker complained, "Over the years, as the debate about property rights
and farmland preservation heated up, the two special interest groups became so inflexible and entrenched in their own dogmas they might more
accurately have been called Oregonians in Traction and 1000 Friends
of Themselves."[30] Thus, from both the pro- and anti-planning communities, Oregon's planning system was pushed into seemingly hardened
winner-takes-all positions, further eroding what remained of the public's
McCall-era enchantment with the grand battle against sprawl.

Some advocates argue that while inflexibility may generate public distaste, this approach may be a defensible and necessary strategy. Robert

Liberty, a former executive director of 1000 Friends of Oregon (and now a Portland Metro councilor) explained this position to us in 2009:

> My experience has shown that the level of political opposition is not calibrated to the level of regulatory rigor. Politicians wrongly think if they weaken the regulations, for example those needed to protect farmland, they can thereby garner enough political support to secure passage of (or defend) the weaker regulations. But in fact, *any* regulations limiting the dividing of properties or building new homes generates serious political controversy. Even ineffective regulations generate controversy. The trap that many politicians don't understand is that by weakening the regulations needed to achieve important outcomes, like protecting farm- and forestlands, or allowing more dense urban development, they may so compromise the efforts that there are no real results from those regulations. And when there are no real results there is no constituency supporting the regulations. In Oregon the rigor of the regulations for rural land conservation was essential to achieving our publicly stated outcomes. Because those regulations saved farm- and forestlands and rangelands, they created a constituency that fought—successfully—the political battles needed to maintain the system. A milquetoast system still has many enemies, but it lacks any useful friends.[31]

Nevertheless, in the aftermath of Oregon's turbulent land use politics of the early 2000s, among land use planners and advocates compromise and accommodation seemed to be the prevailing mood at the end of the decade. Measure 49 itself represented the most significant compromise in the history of Oregon's land use planning system—not by choice, but, in the words of former legislator and land use planning advocate Nancie Fadeley, because "it was the best we could get." When we asked 1000 Friends executive director Bob Stacey whether the inclusion in Measure 49 of requirements for compensation for future regulations was good policy, he replied that at the time "it was *necessary*." For good or ill, through Measure 37 property rights activists in Oregon forcibly ushered in a new politics of compromise in the state's planning system. That kind of new politics, in the view of many of our informants, resulted in large part from the ascendance of the voter initiative system as a form of public policy making.

Ballot Box Politics

In the 1990s and mid-2000s, power in Oregon's state government was divided between the major political parties (until 2007, when Democrats took control of all branches of elective state office). "Hot-button" topics (in Oregon, land use is among them) often faced gridlock. For example, during the 1990s then-governor John Kitzhaber (a former emergency department physician) earned the moniker "Dr. No" among property rights activists for his repeated vetoes of property rights legislation. In the mid-2000s, a split between the Democrat-controlled state senate and the Republican-controlled state house of representatives prevented land use legislation from even moving out of the legislature. However, many political groups in Oregon found they could circumnavigate such barriers by taking their case directly to the public through the state's ballot initiative process. While the initiative process did not create the underlying conditions (as discussed above) that favored changes in the state's planning system, there is almost no doubt that *without* the initiative process such rapid, dramatic policy shifts would have been less likely.

Oregon's statewide voter initiative system is one of the oldest in the country, but the merits and possible flaws in the system have been debated intensely in recent years. In 1902, Oregon was the third state in the nation to authorize statewide voter initiatives, and the first in the nation (in 1904) to actually vote in a statewide ballot initiative, developing what became known around the nation as the "Oregon System"—a key political reform of the progressive era (see Schmidt 1989). At the dawn of the twentieth century, with institutionalized governance deeply corrupted by moneyed interests, the initiative system offered a democratic safety mechanism to put a brake on crony capitalism and politicians for hire. It is a system endorsed by populist crusaders of the 1960s and 1970s, including left-leaning consumer advocate Ralph Nader and right-leaning tax reformer Howard Jarvis in California (whose Proposition 13 tax limitations profoundly shaped that state's future). The initiative process fit the populist ideal of the American West as a place where the people rule, and it is still used most extensively in western states.[32]

In recent decades the voter initiative system in Oregon has often been used to decide controversial political issues on which any elected official with a healthy instinct for self-preservation might dread to vote, including physician-assisted suicide (the first law of its kind in the nation, approved in 1994), gay rights (supported and rejected multiple times since the 1980s, including successful Measure 36 in November 2004 banning gay marriage), term limits for statewide offices (approved in 1992), legalization of medical marijuana (approved in 1998), abortion rights limitations (mostly rejected in multiple initiatives), and, in nearly *every* election, tax-related initiatives. Notably, the state's initiative process itself has been the subject of repeated ballot initiatives in recent decades, mostly to promote greater transparency and integrity in the process. In the 1990s, Oregonians voted on more than 100 initiatives. In the 2000s, voters made choices on 90 initiatives, of which they approved 35—including Measures 7, 37, and 49 on land use.

Much debate has taken place in recent years in Oregon about whether the initiative process empowers citizens, or narrow special interest groups, and whether the process itself is open to manipulation and abuse. Much attention was focused on anti-tax activist Bill Sizemore, who has placed dozens of initiatives on the ballot since the 1990s but was frequently accused, and later found guilty, of unethical and illegal practices in his campaigns. These included filing falsified campaign finance reports, forging petition signatures, and pocketing campaign funds for personal use. In 2002, a Multnomah County jury found Sizemore guilty of racketeering. In 2006 the court of appeals upheld the ruling, declaring Sizemore guilty of "calculated criminal manipulations of the democratic process."[33] The Oregon Supreme Court upheld the ruling in 2008. Yet Sizemore still operates politically in Oregon, filing 13 initiatives for the 2010 ballot[34] and declaring his candidacy for the 2010 Republican nomination for Oregon governor. Sizemore almost surely did more than any single person in recent history to discredit Oregon's tradition of citizen initiatives. Other conservative activists such as former Oregonians in Action attorney Ross Day have worked hard recently to reestablish trust in a process that offers hope for conservatives in a state that has turned a deeper shade of blue in each recent election cycle.

With respect to land use policy, however, questions about the initiative system are arguably more profound than questions of the potential for fraud and abuse. Even with a completely "clean" election, a voter initiative may be an inappropriate way to decide issues as complex as land use planning. With issues such as gay rights or assisted suicide, the outcomes of a ballot choice may arguably be easier to understand for nonspecialist citizens. In contrast, an argument can be made that in Measure 37 and Measure 49 voters had only vague ideas of what the ultimate outcomes of their votes would be (in its sweeping nature, Measure 7 may have been somewhat easier to grasp). To take one of many possible examples, in Jackson County property owner Rick Sawyer recalled that he had only a vague idea that Measure 37 would benefit an elderly lady wanting to develop a few houses on her land, and "Why wouldn't you vote for it?" Twelve days after the 2004 election, Sawyer could not recall how he voted on Measure 37 and complained that, "like so many people in the state or county, there are very few people who know how to vote on these issues. The initiative process and all the ballots we face drive us all nuts."[35] In fact, some land use attorneys who helped to craft these initiatives acknowledged to us that even *they* had only an incomplete understanding of how these measures would work in practice. How reasonable, or even responsible, is it for a democracy to make critically important decisions in such a manner?

Many have also complained about the relative ease with which petitions, even for confusing or badly conceived initiatives, can reach the voters. Michael Cavallaro, the executive director of the Rogue Valley Council of Governments in southern Oregon, describes this concern with mocking exaggeration: "All you need are twelve signatures and you've got a ballot initiative. You can make enough people convinced about almost anything if you yell loudly enough and you couch it in the right way. 'You don't want government controlling your life, do you? Well, sign here.' [It] contributes to the [land use policy] mess we have now."[36] Concerns about the way initiatives reach voters are compounded by concerns about the kinds of information available to voters to make well-informed decisions once an initiative reaches the ballot.

With a subject matter as complex as land use planning and only an incomplete understanding of the ultimate outcomes of policy initiatives, an enormous amount rides on the writing of the ballot title and summary statement for each initiative that is written into the official "voters' pamphlet" (an odd word for a document that often runs to hundreds of pages) (see Bassett 2009). In an age of information overload and heated campaign rhetoric, these official statements are often the only place voters can turn for reasonably sound and objective information. The title and summary statements are particularly important because the volume of information available to voters is often overwhelming. In 2004, volume 1 of the state voters' pamphlet, covering state measures, was 156 pages long. The section of this volume devoted to Measure 37 alone was 30 pages. In 2007, the section of the voters' pamphlet devoted to Measure 49 alone was 55 pages.

There is general consensus among parties on all sides of the issues that, at best, voters rarely read more than the one-page summary statement for each measure. Therefore, the precise wording of these statements is critical. Yet, even if an initiative is a product of true "grassroots" citizen action, the choices that shape the official information the public relies upon to help them make good choices are very much an insiders' game—typically between attorneys for the petitioners and the secretary of state. If democracy is not simply about choice, but about well-*reasoned* and *informed* choice, the democratic credentials of Oregon's initiative system are open to question.

Indeed, judging from the reactions of opponents of *both* Measure 37 and Measure 49, reasoned and informed public choice through the initiative process never stood much of a chance. The ballot title of Measure 37 read as follows: "Governments must pay owners, or forgo enforcement, when certain land use restrictions reduce property value." Some of our informants who opposed Measure 37 complained that from the words "Governments must pay," their cause was lost. Opponents claimed that most voters expected Measure 37 to benefit their neighbors who had been restricted from building a second home for their children—but that they certainly did not intend to vote to allow their neighbors to build commercial establishments or large-scale subdivisions. Even more important, nor *could* voters have reasonably been expected to have known this was a realistic possibility based on the information that was presented to them in the voters' pamphlet. Conversely, in 2007 opponents of Measure 49 complained that (among other things) the wording of the ballot title indicated that Measure 49 would "clarify" rather than, in their view, largely repeal, Measure 37. Oregonians in Action sued to block certification of the ballot title, arguing that the title and explanatory statement in the voters' pamphlet were "factually inaccurate, unfair and underhanded" (the suit was dismissed).

A system in which there is, if nothing else, even a perception that those who can best manipulate the official information voters receive will win is a fundamentally bad way to run a citizens' democratic process. Even in the (seemingly unlikely) event that citizens do break through the clutter and make reasoned and informed (or, at least, reasonably informed) choices, the present system seems to virtually guarantee that the losing side in any ballot initiative will believe (or at least be able to claim) that their opponents won through trickery and gaming the system. Responding to such concerns, Oregon recently passed into law pilot legislation (initiated by policy students at the University of Oregon) that creates panels of randomly selected citizens (similar to the "jury of peers" concept) who reviewed evidence from all sides and wrote official explanatory statements for several initiatives on the 2010 ballot.[37]

"A Different Time"

When we interviewed scholars, activists, and political leaders and asked why, in their view, Measure 37 (and Measure 7 before it) succeeded in Oregon—a state that had been widely viewed as a "model" of effective land use planning—another common category of responses was the view that, in various tangible or intangible ways, the political climate had changed over the decades. For example, former state representative Nancie Fadeley, who helped pass the state's landmark land use legislation in 1973, replied to our question by observing that, first of all, the political fight for planning in Oregon "was never easy," but that the 1970s "was a time when people were more open to it. . . . The Reagan years affected us . . . the idea that government is the enemy, which [Reagan] very much popularized, that made it harder."[38] In chapter 3 we discussed the view, common among those who participated in the creation of Oregon's planning system in the 1970s, that the political mood of that time was possibly a contributing factor but was probably secondary to pragmatic, largely economic, concerns. When we asked, for example, about the national environmentalist mood of the 1970s, Hector Macpherson Jr., the architect of the state's planning system, stated flatly, "I don't think it had much effect"[39] in the creation of the planning program, which he saw primarily as an outgrowth of pragmatic concerns by farmers.

Yet, in several ways the changing time and prevailing political climate could be said to have had, if not a direct effect, then certainly indirect and possibly important consequences. First, there is a matter of generational change and the fading of social memories of the 1970s struggle for land use planning. As Oregon historian William Robbins told us, "Many people in Oregon today don't remember the experience of fighting for the land use protections we have today. They don't remember why we have the system we have."[40] Like most western states, Oregon has experienced very rapid in-migration in recent decades. In 2000 (the year Measure 7 passed), 55 percent of Oregon's population was born outside the state. In the same year, 48 percent of Oregonians were less than 35 years old.[41]

The proportion of Oregon citizens with direct and clear memories of the fight for quality of life and "livability" through planning in the 1970s is small. For most Oregonians today, the link between the state's still much-noted quality of life and the now-bureaucratized planning system is at best fuzzy. As the desirable effects of planning faded into dim memory, the less desirable effects came to the fore. The campaign for Measure 49 appeared to remind many voters that the weakening of "government intrusion" might actually diminish their quality of life. As Hector Macpherson told us, "You've got to keep educating people about the desirability of planning."[42]

Moreover, although it may be difficult to find clear links between national political ideology and the creation of Oregon's planning system the 1970s, the ascendant conservatism and the Reagan revolution of the 1980s contributed to at least one major, very tangible change in the political landscape of Oregon and the American West: the establishment of a well-organized professional property rights movement. As described to us by several participants in the creation of Oregon's planning system in the 1970s, at the time that Senate Bill 100 was created, there was a voice for property rights "at the table," but for the most part that voice belonged to a *single* individual. As now-retired Georgia Pacific Corporation executive Bill Moshofsky recalled, "I was fearful of the creation of a new land use agency and the power that it would have. . . . So it was natural for me to play an active role in lobbying against Senate Bill 100."[43] Moshofsky has proudly dogged Oregon's planning system ever since and now serves as vice president of the property rights group Oregonians in Action. In the 1970s and through much of the 1980s, however, Moshofsky was, as Hector Macpherson described him to us, "a one-man show."

In 1989, Moshofsky and an eastern Oregon farmer named Frank Nims founded Oregonians in Action, which now devotes itself exclusively to "fighting for property rights and against excessive land use regulations."[44] The organization has become the highly effective de facto representative for all property rights issues in the state and literally has a place at the table for many major land use planning decisions in the state today, often side by side with the long-time planning advocacy group 1000 Friends of Oregon. With the political emergence of Oregonians in Action as an aggressive and effective property rights advocacy group—and in particular with the passage of Measure 37—the political landscape for Oregon's planning system has fundamentally changed. As the current president of Oregonians in Action, Dave Hunnicutt told us, the state now directly consults with his organization on a range of land use policy matters: "I do think it's fair to say that our working relationship with the Department [of Land Conservation and Development] is much better than it was prior to the passage of Measure 37. We worked closely with DLCD last session on House Bill 3225, I serve on a DLCD task force relating to religious uses in [exclusive farm use] zones, Richard Whitman [the DLCD director] has presented at our last two land use forums, and I'm currently working with Richard on a bill for the 2010 special session. This would have been unthinkable prior to Measure 37."[45]

Hunnicutt also explained to us that his organization is Oregon grown and did not emerge out of the broader national property rights movement since 1980s and 1990s. However, to the extent that a generalized national conservative political trend since the Reagan administration helped to motivate property rights activism across the nation, and given the socio-demographics of the state as described above, the property rights movement in Oregon did not stand alone—and thus it is probably fair to say, as many of our informants do, that Oregon's land use politics to some degree tracked these broader shifts in the national political mood.

An example of Oregon tracking national political trends is the deep partisan split on environment and land use planning. As described in chapter 3, Oregon's unique planning system emerged mainly from Republican leadership, with strong Democratic support, particularly in urban areas. By the late 1970s, however, land use planning had become a partisan issue, with Republicans aiming to dismantle or weaken the state planning structure, and Democrats fighting to support and strengthen it. As with national politics, the culture of partisanship in state elective office in Oregon is widely noted with alarm, especially among those who remember the creation of the state's landmark environmental laws (including the Bottle Bill and the Beach Bill) as high-water marks for the achievements possible through bipartisanship. Again tracking national trends, the Republican Party in Oregon today has largely abandoned its former pragmatic, conservation-minded conservatism. A few pro-planning Republicans such as former Governor Vic Atiyeh and former DLCD director Lane Shetterly wistfully describe themselves as "anachronisms."

Finally, and perhaps most importantly, the Oregon planning system faces "a different time" today in that it seems to have lost its vital commitment to meaningful public engagement that characterized the program in its early years. In 1974, when the staff of the brand-new Oregon Department of Land Conservation and Development (DLCD) climbed into vans and set out on a 15-month series of public meetings with thousands of Oregonians to let the public decide on the goals that would define the future of planning in the state, "citizen involvement" became, literally, Goal 1. In the years since, the planning system has struggled, and often failed, to carry out that goal in a meaningful way. We devote the remainder of this chapter to a recent well-intentioned but flawed effort to reengage the Oregon public with the state's land use planning system.

Public Engagement and the "Big Look"

Senate Bill 100 wasn't just a bill. It was a new worldview. . . . It came about because leaders such as Gov. Tom McCall engaged in massive public outreach. Thousands of Oregonians saw what was at stake. . . . Civic engagement—the loud "yes" of Oregonians—was the driving force behind the success of the program.
—*Portland Oregonian* editorial, 2005[46]

The strength of land use planning in Oregon was really founded on the ability to engage thousands of people. The goal-setting process that took place after the passage of Senate Bill 100, as much as anything, was the [process] that created some excitement and enthusiasm for what this means. Had that not happened, and the Legislature stopped with the legislation and said to the counties, "You will do some planning," people would just not have gotten engaged. They would not have understood.

—Mike Thorne, chair of the Oregon Big Look task force, 2009[47]

In Oregon, the town of Burns could be said to be nearly as far away as one can get from the Willamette Valley, where the state's land use planning system was created. To reach Burns from almost anywhere in western Oregon requires a day's drive eastward through high desert sagebrush, including hours at a time when virtually no human feature (save for scattered cattle) is visible (Figure 7). It is nearly as geographically, economically, culturally, and ecologically different as one can get in Oregon from the moist, green, politically dominant and left-leaning urbanized corridor of the Willamette Valley west of the Cascades mountains. The rapid growth and threats to the agricultural economy, as well as environmental and aesthetic concerns that stimulated the creation of Oregon's planning system in the Willamette Valley, have never applied in the same way in remote communities such as Burns. In important ways, however, Burns is emblematic of some of the most important problems with the state's planning system today.

With the goal of better understanding such problems in the wake of the passage of Measure 37 in November 2004, in 2005 Oregon Governor Ted Kulongoski, Oregon house speaker Karen Minnis, and Oregon senate president Peter Courtney appointed a 10-member group of leaders from agriculture, business, law, and local government as the Oregon Task Force on Land Use Planning (better known as the "Big Look" task force). Under the terms of the legislation that created it, the task force sought to study and make recommendations on the effectiveness of Oregon's land use planning system for all Oregonians, "current and future," in "all parts of the state."[48] The task force conducted 11 public "town hall" meetings in 10 Oregon cities and towns in September and October 2008. On October 1, the task force held its first and only meet-

Figure 7   On the road to Burns, Oregon, sprawl seems under control
(P. Walker 2008)

ing in southeastern Oregon, in the Armory Building in quiet downtown
Burns (Figure 8).

As in all other locations, the Big Look town hall meeting in Burns was
attended mostly by local landowners, business leaders, and local government officials. On that warm Wednesday evening in Burns, the audience
was (generously) estimated by DLCD staff at 70 people. Big Look town
hall meetings were organized by staff from the Oregon DLCD and facilitated by a professional planning consultancy, Fregonese Associates, based
in Portland. Most members of the task force attended only selected town
hall meetings, but the meeting in Burns was officiated by Big Look task
force chairman Mike Thorne and attended by Oregon DLCD director
Richard Whitman.

What Thorne and Whitman observed in Burns may have been un-
surprising to them, and certainly was similar to other Big Look town
hall meetings throughout the state. But the feel of the evening in Burns

Figure 8   The Big Look town hall meeting in Burns was a low-key affair
(P. Walker 2008)

was odd. Oregon land use politics elicits strong emotions and, not infrequently, strong tempers. The audience in Burns, however, was quiet, even subdued. Like all the Big Look town hall meetings, the evening was tightly structured. Private consultant and facilitator Sorin Garber showed the finely produced "Big Look video," gave a PowerPoint lecture, and facilitated discussion on three main topics identified in advance by the task force. The video, PowerPoint slide show, and discussion topics were the same in every town hall meeting in every part of the state: protecting farms, forests, and natural areas under pressure from urban growth; promoting "livability" in urban areas; and fostering public participation in land use planning. These are issues of great concern in the Willamette Valley, the Interstate 5 corridor, and the Columbia Gorge region—home to all but two of the task force members.

In Burns, however, the fit of this structured presentation seemed "off." The population of Burns (3,064 in the 2000 U.S. Census) has been essentially stable or declining since 1950. Burns is located in Harney County, the largest county in the state in land area and smallest in population. Harney County had 7,609 residents in 2000, essentially unchanged from 1970 and significantly less than in 1980. The task force's preselected "town hall" discussion topics of containing urban sprawl and financing expansion of urban infrastructure are simply not pressing issues in any way like the rapidly growing Willamette Valley. As for the preselected topic of public participation in planning, members of the Big Look audience in Burns grumbled quietly about the sincerity and motivations of their visitors from Fregonese Associates and the DLCD (based in Portland and Salem—the state capitol—respectively). Some members of the audience in Burns found it amusing that the Big Look task force asked them whether "e-blasts" or RSS feeds were a preferred option for enhancing public engagement.

Perhaps the most poignant moment of the evening occurred during the facilitator's PowerPoint presentation. A member of the audience raised a hand and asked the facilitator to go back to a previous slide that showed a map of private land in the state. The audience member pointed out that the legend of the map (indicating differing types of private ownership) covered a large portion of southeastern Oregon (Harney and Malheur counties)—literally making that part of the state invisible. The facilitator from Portland responded, "It's because the graphic artist made an artistic decision, and obviously it wasn't a very good one. I apologize for that," and quickly moved on with the presentation, seemingly unaware that some audience members regarded this graphic insult as more than an "artistic decision." To many in the audience, this map graphically reinforced their longstanding view that Oregon's powerful "elites" barely even think about the people and land outside the Willamette Valley. This same map was used in every presentation in all 10 Oregon locations where Big Look town hall meetings were held. The facilitator's response to the question about the map legend obscuring their region sent murmurs and soft groans rippling though the Burns audience. A local municipal official leaned over to one of the researchers for this book and whispered, "We're *used* to being invisible to those people."

In many respects the town of Burns is exceptional, but the skepticism by the Burns audience about the sincerity of the state government's desire to "listen" to the public was shared at almost every Big Look town hall meeting. To be sure, like most westerners, many Oregonians approach *all* interactions with government with suspicion. Yet, the manner in which the public engagement component of the Big Look process was handled often deepened such suspicions. We attended and participated in eight of the 11 Big Look town hall meetings and reviewed audio recordings of the other three. The unanimous opinion of the participants with whom we spoke during and after the Big Look town hall meetings was that, whether intentionally or not (opinions differed), the heavily structured format of these meetings unduly limited public input.

The Big Look town hall meetings followed the same format in nearly every meeting location.[49] Usually between two and four of the 10 Big Look task force members attended the meetings and made introductory welcoming comments to the audience. The handling of the meetings was then given over to a private consultant and facilitator from Fregonese Associates. The meetings were organized around four parts: an introduction, followed by a presentation and discussion on the three main issue areas identified in advance by the task force (farm, forest, and natural areas; "livable communities"; and public participation). For each of these parts, the facilitator showed a segment of the specially produced Big Look video, followed by a PowerPoint presentation, and, finally, audience discussion and questions.

The structure of these events limited both the scope of topics discussed and the amount of time for public questions and comments, often resulting in great frustration and even anger among participants. Meetings were scheduled for two hours each (6:30–8:30 p.m.). With the introduction, video, PowerPoint slides, and approximately five-minute "table discussions" by participants on the first topic area ("farm, forest, and natural areas"), audiences usually could not address the task force in open discussion until approximately 30–45 minutes into the meetings. The same steps (video showing, PowerPoint presentation, and "table discussions") were then repeated for the other two main issue areas identified by the task force ("livable communities" and "participation and coordination"). Typically the meetings would fall behind schedule, allowing for a total of 45 minutes or less out of a two-hour program for as many as 350 citizens at a time (at the Portland town hall meeting) to address the task force.

Even more problematic, the scope of the topics and questions to which the Big Look staff asked members of the public to respond were so limited and confining that many participants immediately dismissed the entire process as a sham. For example, on the topic of urban infill, audiences were asked to respond to a question on how best to pay for urban infill (i.e., to promote density of urban areas, vs. "sprawl"). Participants were asked to choose between only two options: (1) rely on market forces or (2) pay more in taxes for public investments in infrastructure. As one audience member at the Portland Big Look town hall meeting observed, any question about raising taxes when stated in the abstract is "loaded" against taxation. The task force did not ask participants to discuss the beneficial uses to which the money might be put. The audience member went on to complain that "these are narrow questions designed to elicit a specific response. I find that deeply disturbing. This is not what I would call public input. If you are looking to increase public participation, I would suggest that you give us a chance to provide real input, not answers to limited and loaded questions." On the same topic, a participant in the town hall meeting in Coos Bay observed that she disagreed with the underlying premise that urban density is desirable. The participant suggested that rural development allows children to grow up in small communities where they can play in and explore open spaces. Every member of the public attending a Big Look meeting was given a questionnaire with the same tightly worded and conceptually confining questions. There was literally and figuratively no place for the public to raise more fundamental questions such as these—the kinds of "big" questions that seemed clearly implied in the idea that the state should take a "big look" at the planning system.

Many comments and complaints voiced by members of the public at the Big Look town hall meetings were heartfelt and thoughtful—and they revealed fundamental flaws in the conceptualization and implementation of the public outreach effort by state planners. *Every* topic on the official agenda for discussion in the Big Look public engagement effort was narrowly framed, and the range of answers was confined. Potential solutions offered in the Big Look questionnaire were literally presented in a multiple-choice format, some lacking even an option to choose "none of the above" (which greatly angered many participants). In the language of academic research on participatory planning, public participation in the Big Look was strongly "contained" (Few 2001), to the extent that other ideas had no point of entry into the process.

The fundamental flaw was not necessarily in the "containment" of the process—there are times when a contained public participation process may be appropriate or required. The fundamental flaw with the Big Look public outreach was the mismatch between the expectations among the participants and the task force about what the purpose of public participation should be. Most members of the public who participated in the Big Look town hall meetings came with the expectation that they were invited to help the Big Look task force to take *a big look* at the planning system. For example, many participants learned of the Big Look town hall meetings from 500,000 newspaper inserts (and subsequent media coverage) that invited members of the public to "join the conversation about Oregon's land use planning system. Are there changes you would like to see or would support?" Big Look task force members repeated this kind of broad invitation in the introduction to every town hall meeting.

At the first town hall meeting, in Tillamook, task force member and then-mayor of Lake Oswego (a Portland suburb) Judie Hammerstad stated that the purpose of the town hall meetings was to take the Big Look process "to the people in Oregon . . . our purpose is to get feedback from you. It is not to tell you what we want to do . . . we really want to hear from the wisdom of the people who live in Oregon." To many participants, these words conveyed the idea that they were being invited to be full participants in taking a *big* look at the state's land use planning system. Some were skeptical of the state's sincerity. What they did not understand, however, was that while the invitation was sincere, the role that the Big Look officials expected the public to play was actually to provide feedback on a relatively *narrow* (not "big") set of issues and options that the task force had already identified as its priorities. This was not intentional deception of the public. Rather, it was a failure of the Big Look public engagement effort to adequately communicate its expectations. In our direct observation in eight town hall meetings, virtually no members of the public understood that the task force intended that the general public should play a rather limited role in the Big Look. The resulting clash of expectations and palpable public anger at nearly every

Big Look town hall meeting almost certainly undermined Oregonians' sense of engagement and ownership of their state's unique land use planning system.

Right or wrong, the choice by the task force to limit the role of the general public was made quite deliberately and for practical and defensible reasons. At the first internal meeting of the Big Look task force members in March 2006, there was a keen awareness of the limited time and resources available to carry out such a large-scale review. Governor Kulongoski attended that first meeting and noted that Measure 37 would soon come into effect, and then-director of the DLCD commission, Lane Shetterly, warned that conducting public meetings might take too much time. The task force chose a strategy of "targeted research," involving meetings with key "stakeholders" and travel to specific sites around the state where land use conflicts had occurred. The work plan for the task force that was adopted on May 26, 2006, specifically emphasized that engagement with the general public should *follow* identification of major issues and options by the task force and should "be organized around specific questions and issues and would include the framing of trade-offs, *not* open-ended generalities" (emphasis original).[50]

As Big Look chairman Mike Thorne explained later, the task force's research and meetings with experts and stakeholders, conducted from March 2006 to September 2008, "laid the foundation that led us to some conclusions that we wanted to formalize at town hall meetings." The function of the meetings would be to "either confirm what we thought or help us better define where we were going"—to "validate assumptions" that the task force had formed in the previous two years of work.[51] Chairman Thorne also observed, however, that he was unable to think of a single example in which task force members changed their minds as a result of something said in a public meeting, and noted that in any event most people who attended came with "strong feelings"—implying that the views expressed at meetings of the general public were not necessarily useful or even representative of general public attitudes. The task force made a considered decision that directly engaging the general public was not an effective path to identifying critical issues and solutions to address problems with the state's planning system. In other words, the general public's lack of trust in the representatives of the state's land use planning system—evident in Big Look town hall meetings across the state—was reciprocated.

Bob Stacey, executive director of 1000 Friends of Oregon, described the philosophy of the Big Look task force this way:

> The members of the task force, somewhat understandably, tried to avoid eruptions of passionate disagreement around fundamental issues, like the role of government. They looked for internal cohesion on issues that they could study. . . . [Some members of the task force] fundamentally distrust public process.
>
> [Characterizing the view of the committee:] "If you want a bunch of pabulum, a bunch of meaningless input, we can do that. But that's not what we're here to do. . . . We're the experts, we're appointed because we're experts, and if we can agree on this disparate task force, then the answers must be right for all Oregonians. So, we'll engage the public when we've made up our minds what we're going to propose, and in the last phase let them respond. But we're not going to waste time with that kind of silliness: we don't need a big research agenda. Those of us around the table have enough experience that we don't need outside experts telling us how the system has performed, and we certainly don't need to engage a bunch of people in he-said-she-said testimony about these controversial issues. We know there are things that can be fixed, let's go fix them."
>
> So it became a utilitarian, technocratic exercise with no opportunity to change the way Oregonians think about the land use planning system, the future of the state, or the relationship between the two—which is what I was in it for, and what a lot of Oregonians would have supported if they had the chance.[52]

If there is a lack of public understanding of what the land use planning system does to benefit citizens as well as a certain level of distrust between the state and the public on this topic, the Big Look public engagement effort may have damaged the relationship even further. Few participants gave up an evening of their lives with the desire to "validate" someone else's "assumptions." Worse, the failure of the Big Look leadership to display genuine respect for ordinary citizens deepened hostility even among people who should be the planning system's political "base."

In the Big Look town hall meeting in The Dalles (a fast-growing area in the Columbia River gorge), audience member Ken Maddox complained, rightly, that "the recommendations were written four months ago, and tonight we're being asked for public input" (only a few weeks before the recommendations would go to the state legislature). As to the survey, "that's public participation of a kind I suppose, if we're all pigeons. Because we've all been put into pigeon holes by the survey."[53] Facilitators seemed at a loss when faced with such basic questions. John Fregonese, president of Fregonese Associates, led the meeting in The Dalles. After reminding the audience that "we want you to stick to the topic," the frustrated facilitator asked,

FREGONESE: Ok, what would *you* do about the state's land use system?

MADDOX: Oh, now that's a good *open* question! How long do we have? Where should we start?

FREGONESE: I think I should take that back.

MADDOX: I think you probably should.[54]

We heard similar frustration in almost every Big Look town hall meeting we attended. Most often, when members of the public expressed such frustration about these conceptual and procedural constraints, Big Look facilitators simply thanked the speaker in a polite but somewhat patronizing manner and moved on with no substantive response.

The public frustration at the substantive constraints built into the Big Look public engagement process was compounded by numerous logistical blunders. Nearly every Big Look town hall meeting was marred by technological problems (noisy feedback or incorrect volume on microphones being the most common). As experienced classroom lecturers as well as researchers, we can testify to how quickly a failure to control presentation technology causes an audience to lose patience and confidence. The facilitators also displayed surprising insensitivity to local culture. In the Big Look town hall meeting in deeply conservative Klamath Falls, the Portland-based facilitator wore a blue blazer, shiny loafers, and a diamond stud in his ear, in a room full of Wrangler jeans and cowboy hats. Possibly the worst mishandling of any town hall meeting occurred in Medford, where the room selected by the organizers was far too small for the number of citizens wishing to participate. Many came from long distances in rural areas to participate, only to find themselves literally shut out. For many would-be participants, this only reaffirmed the perception that the state did not really want to hear their ideas.[55] We do *not* agree with the view of some participants that this was an intentional effort to suppress public input. Yet, perceptions matter, and the avoidable problems that occurred at these meetings inexcusably reinforced already-existing antipathy toward, and alienation from, the state's planning system.

Some critics have suggested, however, that these procedural and stylistic problems also deafened the Big Look leadership to practical options for reducing problems that have emerged in the planning program. The Big Look process led to legislation that may eventually provide more flexibility in the planning system by allowing counties to rezone rural land with state approval.[56] However, the legislature did not provide funding for the costly and time-consuming process of reassessing rural land, and any such changes may take years, if they happen at all (particularly in a time of budget crisis). In the meantime, immediate problems that the public pleaded for the Big Look leadership to hear at every town hall meeting remain unaddressed. 1000 Friends founder Henry Richmond complained that there are many things the task force could have done to provide immediate relief, and that "somebody who went to [the Big Look town hall meetings] and made a legitimate complaint, they would read the report of the task force and say, 'What the hell does that have to do with *me?*' Nothing. People are just going to be more burned up than they were before."[57]

This unintentional alienation of the public was possibly the last thing the state planning system needed. It may be useful for leaders who tend to see little value in deep public engagement to remember that the Oregon land use planning system would almost certainly not exist today—and may not be politically sustainable in the future—without a high level of public involvement, even a sense of pride and ownership in the vision and accomplishments of Oregon's unique way of protecting its landscapes. Former state senator Hector Macpherson observed that when he began drafting Senate Bill 100, "the legislature didn't want to touch it" (Walth 1994: 353). What made the difference politically was widespread *public* support, harnessed through a great deal of work by a politician with a gift for communicating with the public—then-governor Tom McCall.

The conventional wisdom among Oregon planning advocates in the 2000s seems to be that McCall had a special talent that is absent today. This view misses a fundamental lesson of history. McCall worked very hard to win public support for the planning system, by taking his case directly—and *sincerely*—to the people of the state. In the lead-up to the vote in 1973 for Senate Bill 100, McCall presented scenarios for growth directly to the public before 275 civic groups and town hall meetings. As Macpherson noted, "Tom was a master with words. . . . He was not a nuts-and-bolts man. . . . But this is the kind of thing we needed. He prepared the public for the legislators back home and helped create that groundswell" (Walth 1994: 355). Even then, the bill passed the legislature only because negotiator L.B. Day agreed to include provisions that the core "goals" of the planning system would be established not by politicians or bureaucrats but by the general public through a series of local meetings that engaged thousands of Oregonians.

To be fair, the Big Look task force had neither the budget nor the mandate to repeat the ground-breaking public engagement of the early 1970s. But the insular, technocratic mindset of the state's planning leadership displayed in the Big Look process revealed a fundamental problem. When Oregon planning advocates today complain about the absence of "a Tom McCall" for our time, they fail to understand that McCall was not a magician; McCall simply understood the power of making himself a catalyst for *public* pride and vision about the special quality of the place we call home, the place called Oregon. When called upon to validate the planning system through ballot measures in 1970 (in response to SB 10, the unsuccessful precursor to SB 100), 1976, 1978, and 1982 (in response to SB 100), Oregonians voted decisively to uphold statewide planning. McCall certainly contributed to these successes, and now he is gone. But strong evidence suggests that the values and vision he tapped into are alive and well. The 62 percent vote in favor of Measure 49 in 2007 (along with gigabytes of polling data that went into the Measure 49 campaign) indicates that Oregonians today are no less supportive of fair planning policies that maintain the special qualities of living in Oregon than they were in McCall's day.

The power of vision and deep public engagement is a power that leaders of the state's planning system today underestimate at their peril. Planning advocates would do well to learn from history that the power of the public imagination and serious, deep, and sustained public engagement was at the core of the state's planning system from the beginning. Far from being an obstacle to successful planning, deep and sustained public engagement may be indispensable to the future viability of the planning system. In the end the Big Look process created worthy legislation that may eventually allow greater flexibility in the system. Certainly in places like Burns—far from the green Willamette Valley and the economy and culture that gave birth to the state's planning system—such flexibility is needed. Yet, the even bigger problem that we observed in close observation of the Big Look process was the absence of trust and sincere dialog between planning leaders and the public—the public that ultimately owns this process and decides its fate and the citizens who own the landscapes that make the place called Oregon. While flexibility is very important, public vision, engagement, and sense of ownership—a sense of why we have the unique system we have to begin with—may be even *more* important.

"Not as Bad as It Could Have Been"

Advocates of Oregon's land use planning system should consider themselves lucky—*very* lucky. Twice in a single decade Oregon voters approved ballot initiatives (Measures 7 and 37) that would have fundamentally weakened the state planning system. Twice the planning system survived by essentially mere flukes. In December 2000 a Marion County judge blocked Measure 7 from taking effect on a technicality, a decision that was later upheld by the state supreme court before the measure ever took effect. In October 2005 another Marion County judge blocked Measure 37 on constitutional grounds. The state supreme court overturned the lower court decision in February 2006, but the delay gave opponents of Measure 37 time to regroup. Moreover, with ambiguity in Measure 37 on the question of transferability of development rights, few developers, banks, or insurance companies were willing to invest in Measure 37 claims without greater certainty from the courts or the legislature. In the meantime, the economy crashed. Very few approved Measure 37 claims became actual brick-and-mortar construction.[58] However, enough developments were approved to remind the public why removing development restrictions might not be a cost-free idea, and the Measure 49 campaign was able to turn public anxieties about excessive development into electoral victory. Many of the planning advocates with whom we spoke noted that, from their perspective, the Measure 37 experience was "not as bad as it could have been."

From their perspective that is certainly true, but if planning advocates believe that the state planning system is secure, they may be as short-sighted as they were when Measure 7 was overturned by the courts in October 2002—and the planning community popped champagne corks and went back to business as usual. In the 2007 vote for Measure 49, voters reacted against the threat of uncontrolled development that Measure 37 appeared to pose, but it is far from clear that the public warmly embraced the state's still politically weak, still unfair, still bureaucratized, still technocratic and insular planning system. And in the meantime, the state has taken only very modest steps to address the kinds of widespread concerns and weaknesses in the planning system that we have described in this chapter. In 2009 the state passed legislation based on the recommendations of the Big Look task force that gives modest additional flexibility to counties to reconsider what lands are zoned farmland and forestland and refines how counties and local governments can engage in "regional problem solving" (see chapter 8). Land use attorney William Van Vactor summed up the results of the Big Look this way:

> [It] did little to remove the complexity that has developed over the last 35 years or to create more flexibility in how land use regulations are implemented. Further, [the Big Look legislation] does little to address improving citizen participation, or improving coordination among planning efforts for transportation, infrastructure, and economic development. Perhaps this is the result of Oregon's land use system taking a back seat to the more pressing issues facing the 2009 legislature as a result of the recession. Or conceivably, the result is the legislature's way of saying that the Oregon land use system is in need of only minor tweaks.[59]

In either case, the state failed to come firmly to grips with the genuine problems that still exist in the land use planning system—which we have briefly described in this chapter. In the next three chapters we explore these issues in more depth in specific regions of the state (Portland Metro, Central Oregon, and southern Oregon). In each of our regional case studies we examine the on-the-ground realities that indicate to us that the planning system still needs much serious attention. If supporters of the state's land use planning system doubt this, perhaps they should just wait until the end of the current economic recession for the next Measure 37.

6 Metro Visions

Oregon has not adopted a plan to stop growth. We know that growth is going to happen. If we foreclose development of agricultural land then we have to ensure that land within the cities is developed properly to accommodate the growth that we will experience. . . . If the part of our planning program that determines where growth is supposed to go doesn't work, then we open up the dam. The whole planning program will go down the drain, inevitably.

—Henry Richmond, founder of 1000 Friends of Oregon, 1978[1]

We've done a horrible job. If we don't figure out how to do density and infill, that's where the system's going to fall apart.

—Jon Chandler, Oregon Building Industry Association, 1999[2]

The one thing about Damascus that I want you all to understand, is that Damascus has been rural for a long time, and they'd like to retain their rural character.

—Dee Wescott, mayor Damascus, Oregon, 2002[3]

They didn't ask us in Damascus!

—Rallying cry for the Damascus Community Coalition, 2006[4]

When flying into Portland International Airport on a clear day (they do happen), a visitor is likely to be struck by the majestic natural beauty of snow-covered Mount Hood, Mount Adams, and Mount St. Helens (the nearest in the chain of volcanic peaks that forms the Cascades Mountains in Oregon and Washington). One is also likely to be struck by the magnificent Columbia River Gorge (and, because the airport sits on the riverbank, perhaps by the fact that your airplane appears headed to land in the great river itself).

Surrounded by so much natural beauty, one might fail to notice the remarkable human signature on the landscape. The authors have not flown from Phoenix to Portland. It would be an interesting flight. From the air, the Phoenix metropolitan area, with 14,598 square miles and 3.2 million people in the 2000 U.S. Census, seems to roll out into the desert like an endless carpet of suburbia. In contrast, the Portland metropolitan area had 5,133 square miles and 1.9 million people in the 2000 Census.[5] Thus, Phoenix is home to about two-thirds more people but occupies three times more land than Portland. Even more remarkable, seen from the air Phoenix seems intent to expand forever, whereas Portland quite deliberately comes to a visible abrupt stop. The urban growth boundary (UGB; see chapter 2) that separates rural from urban areas around Portland (and all Oregon cities) forms a very bright line. In urban areas like Portland that are pressing up against their growth boundaries, when you have crossed into, or out of, the UGB, you *know* it. It is an unmistakable physical manifestation of Oregon's unique land use politics.

Descending from cruising altitude as you approach the Portland airport, it looks serene enough. You probably will not hear the verbal battles taking place over these bright lines down below, in small places with odd names like Happy Valley, Boring, and Damascus.

City of Green Dreams

On the ground, you might wander into Portland's Pearl District, walking distance from the heart of the city center—an area the *New York Times* describes as "Portland's answer to SoHo, [that] has evolved rapidly from a raw industrial zone into a neighborhood of galleries, parks and condos," part of the city's "vibrant downtown, overflow[ing] with urban pleasures like chic restaurants, funky nightclubs and spritely neighborhoods crackling with youthful energy."[6] The district has also been described as "one of the best-known urban reclamation projects in the country" and a product of "a growing appreciation for urban life." (The district was named for the "pearls" of economic activity and artistic creativity taking place inside the crusty exteriors of reclaimed former industrial buildings.)[7] But the district is more than a playground for next-generation young urban professionals: it is also home for an intended 12,500 people (many living in converted warehouse lofts and high-rise condominiums) and future professional workspaces that will allow still more residents to live and work in the district without cars.

The humming, high-energy, high-density Pearl District may seem unconnected to the sleepy small towns at the edge of Portland's metropolitan area, but it is not: it is part-and-parcel of the city's vision for tightly limiting urban expansion. Portlanders know, and are justifiably proud of the fact, that their vital, economically and aesthetically attractive urban core makes it possible to minimize growth around the urban edges. As Pearl District resident Patricia Gardner told the *Portland Oregonian*, "I always say the Pearl is all about the urban growth boundary. Every bit of housing we put here allows us to not expand. I think there's a duty—particularly of downtown areas with transit—to take as many people as possible."[8] Model districts like the Pearl are very much a part of a broader vision of Portland as a sustainable, "green" city of the future.

And, as the Green Rush of the 2000s got under way, Portland could plausibly claim the mantle of "sustainability" mother lode. By various rankings of the most "sustainable" cities in the country, Portland is consistently at or near the top of almost every list.[9] Among these, SustainLane .com offers the nation's most-cited rankings, based on an annual peer-reviewed survey of America's 50 most populous cities ranked according 16 criteria, self-described as "the most comprehensive and credible benchmarking of sustainability in America."[10] The rankings are cited in popular media such as the *Wall Street Journal*, CNBC, CNN, National Public Radio, and the *New York Times*. To date, Portland has placed number 1 every year since the survey was created in 2005.[11] In awarding the 2008 prize, SustainLane.com lauded then-mayor of Portland Tom Potter's declaration that "Portland's support of local farmers and farmers' markets; its explosion of green buildings and commitment to renewable energy, and its emphasis on mass transportation, including light rail and bicycles, shows that a city can not only be kind to the earth, but also flourish economically and grow by being green."[12]

Some "sustainable city" runners-up noted a bit ungraciously but correctly that in a sense Portland had a 30-year head start. Among SustainLane

.com's and other indices' criteria for "sustainability" are such indicators as planning and land use, a "green economy," "green building," and "city innovation" — all areas in which Portland ranked at or near the top among all American cities. To some extent these "green" virtues could be said to have been not entirely choices, but requirements of being by far the largest metropolitan area in a state often described as having the most stringent urban growth policies in the nation. Under Oregon law the Portland Metro area had no choice but to pursue rigorous land use planning.

Nonetheless, Portlanders on the whole have unquestionably embraced a strong pro-environmental and pro–land use planning ethic for decades. It was no coincidence that when Republican state senator Hector Macpherson Jr. needed a cosponsor for his 1973 Senate Bill 100, he turned to and received enthusiastic sponsorship from Portland Democratic state senator Ted Hallock (chapter 3). While Hallock himself has been described as not a particularly strong environmentalist personally,[13] he was by all accounts an extremely savvy politician who understood his constituents' views. Portland was not the spawning ground of Oregon's statewide land use planning system, but it has almost certainly been the most important and consistent block of public support for the state planning system ever since. In 2007, pro-planning Ballot Measure 49 passed in Multnomah County (the center of the Portland metropolitan area) by a remarkable 79 percent, compared to 62 percent approval statewide. And because the three counties of the Portland metropolitan area (Multnomah, Washington, and Clackamas) make up 43 percent the state's population,[14] the region's "green" politics have an enormous influence on the state's voting patterns. Had the three Portland area counties not voted, Measure 49 would have passed with a less politically potent approval of 55 percent.[15]

The greater Portland metropolitan area and its 25 cities are governed by a unique elected regional authority, the Portland Metro Council ("Metro"; see chapter 2). In recent decades Portland area voters have consistently elected Metro councilors who strongly support urban revitalization, "infill," public transportation, and tight limitations on growth around the urban area. For example, in 2009–2010, when Metro initiated a long-term planning exercise to designate "urban reserves" (areas where the current Portland UGB might be expanded in the future to accommodate population growth), the importance (if not the precise amount) of urban infill and increased population density, as opposed to expansion of the UGB, was not in dispute. The region previously accommodated almost all growth within the UGB created three decades earlier, in 1979 (with some small expansions). In March 2009, however, Metro released population and employment projections showing that new policies and zoning would be required to cope with predicted growth of one million people in the Metro area by 2030, and both significantly expanding the UGB (growing "out") and promoting greater urban density (growing "up") would have to be considered.

The political winds clearly favored growing "up." These views were illustrated clearly in a public forum in December 2009[16] on regional growth policy with the chair of the Washington County Board of Commissioners, Tom Brian, and Portland mayor Sam Adams. Chairman Brian argued that "at some time as we face the million or so people coming our way in the next 25 years, I think after we do everything we can we will still need to expand the urban growth boundary." Brian also acknowledged, however, the regional demand for compact growth:

It's not an "or" situation, it's an "and" situation. We need to have a vital core city . . . but it's an issue of choice. There are people who feel very strongly about their neighborhoods and having a yard for their kids and so forth. Others would very much rather have an urban setting and a vital city and be in a condo or a row house or other densities. There's no "wrong." We really need to figure out how to do both to meet choices [people want] and at the same time do it well enough to minimize expansion onto the farmland.

In Oregon, however, "expansion onto farmland" are fighting words. Mayor Adams aptly represented the pro-planning community's uncompromising vision:

My vision for the region includes taking care of what's already here before we unrealistically and fancifully expand the boundaries. When I say fanciful, [I mean] we have not used what we have already annexed since 1990. Our current cities don't have the resources both within Washington County and the other counties of the region to fix and repair and replace what we already have. And I think that the growth should be focused on "mainstreets," and change some of these auto[mobile]-oriented strip malls in areas of both my city and other cities across the region into something that are more 20-minute complete neighborhoods. . . . So, [my visions is] an even better Washington County within the boundaries that are *already* here.

To critics, such uncompromising visions indicate that Portland's anti-expansion "true believers" had "drunk too much of their own Kool-Aid."[17] This reference (apparently to the tragic story of Jim Jones and his People's Temple cult in Guyana in 1978, when more than 900 people drank cyanide-laced Kool-Aid) became popular among critics of anti-expansion policies, implying an almost cultlike, dogmatic adherence to an unrealistic vision. It also seemed to imply intolerance for differing views.

On the other side, however, the "believers" steadfastly maintained that it was the advocates of UGB expansion who were being unrealistic. The "up and not out" advocates argued that significant UGB expansion was not even possible in the prevailing economic climate, due largely to the absence of funding for new infrastructure. To drive home this point, Mayor Adams pointed to the most recent previous attempt to expand the Metro growth boundary, in 2002: "If you're going to expand the region, there's planning and then there's implementation. If you continue to expand the region there's a finite amount of money you can spend on transportation, you're stretching your dollars thinner and thinner. And that's a big reason why there are 15,000 acres ready to go [but] unbuilt, unused, the way it was zoned and brought into the UGB—15,000 acres that haven't been used. We don't have the money to get the infrastructure there."

Most members of the audience at the forum with Chairman Brian and Mayor Adams needed no explanation of Adams's reference to 15,000 acres of "unused" land already within the Metro UGB. Most of those acres were in a single place: an aging, quiet, and conservative semirural community at Portland's southeast edge that, in 2002, became famous when it found itself designated to become the center of the largest planned urban expansion in Oregon's history. The expansion would be described heatedly as an example of the inflexibility, inequity, and just plain "stu-pidity" of Oregon's statewide planning system. Some members of the community would bitterly decry what they saw as an imperialistic Metro vision of their land as "a blank slate." Years later, that community re-mained a symbol in a wider battle of visions for Metro's future.

The Road to Damascus

In 1867 Euro-American settlers in the eight-year-old state of Oregon es-tablished a post office in a community near the Oregon Trail. They opti-mistically called it Damascus—a biblical reference to a place of new be-ginnings, in reference to the Apostle Paul's conversion experience on the road to Damascus (McArthur and McArthur 2003: 266–267). The timing could have been better: two years later, the completion of the transcon-tinental railroad drastically reduced passage on the Oregon Trail. Hopes for growth in Damascus faded. In 1904, the Damascus post office closed and moved to the nearby community of Boring. In 2000, the community's population was not counted by the U.S. Census but was almost certainly less than 8,000. In the intervening years, it appears nothing of regional significance happened in Damascus (except hosting a state centennial celebration in 1959). Nor is there much indication that Damascus resi-dents wished it otherwise. But this uneventful history changed in 2002. Damascus is 17.5 miles southeast of the Portland Metro headquarters, a fateful proximity for a small town on the city's edge (Figure 9).

Damascus is located in Clackamas County, halfway between the small towns of Happy Valley and Boring.[18] Damascus sits in the middle of a cluster of numerous buttes and small cone- or dome-shaped hills known as the Boring volcanoes, a swarm of volcanic vents that were active 1.2–3.9 million years ago but are now obscured by heavy tree cover (Loy et al. 2001: 122). For this reason, the area in and around Damascus is characterized by many small hills with steep slopes. The U.S. Department of Agriculture's Natural Resources and Conservation Service identifies soils in eight "capability" classes, from class I (with almost no agricul-tural limitations) to class VIII (with little or no value for agriculture). Soils in and around Damascus fall almost entirely into classes III and higher (meaning significant agricultural limitations). By comparison, land

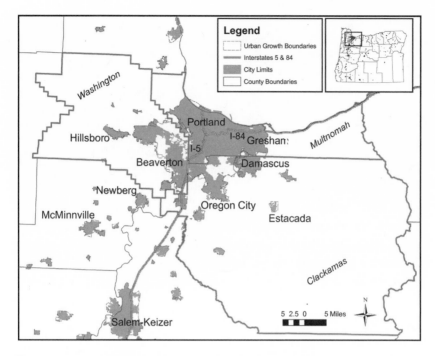

Figure 9   Portland metropolitan area (P. Hurley 2010)

in nearby Washington County that has also been considered by Portland Metro for urban expansion falls mostly into class II, with even considerable areas of class I soils.[19]

To some extent, soils and topography made the history of Damascus. The settler said to have proposed the name "Damascus" in 1867 was not a farmer but a potter, who valued the heavy clay soil in the area. Farming was always marginal, keeping the area relatively underdeveloped for many decades. Yet, it was precisely the same natural resource limitations that had slowed growth in the area for a century and a half that would, at the dawn of the twenty-first century, make Damascus ground zero for the largest proposed urban expansion in the state's history. According to the state's rules for prioritizing areas for urban expansion (see chapter 2), the relatively poor soils and low value for farming (in contrast to the flat, fertile lands to the west in Washington County) made Damascus the

Figure 10   Road to Damascus—no solutions to chronic traffic congestion were in sight when planners proposed to expand the population by 10 times or more (P. Walker 2010)

logical area to accommodate Portland's growth. Metro targeted Damascus, with less than 10,000 people, to receive as many as 150,000 new residents in the next decades. A place named for "new beginnings" would finally, and quite dramatically, live up to its name.

And the conversion would begin, literally, on the road to Damascus. Today, the main urban area in Damascus is sliced through the middle by the busy two-lane U.S. Highway 212, the only highway link to the area. Damascus City Hall and its neighbors (including a McDonald's restaurant and a Bi-Mart) occupy a strip mall along Highway 212, providing a front-row view of traffic jams that regularly seem to back up for miles (Figure 10). As early as 1987, such political heavyweights as then-governor Neil Goldschmidt and U.S. representative Ron Wyden (now a U.S. senator) spoke passionately of the need for road improvements to Portland's southeast suburbs to stimulate economic development. In proposing a new "Sunrise Corridor," Wyden proclaimed, "You can't have big-league growth with a little-league transportation system."

A pattern was begun: grand visions for Damascus were offered by those outside the community, but questions about the logistical and political feasibility of such visions were put aside—including the question of what the people of Damascus themselves wanted. Some local residents strongly supported the Sunrise Corridor because of the economic opportunities that, they believed, would follow. Most Damascus residents, however, wanted no part of new development. Many residents came to the area from California or elsewhere because of the area's rural qualities. In some cases these residents intentionally purchased property outside the Portland UGB precisely because they believed the UGB would protect them from unwanted growth and development. They feared bigger roads would lead to expansion of the UGB.

Ironically, in the end the Sunrise Corridor never came, but UGB expansion happened anyway. And inadequate transportation, it would turn out, was only the first of many obstacles on the road to a grand city of new beginnings. Even today, signs in the restrooms of business establishments in the main urban area of Damascus implore customers to handle the plumbing with care because the city—including its largest businesses—lacks funds for sewers and depends on septic tanks. From its beginning, big visions and reality met awkwardly in Damascus.

But such obstacles proved no impediment to grand visions. In 1993, the Portland Metro Council hired famed San Francisco landscape architect Peter Calthorpe to help develop a 50-year plan for the Portland Metro region to accommodate as many as one million new residents, as part of the regional government's "Region 2040" planning project. The Region 2040 project responded to state laws requiring planners to accommodate 20 years of projected growth. Region 2040 sought to meet this goal by directing new development to be located within the UGB around existing "town centers" (e.g., Gresham and Troutdale); reducing the size of new lots inside the UGB; adding more housing in the form of apartments and multistory buildings along existing transit corridors; *and* a relatively small expansion of the UGB—most of it in the Damascus area.

The Region 2040 goal for Damascus was to fill the relatively sparsely populated area with a population of as many as 150,000 residents by building as many as eight homes per acre. Calthorpe envisioned a cluster of small "villages" in Damascus separated by green spaces, and he defended the plan against critics of urban infill by describing this high-density village concept as "a return to the idea of the neighborhood."[20] Some Damascus residents complained that they already liked their neighborhoods. Debra Stevens, who lived on 10 acres with her husband, a Portland firefighter, and their two children, wistfully told the *Portland Oregonian*, "You can see the stars at night."[21] Many residents argued that the rural feel of the area justified long commutes to Portland, and they had no desire to see the city follow them to the country.

Still, by 1995 the vision began to transform into policy and immediately ran into real-world logistical obstacles and local resistance. Having adopted the Region 2040 plan, Metro began sending letters to the owners of property within the proposed Damascus expansion area notifying them of the proposed conversion of their semirural community into a highly planned urban growth target. Since the Portland UGB was created in 1979, nothing like it had been done before.

Almost immediately battle lines began to be drawn. Developers, home builders, and some residents saw economic opportunity. Even with no formal zoning changes yet in place, property values skyrocketed. At the same time, farmers and many rural residents were alarmed that their livelihoods and lifestyles could be lost. And no solution to the problems of poor roads and lack of adequate water, sewer, and other infrastructure was in sight.

When Metro produced maps showing the per-housing unit costs of infrastructure development, the Damascus area literally floated in a sea of red ink—indicating the highest infrastructure costs (owing partly to the area's difficult topography). Metro responded by changing the maps' color scheme.[22] In 1995, the total estimated infrastructure cost to meet Metro's goals for Damascus stood at a staggering $15.8 billion.[23] Recoloring Metro's maps did little to lessen local fears that infrastructure needs would force new taxes to support development that most local residents did not want. At public hearings on the proposed UGB expansion in autumn 1995, Metro heard "overwhelming opposition" to the proposed expansion.[24]

However, Metro officials, then and now, maintain that they had little choice but to push forward with expansion into Damascus. Metro leaders argue that local politics and even practical infrastructural problems were a less immediate imperative than the demands of state land use law. As described in chapter 2, Oregon's state planning law does not seek to limit growth—rather, it requires local governments to establish plans that limit the *impacts* of growth on agriculture, forestry, and natural areas. When state population projections showed that the Portland Metro area could expand by one million people, state law required Metro to establish a plan to accommodate this growth. Failure to comply with state law could result in official sanctions or citizen lawsuits. In 1995, Portland Metro executive officer Mike Burton argued that this was precisely the prospect his regional government faced: home builders indicated that if Metro did not expand the UGB, they might sue Metro to force an expansion in compliance with state law to accommodate projected population growth.[25] Burton argued that by establishing a relatively small expansion (mainly around Damascus), Metro could preempt the larger expansion that home builders wanted—and might have won, if the matter went to court.

At the same time that the Metro regional government faced pressure from the political right to formally plan for growth, it faced pressure from farmers and the political left to *not* expand onto high-value farmland. On March 27, 1997, the Oregon Department of Agriculture along with the Land Conservation and Development Commission, the Oregon Farm Bureau, the Washington County Farm Bureau, 1000 Friends of Oregon, and others filed appeals against the Region 2040 plan with the Oregon Land Use Board of Appeals (LUBA), complaining that Metro had failed to adequately justify even small proposed expansions onto prime farmland in Washington County. LUBA ruled in favor of the plaintiffs. In January 2000 the LUBA ruling was upheld by the Oregon Court of Appeals. The state's highest land use adjudication authorities had spoken loudly and clearly that they would strictly uphold the spirit and letter of Senate Bill 100's provisions to protect farmland.

This was bad news for opponents of the proposed UGB expansion into Damascus. When Metro was again ready to try to expand the UGB in 2002, the 2000 legal decisions weighed heavily. Because the Damascus area has very little prime farmland, it became, essentially by default, the only area where Metro could expand the UGB without risking further lawsuits by farmers and land use planning advocates. Likewise, it was the only area that had sufficient available land to allow expansion on enough acreage to avoid potential lawsuits by developers and home builders. In 2009, Metro president David Bragdon told us flatly that geography and state land use law had joined forces in favor of a major expansion in Damascus—Metro had "no discretion."[26] In December 2002, the Portland Metro Council voted in favor of an unprecedented 18,600-acre expansion of the UGB—two-thirds of it in Damascus. In June 2003, the state's Land Conservation and Development Commission strongly endorsed the Metro expansion plan.

One could forgive the Metro council and their staff for, at least briefly, breathing a sigh of relief that their long effort to comply with the state's growth laws appeared to have come to an end, and that their journey on the road to Damascus had delivered them to a place of new beginnings.

But this sense of arrival would not last long—Metro's expansion headaches were just beginning. With the 2002 UGB expansion formally approved, the practical realities of infrastructure costs and local political resistance that had been put on the back burner could no longer be ignored. Since 1993, when Damascus was first actively considered as a location for UGB expansion, there had been essentially no resolution of questions about how to provide new roads and infrastructure to the area, no solution to the absence of local jobs for new residents, and no adequate effort to respond to local political resistance.

Local resistance to urban expansion took multiple forms, but one of the most remarkable and important was not protests in the streets or at planning meetings but, instead, a successful local grassroots effort to incorporate Damascus as a full-fledged city, with its own government that could give Damascus residents a degree of institutional voice they had lacked as an unincorporated area. This problem of lack of representation of Damascus in the planning process was widely recognized early on. In 1997, even Metro acknowledged a significant problem: the lives of residents on the "exurban" fringe could be turned upside down by the planning choices made by urban planners, but under the Metro charter, unincorporated areas outside the UGB had no representation in Metro's decision making. This matter of urbanization without representation was not exactly lost on Damascus residents.

By 2000, local organizers concluded that stopping growth from Metro was no longer possible. One local cityhood advocate reported asking a Clackamas County commissioner, "If all of the residents of Damascus stood on their chairs and stomped their feet, could we stop growth?" The commissioner's answer was a blunt, "No."[27] As a city, however, Metro would be required to delegate some planning decisions to Damascus. Cityhood activists argued that the only other choice was to accept annexation to another existing city (most likely Happy Valley) and be subject to the planning ideas of a different community. As a result, despite the area's dominant conservative and anti-government values, local activists of diverse political persuasions saw cityhood as the only way to give the area some autonomy in deciding how growth would occur.

Autonomy was a concern for Damascus residents because it seemed that nearly everyone *else* had ideas for how Damascus should grow. Damascus was something of a planner's dream come true. The area presented an opportunity to create a city "from scratch" in a place often described (problematically) as a "blank slate." The opportunity to plan a new beginning in Damascus, using the most "progressive" planning principles, would be unprecedented. But as early as 1993, when Metro brought in landscape architect Peter Calthorpe to plan Metro's vision, Damascus residents wondered why planners did not begin by asking *them* what they wanted for *their* community. To many residents, it appeared that outsiders' visions were being imposed upon them. Some planners did not disagree but pointed out that state law prioritizing expansion into low-farm-value area would eventually push urban expansion into Damascus regardless of local opinion, and therefore planners tended to brush off local resistance with statements such as " 'Thanks . . . your input is very important to our process' " (Apostol and Yap 2009: 4).

Among those most active in visioning a new future for Damascus was the group 1000 Friends of Oregon. Although the group had previously called the UGB expansion a mistake, by the time the expansion into Damascus seemed all but inevitable in the early 2000s, 1000 Friends took a leading role in the planning and visioning process. In 2002, 1000 Friends director Robert Liberty described Damascus as an opportunity to create a "model community," and his group sponsored a more than $300,000 planning project employing professional planners and landscape architects to plan compact, ecologically sound "livable futures" concepts to offer to the community—free of charge. Damascus residents did not by any means reject these visions. Some, however, such as Dee Wescott—the future first mayor of Damascus—complained that the visioning process "doesn't appear to be locally driven."[28] Damascus resident and landscape architect Dean Apostol said, "I hope this project is not presented as being from our community. It's not."[29]

1000 Friends was not alone. In September 2003, after Damascus was brought into the UGB, Clackamas County together with Metro and the Department of Transportation began creating a "concept plan" that would decide where new homes, roads, business districts, parks, open space, and other features should be located. The plan was scheduled to be completed in 2005. Clackamas County planners took the lead and actively sought comments from the community through public forums and town hall–style meetings. However, these meetings typically consisted of planners presenting precooked "scenarios," or "options," to the community for public comment rather than starting from square one by soliciting the community's own ideas. And with no city government at first, local participation in the concept planning was rather ad hoc and dependent on which community members could attend the meetings.

The plethora of high-minded, outsider efforts to advise Damascus about what kind of "livable future" and "concept plan" it should have helped propel the long-discussed idea of cityhood to takeoff velocity. In response to this sense of their marginalization in the visioning process, in early 2002 around 150 Damascus residents met to form the Committee to Incorporate Damascus. Over the next few years, as frustration increased, local residents became more determined to develop their *own* way. Overcoming significant concerns about inevitable city taxes (always a concern in conservative Clackamas County), in November 2004, 65 percent of Damascus voters chose to establish the first new city in Oregon in 22 years.

The birth of the new City of Damascus would not, however, lead to any unified vision of the area's future. In recent decades, extensive research across the globe has shown that people within local communities are usually not of a single, like mind, and devolving decision-making authority to the "local" level can lead to intense struggles to define the meaning of the community and the proper path to development (Agrawal and Gibson

1999). The new City of Damascus was no exception. Local control in Damascus meant that decisions by the new city about where and what to build, or not to build, had enormous consequences for landowners. Divisive local political conflicts within the community quickly ensued. At one level these politics had to do with the unleashing of mundane economic opportunism associated with the prospects of new development—as well as the predictable disappointments that, under a regulatory land use planning authority (albeit a "local" one), not everyone would benefit. In public meetings in 2005, local residents whose development opportunities were blocked by city plans accused the new mayor (a 78-year-old local patriarch and auto shop owner) and city council members of drawing development maps to secure personal economic gain.

Another key set of local disputes emerged over green space policy, leading to a backlash with profound implications for the policy of the city, Metro, and possibly even state policy. With cityhood, the City of Damascus became, as intended, the key player in drafting the new "concept plan" for development. Certain areas of the city were designated by the new government as green space and off limits to high-density development. The expectations of development and financial opportunities for some landowners were, literally, wiped off the map. Specifically, owners of land on top of the Damascus area's many buttes found that their properties were designated as green space. Steven and Cindy Spinnett complained that they wanted to build homes for their three children (a claim that planning advocates claim often masks more strictly monetary motives) but were prohibited by the concept plan. After getting no satisfactory response from the city, the Spinnetts helped to form the Damascus Community Coalition and circulated petitions asking the city to eliminate the greenspace system. As Cindy Spinnett explained her view, "This is not American. This is not equal property rights for everyone."[30]

However, some local activists saw cityhood as a different kind of opportunity. Cityhood created a political tool to potentially block both Metro *and* local development policies—including tax and zoning policies. Having failed to steer the city onto a more pro-development course, some of the same local critics of the Damascus concept plan broadened their political strategy, aiming directly at the taxation and land use regulatory authority of the new city. As with statewide land use Measures 7,

37, and 49 (see chapter 4), Oregon's ballot initiative system would play a central role. Dan Phegley, who lives in Damascus on the 2.5-acre parcel he has owned since 1993, commutes to his Portland insurance agency and might be described as typical "exurban" commuter. He is also the leader of one of Oregon's most effective insurgent populist anti-tax and anti-regulatory grassroots organizations. In 2009 we interviewed Phegley in his Portland office, where his wall is decorated with a photo of former Republican vice presidential candidate Sarah Palin, and his desk is strewn with publications by conservative radio commentator Rush Limbaugh. When we asked whether he would describe himself as anti–land use planning, he explained that he is "pro-democracy." "Our goal," he said, is to change the city charter, "to more reflect [in his view] the will of ordinary citizens."[31] His organization is called Ask Damascus.

In 2008, Ask Damascus scored one of the most remarkable populist conservative political victories since the passage of Measure 37 in 2004. Channeling deep pockets of local resentment against government in general and land use planning in particular, Phegley's group put three initiatives on the new city ballot. The first would prohibit the City of Damascus from creating any new taxes, fees, or charges without a public vote. The second was essentially a local-scale Measure 37 copycat law— requiring the city to give "full compensation"[32] to property owners for any reduction in property values resulting from city regulations. The third would prohibit the city from condemning private property and transferring the ownership to another private owner.[33] All of the Ask Damascus initiatives passed, with overwhelming margins of victory—70 percent, 67 percent, and 76 percent, respectively.

On the morning after the election, the four-year-old City of Damascus, already struggling, faced a difficult new political reality. Lacking authority to raise even a dog license fee without a public vote, the probability of the city contributing in any significant way to the funding of the massive infrastructure costs required to build a new city of 100,000 people or more appeared to be somewhere between miniscule and zero. In addition, the city would be required to compensate landowners for any policy (pro- or anti-development) shown to reduce property values. And using eminent domain to put property in the hands of those with the capital for development is prohibited. As Damascus mayor Jim Wright stated bluntly to the *Portland Oregonian* newspaper in 2009, "At this point, we're pretty much dead in the water."[34] The *Portland Oregonian* went on to observe that, with this "Damascus debacle," the metropolitan area "once deemed most likely to develop appears to be the place where [growth] is least likely to occur." In 2009, Damascus community development director Anita Yap confirmed to us that since Damascus was pulled into the Portland UGB in 2002, scarcely a shovel of new dirt has been turned for development.[35] The grand visions of a "new beginning" in Damascus all but disappeared, replaced with the all-too-clear realities of enormous political and logistical barriers.

Rurbanistas

In the crumbled ruins of the vanquished (or at least postponed) visions for a grand new beginning in Damascus, however, some truly homespun and vibrant new local visions began to grow. The UGB has long been considered the core of Oregon's land use planning system, and many have linked the viability of the state's planning system as a whole to the ability not only to prohibit development outside the boundary but also to promote urbanization inside it. For planning professionals in Oregon, the so-called Damascus debacle undermined confidence in the ability of cities to fulfill that task. But if anyone had chosen to bet that Damascus would be satisfied with taking a hammer to just one of the conceptual pillars of Oregon's planning system, they would have lost. Damascus also appeared to be determined to go after nothing less than the Holy Grail of Oregon planning: the separation of farm and city.

With plans for large-scale development at least postponed for the foreseeable future, the new City of Damascus has chosen to encourage its small but vibrant specialty farming sector *inside* the new UGB. We should pause to observe that, having spent years talking with Oregon planners, it would be no exaggeration to observe that for many planners the sanctity of the principles defined in Statewide Planning Goal 14 (requiring separation of farm, forest, and urban spaces) takes on a nearly religious dimension. It is often said that if Oregon's planning system has done nothing else, it has successfully established a bright line between farms and cities. This served to protect both farms *and* cities: farmers could operate with-

out conflicts and pressure on property values from urban neighbors, and
cities would thrive because they would be forced to contain city-center-
killing sprawl. Under the Senate Bill 100 model, farms and cities in Oregon are geographically separated but functionally interdependent.

Yet, with the odd phenomenon of presently nonurbanizable space
within the Portland UGB around Damascus, new configurations of land
use and new *visions* have sprouted. Literally. Some relatively small but
successful farmers in Damascus who grow for urban "niche" markets
just want to do their work and make a modest living in peace. With the
pulling of the Metro UGB over Damascus in 2002, that option appeared
threatened. With the single largest UGB expansion in state history, the
Damascus expansion swallowed whole farms alive. In some cases, neither
the farmers nor local planners were prepared to see their farms converted
to urban use.

In Damascus one of the most celebrated cases is farmer Larry Thompson. Suddenly, Thompson's 77-acre mixed fruit and produce acreage became an *urban* farm—squarely within the boundaries of the new City of
Damascus and the Portland Metro UGB. In Oregon's planning orthodoxy,
that would mean that Thompson's farm is *planned* to no longer be a farm
in the future. Both Thompson and the City of Damascus had different
ideas: as Thompson argues, the city can not only grow around the farm,
but grow "with" the farm.[36] Thompson proposes to retain 20–30 acres
of his most fertile land in farming, while building a restaurant that serves
his own organic food on land nearby, as well as a community garden and
produce stands. Homesites would go on the remainder of his land. The
farm would provide local, vine-ripened organic food for the community
with minimal transportation, and enhanced assurance of food safety and
reduced reliance on globalized food production and trade. In Thompson's
vision, the farm becomes a *part of*, rather than apart from, the city—both
geographically and, in an enhanced way, functionally.

Thompson became something of a local hero to advocates of various
related alternative foods movements—community-supported agriculture,
urban farming, slow foods, and others. And, at least since the mid-1990s,
small-acreage specialty "rurban" farms serving mainly the local metropolitan market have been a remarkable bright spot in the state's farm
economy. As one local blogger noted, "We may have an opportunity to

build community and keep growth contained and eat some good food."
The blogger used the Web name "Rurbanista."[37]

This new "rurban" vision does not, however, fit comfortably with Oregon's older vision of separation of farm and city. As City of Damascus community development director Anita Yap explained to us, this new vision has received much resistance from state regulators, who see it as opening "a can of worms."[38] Advocates of the conventional Oregon land use planning model question whether urban farming might reduce the efficiency of road building, sewers, and other infrastructure by creating relatively large uninhabited areas inside urban boundaries. Worse, if urban farming reduces overall residential density within the urban area, it might create additional pressure to expand cities outward, threatening more (and typically larger) farms—the very problem that Oregon's planning system was created in 1973 to prevent. Richard Whitman, the director of Oregon's Department of Land Conservation and Development, does not reject the idea but warns that urban farming cannot reduce urban overall density or be used to excuse further expansion of the growth boundary.[39]

However, the Portland metropolitan area seems safe from further UGB expansions, at least for now. With large areas of undeveloped land inside the Portland UGB around Damascus, and the memory of seemingly insurmountable infrastructure problems and political backlash fresh in minds of Portland's planners, further expansion of the Portland UGB appears unlikely at present. Indeed, the experience of the "Damascus debacle" challenged long-held visions among Oregon's planners. Arguably, a reexamination and revitalization of Oregon's planning vision was needed.

Revisioning the City

The failure (so far) of the urbanization proposed for Damascus in 2002 could be seen as a dramatic example of what land use scholar John Echeverria calls the "sclerotic" character of Oregon's land use planning system (see chapter 9). Merriam Webster's dictionary defines "sclerosis" as a pathological hardening, or an inability to be flexible or compromising.

Evidence for this claim can be found in the odd fact that very few people actually *wanted* Damascus to urbanize. Surveys consistently found that residents of Damascus were by and large happy with their quasi-rural lifestyle and did not want their way of life changed (Apostol and Yap 2009). The overwhelming public support for ballot initiatives that stripped the new City of Damascus of its powers to tax and impose new regulations to implement development showed that resistance to change went well beyond a small group of right-wing activists.

More surprising, perhaps, is the fact that even the Metro government that enacted the expansion policy for Damascus seemed to be simply following rules, rather than pursuing a vision—or even sound policy. As Metro officials explained it to us, they expanded the UGB over Damascus to comply with state laws that required expansion of the UGB to accommodate projected population growth, but they had no particular desire to see Damascus become a city. In fact, no less important a figure than John VanLandingham, the chair of the Oregon Land Conservation and Development Commission (LCDC; the appointed citizen committee that oversees the state planning system) stated to us in 2009 that "some of our [LCDC] members are concerned that Metro never had any real intent to develop Damascus . . . there's a sort of reverse concern from the development community that Metro didn't want to develop [the towns of] Bethany and Damascus and threw it out there knowing it would never happen, as part of the 'left's goal of not having any growth."[40] To be clear, neither the LCDC chair nor we are suggesting any conspiracy—unless one counts as a "conspiracy" a begrudging compliance with state laws that one knows are unlikely to succeed. As Metro president (and, in 2002, councilor), David Bragdon explained to us, it came as "no surprise" to him that the Damascus expansion failed.

The real problem in Damascus, we suggest, was something more powerful and insidious than a "conspiracy." It could be described as the unguided force of an out-of-date vision operating on institutional autopilot. When state senator Hector Macpherson drew the blueprints for Oregon's planning system in 1973, he took as his point of departure the Model Code of the American Law Institute (see chapter 3). At the time, this model made sense. Populations grew in certain ways; cities and regions could respond to growth through expansion of the UGB, and infrastructure would be provided by federal or other sources. Local resistance may have been present but did not have the organizational capacities (and perhaps not the anti-government fervor) that some groups have today. Transportation problems were less severe. And alternative options for accommodating growth with less horizontal expansion had not been fully conceived. By 2002, all of these (and other) conditions had changed. Yet, state land use laws were still essentially operating on a 1973 model that mandated unrealistic policy choices in particular geographic contexts. The result was a time- and resource-consuming, politically divisive non-expansion expansion that hardly anyone wanted. Even those who *did* want it ended up disappointed!

At one level, the "lessons" of Damascus for Oregon's statewide planning system seem clear and simple. To start, an expand-and-pray approach to infrastructure provision does not work in the twenty-first century. As Metro president David Bragdon explained to us in 2009, "We were just acting under the state statute that says you have to expand the urban growth boundary. State statute didn't say somebody had to *pay* for all the services. . . . The lesson [of recent UGB expansions including Damascus] is that we can bring land into the urban growth boundary, but unless the property owner or the developers are willing to pay for the sewer and water and parks and roads and other things that are needed, then the land's not going to develop."[41]

Another key lesson from Damascus is that local politics and questions of equity matter. To be more accurate, this should be described as a "reminder" rather than a "lesson": in the 1970s, Governor Tom McCall and key agency leaders such as Oregon Department of Land Conservation and Development director Arnold Cogan went to Olympian efforts to build public support for the planning program that was both wide and deep. In 1974, the Oregon public literally wrote the statewide planning goals and "owned" the planning system. Today, probably very few ordinary Oregonians could even clearly articulate why Oregon has a UGB policy. Moreover, the political currents pulling against a centralized system of state planning have become far stronger in the wake of the Reagan revolution of the 1980s, the property rights movements of the 1990s, and ascendance of populist conservatism in the 2000s. In the concluding chapter of this book we expand on the question of equity. But, at a minimum, it should have been obvious to anyone promoting planning for the common good in a twenty-first-century era of individualism that deep commitment to, and competent implementation of public engagement in, land use planning is essential. As described by Connie Ozawa (2008), neither was present in regional and county "outreach" efforts to Damascus—in fact, the public outreach efforts were almost shocking in their apparent lack of professionalism and sincerity.[42]

Another (hopefully) obvious lesson from Damascus is that in an era of global climate change and profound national security, health, and other concerns about globalized agriculture, new ways of thinking about farming are urgently needed. While the historical success of Oregon's planning system in supporting commercial farmers should be celebrated, a nearly 40-year-old vision that sees only one kind of "farm" (the kind that is big and incompatible with urban conditions) clearly requires reexamination. With rapidly rising urban consumer demand for fresh, high-quality, environmentally friendly farm produce, a policy that deliberately keeps farms and city dwellers geographically separated seems likely to miss important and profitable opportunities.

To their credit, state planners clearly have absorbed at least some of these lessons. On February 25, 2010, Metro voted for an unprecedented and historic land use blueprint for the next 40–50 years that involves no immediate UGB expansion and only a relatively modest expansion of so-called urban reserves (areas where the UGB *might* be expanded in the future). Most important, following the painful lessons of Damascus and other recent unsuccessful Metro expansions, the state LCDC appeared poised to endorse Metro's new approach. Similarly, state planners have cautiously opened the door, at least a crack, to new ways of incorporating urban farming into the statewide system. And the problems of financing urban infrastructure are high on the state planning system's radar screen, even though solutions remain elusive. It is probably safe to say, however, that the era of "expand and pray" is in the past. Metro leaders and state planners are learning, perhaps haltingly, to revision the city.

There is another lesson from Damascus—but it is far from clear whether state planners have learned it. The "Damascus debacle" did not result simply from any single bad policy. Rather, it resulted from a hardened vision, programmed into a bureaucratic system and maintained by "true believers" fearful of tinkering with a system that has served

Oregon's environmental and agricultural interests and urban planners well for decades. Critics complain that planning advocates in Oregon have become a cultlike community that views Senate Bill 100 in nearly sacred terms—and some planners themselves acknowledge as much. And who can blame them? Oregon *earned* its national reputation for innovative and effective land use planning. Oregon earned its reputation for willingness to pursue policies so bold that no other state has followed. But in recent years Oregon's claim to boldness and innovation seems on far shakier ground. Defending outdated models is neither innovative nor bold. When Metro headed into Damascus, where were the voices willing to say that, law or no law, bad policy is bad policy? Where were the voices demanding—in Tom McCall fashion—a *true* conversation with ordinary citizens? After Damascus (not to mention Measures 7 and 37), how many near-death experiences will it take for Oregon's planning community to accept that the Senate Bill 100 model needs updating?

As we show in the next chapter on protection of the Metolius River basin in Central Oregon in 2009, it is far from clear that Oregon's planning community has absorbed this question, much less resolved it. We argue that the state's planning community should think long and hard about whether past successes and even desirable present outcomes justify policies like the 2002 Damascus UGB expansion that make the planning system look inflexible, unjust, or plain stupid. Measure 37 proved Oregonians have little loyalty to planning per se. We ask, how many public failures and inflammatory choices can Oregon's land use planning system withstand over time?

7 Central Destinations

It's not often that a place as extraordinary as the Metolius River is so unnervingly threatened by plans for massive residential developments. In Oregon, *of all places*, these sorts of things aren't supposed to happen.

—Erik Kancler, Central Oregon Land Watch, 2007[1]

A high school government class that wanted to know how government really works could do much worse than follow the Legislature's attempt to "protect" the Metolius River Basin. . . . Look who's involved. . . . There's nothing like being a NIMBY with clout.

—*Bend (OR) Bulletin* editorial, 2009[2]

Go ahead and pretend that the process makes a difference if it makes you feel better, but make no mistake: Governor Ted Kulongoski wants to ensure, *by whatever means necessary*, that two proposed destination resorts near the Metolius end up in regulatory Siberia.

—*Bend Bulletin* editorial, 2009[3]

Oregonians will be grateful that we did all we could to protect the [Metolius River] basin from large-scale development.

—Mike Carrier, Oregon natural resource policy adviser, 2009[4]

We tried very hard to work with Jefferson County . . . [but] Jefferson County has simply continued to resist the whole notion of an area of critical statewide concern.

—Richard Whitman, DLCD director, 2009[5]

In this chapter, we turn our attention to Central Oregon—specifically Crook, Deschutes, and Jefferson counties—and the intersection of political and economic forces that have characterized the so-called New West, namely, the replacement of natural resource–based economies and cultures by a booming real estate market centered on natural amenities. Specifically, we explore the ways this transformation intersects with Oregon's planning system, and the land use politics that have resulted. We focus on specific land use conflicts centered on the development of so-called destination resorts located outside urban growth boundaries (UGBs), which have generated enormous controversy over the past decade (Figure 11). Some see these resorts as engines of prosperity; others see them as de facto rural subdivisions that violate the spirit of Oregon's land use laws. The story of destination resorts and the politics they have engendered contributes to our overall analysis by demonstrating the extent to which Oregon's planning system has accommodated, albeit unevenly, the development forces associated with the New West. But more important, we document the lengths to which (and ways that) powerful individuals and actors can and will go—while carrying the shield of Tom McCall and the planning system—to steer development away from ecologically and socially important landscapes or, in the language of Oregon planning, "areas of critical state concern."

Sagebrush Subdivisions

In recent decades, economic restructuring and associated declines in natural resource–dependent communities in the American West (Nelson 2001; Jackson and Kuhlken 2006; Travis 2007)[6] have resulted in replacement of economies built on extraction by economies built on rural residences and recreation (Walker and Fortmann 2003; see, e.g., Brogden and Greenberg 2003; Ghose 2004).[7] Amenity migration became an important factor in explaining population growth, particularly differences in growth among counties (Nelson 2006). High-amenity counties in the American West experienced faster rates of growth than did low-amenity counties, with nonmetropolitan areas characterized by much lower density growth than in nearby metropolitan areas and higher density growth than in low-amenity counties (Vias and Carruthers 2005; Nelson 2006).

Crook, Deschutes, and Jefferson counties possess many of the natural amenities that characterize communities elsewhere in the American

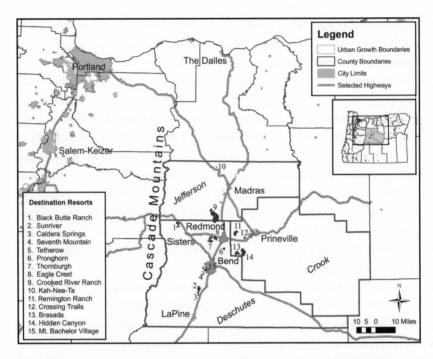

Figure 11   Central Oregon map with destination resorts (P. Hurley 2010)

West that have experienced rapid growth.[8] The three counties are located largely within the Deschutes River Basin and contain significant stretches of the river or its tributaries. Likewise, significant peaks of the Cascade Crest, including Mt. Bachelor, and the high desert of Central Oregon provide an abundance of opportunities for outdoor recreation: world-class fly-fishing, hiking, horseback riding, skiing, mountain biking, and much more. Deschutes County proclaims itself the "outdoor recreation capital of Oregon." Much of this land, and the opportunities it contains, is owned by the federal government and managed by either the U.S. Forest Service or Bureau of Land Management.

In Deschutes County, the population grew from 30,442 in 1970 to 74,958 in 1990. Today, there are an estimated 158,456 people living in the county, with about half of this population living in the City of Bend, Oregon's fastest growing metropolitan area since 2000 and one of the fastest growing metropolitan areas in the United States.[9] In 1970, the population of Jefferson County was 8,548. Today, the population has reached 20,512. Crook County grew from 9,985 in 1970 to 23,023, with more than 34 percent of this growth since 2000.

Population growth and real estate markets centered on residential development—both inside and outside of UGBs—have developed in the three counties that, like many other places in the American West, have transformed the rural and agricultural economies and cultures of the region. Yet, this development, and the degree to which real estate markets and housing development have transformed the three counties, has been rather uneven. Not surprisingly, given the population numbers described above and the county's tremendous recreational opportunities, Deschutes County has experienced the greatest degree of transformation; no longer is the county characterized by an economy reliant primarily on timber or grazing activities. Since the 1980s, tourism, recreation-related services, and construction have anchored the economy of the county.

By contrast, Jefferson County has largely retained its agricultural roots, with the central portion of the county still home to farmers who specialize in the production of grass seed, other seed crops, potatoes, hay, and mint. In eastern Jefferson County, dry wheat farming, cattle grazing, and some timber activity are still present. Similarly, Crook County's economy remains tied in important ways to agriculture, forest products, and livestock, but construction, manufacturing, and tourism and recreation have become essential components as well. Nevertheless, the landscape of western Crook is characterized by irrigated agricultural fields, while the north-central part features higher elevation forests, and the eastern and southeastern parts of the county retain a fair amount of rangelands.

Different land use and ownership patterns as well as economic bases among the three counties reflect diverse land use histories and decisions and competing political priorities. Together with the changed economic and cultural landscape of the region, these divergent histories are central to understanding today's land use contestations. In important ways, the creation of the Oregon land use planning system was a response to rapid partitioning of rural parcels—the rise of the "sagebrush subdivisions," as Tom McCall described it—in the southwestern portion of Deschutes County.[10] Indeed, by the time the state had created the planning system, a large degree of rural land partitioning had occurred throughout the county, a trend in some parts of Oregon that land use planners recognized and accommodated through the creation of the so-called rural exception areas.[11] Further, in the years it would take Deschutes County to finalize a countywide planning document, 5- and 10-acre parcels came to dominate many rural parts of the county, because these low-density minimums became the preferred mechanism among county planners to slow parcelization, and also due to the high degree of demand to create parcels that could later be sold for residential development.[12] It is these densities that, together with the land use rules put in place by the planning system, would largely set the level of potential development entitlements for future projects.

When compared to Deschutes County, rural areas in Crook and Jefferson counties have seen lower levels of residential development. For example, Crook County experienced an interesting period during which county planners asserted their independence by ignoring their own plan and state rules in order to encourage rural development. These so-called renegade development approvals eventually were uncovered by Department of Land Conservation and Development (DLCD) officials and were stopped, but they fostered a new pattern of low-density development in the western portion of Crook County, mainly around an area known as Powell Butte.

By contrast, Jefferson County's 1981 comprehensive plan and decision making closely followed the goals set out by DLCD and the planning system by prioritizing the maintenance of farm and timber lands. This may have been either cause or consequence of the slow population numbers. But as Deschutes County grew during the 1990s, including in its two large cities of Bend and Redmond, as well as on rural parcels outside these UGBs, new development pressures began to spill over into Crook and Jefferson counties. For example, Brooks Resources—a long-time developer in Bend—purchased land in Prineville (Crook County) for new subdivisions, while the City of Madras (Jefferson County) welcomed new housing opportunities. However, these projects were merely precursors for larger and much more controversial proposals to come.

As growth continued to skyrocket through the 1990s and the early 2000s, concerns about future natural resource use, including agriculture and timber, and the quality of the region's environment have grown. For example, national groups, state-level nongovernmental organizations, and regional conservation groups such as the Deschutes Land Trust and the Deschutes River Conservancy expressed the need to protect critical wildlife, such as elk and pronghorn, and the natural habitats characteristic of the region's high desert and forested habitats (e.g., sagebrush steppe, native grasslands, and Ponderosa pine forests); increase instream flows for fish in the Deschutes River and its tributaries; and retain working forests and farms in the region.[13] Particular attention has been paid to the rate of development in Deschutes County and its implications for a number of environmental issues, most prominently water, but also concerns of habitat for deer, elk, and salmonids. Concerns about the environment (outside of debates about forest management and fire safety) in Crook and Jefferson counties generally have not featured prominently in land use debates.

Still, in 1998, Defenders of Wildlife released its book *Oregon Living Landscapes* (Oregon Biodiversity Project 1998), which was intended to serve as a road map for future conservation efforts in the state. Using an ecoregion- or landscape-scale perspective, the report assessed areas of the state, including the East Cascades, Lava Plains, and Blue Mountain ecoregions of Central Oregon, for their biodiversity value, designating so-called conservation opportunities or areas with significant ecological features, with low levels of development and in need of further conservation.[14] In particular, the report noted the high rate of development in Deschutes County and its implications for a number of environmental issues, most prominently water. One area is singled out in the report as particularly important: the Metolius Basin—to which we return shortly.

The Boom in Destination Resorts

With at least 15 major destination resorts (depending on definition) completed or in various stages of development as of 2010,[15] along with many smaller ones, Central Oregon is home to far more destination resorts than any other area in the state. Even Oregon's renowned Willamette Valley wine region did not have one until 2009.[16] Indeed, it is rare to meet an Oregonian—especially one living in western Oregon's populous but soggy Willamette Valley—who has never headed east to escape the rain, and chances are that one of the places they have sought refuge is Sunriver—one of central Oregon's oldest and most widely recognized destination resorts.

Sunriver began as the idea of John Gray and Donald McCallum, who built condominiums on the site of a former army training facility. By the end of the 1960s, Gray and McCallum completed their master plan and began selling lots in the sagebrush. Since the 1960s, the Sunriver area has prospered. Today, it has grown beyond its original borders, and the area is home to numerous newer planned developments. Likewise, many have spent time at Deschutes County's oldest resort, Black Butte Ranch. Acquired in January 1970 by Brooks Resources, a long-time timber company based in Bend, the company embarked on a plan to create a seasonal community, while offering nearby merchants in Sisters encouragement and incentives to redevelop the town with an "Old West" theme look.[17]

Deschutes County's resort destiny

Sunriver and Black Butte Ranch predate the creation of Oregon's Goal 8, which seeks to "satisfy the recreational needs of the citizens of the state and visitors and, where appropriate, to provide for the siting of necessary recreational facilities including destination resorts."[18] It was not until the early 1980s and the onset of an economic downturn and decline of rural timber economies that the idea of destination resorts, largely modeled on Sunriver and Black Butte Ranch, became an official economic growth policy and planning tool. And it is really only over the past decade that a new boom era in resorts has come to characterize the county's growth and changes to its landscapes. Each resort has its own story and suite of amenities to market to would-be homeowners and tourists.

In the view of supporters, these resorts provide short-term construction jobs and longer term service jobs and increased property tax bases. Not surprisingly, the Central Oregon Association of Realtors wrote in a letter to the Deschutes County Planning Commission that "Central Oregon's experience with destination resorts has demonstrated unequivocally the benefits of this land use."[19] Opponents dispute claims about the scale and types of economic benefits provided by destination resorts and express concerns about the impacts of these developments on roads, infrastructure, resources (especially water), and ecological and aesthetic integrity.[20]

For example, residents in the small town of Tumalo have been outspoken against the approval of the Thornburgh resort, arguing that this project and others threaten the open space and the rural lifestyle that define Central Oregon, given the construction of a large number of resorts in the green belts outside the UGB—in contradiction to the core principles of the Oregon planning system.[21] In a letter to the editor, one opponent of the Thornburgh project observed that much of the county is mapped as eligible for resorts and warned, "There's a destination resort coming to a neighborhood near you. If you think it's not your problem, you're wrong."[22] But so far, opponents' challenges filed with the Land Use Board of Appeals (LUBA) have largely proved unsuccessful.

However, not all resort proposals have been approved by Deschutes County, illustrating that there are some situations in which this approach is viewed as problematic. For example, in the late 1990s, developers acquired several ranches on the west side of Smith Rock State Park, an iconic volcanic landscape and popular hiking and rock-climbing destination, as part of a strategy to build a project. Early proposals for a Rimrock Resort destination resort project, which would have featured the typical overnight units and residential homes, stalled when it was determined that state law prohibited resorts in close proximity to high-value farmland. Appeals to the state legislature, including a bill in 1997 to change state law, resulted in an early regional battle, and ultimately the resort was defeated.

The result, instead, was a smaller residential "planned unit development" that resulted in 60 residential units and a gated "preservation ranch." Using the county code for clustered development, the resulting community, Ranch at the Canyons, included 600 acres of irrigated land managed for hay, fruit, and grape production. Since its completion, the Ranch at the Canyons' owners donated the development rights for 550 acres on the north side of Smith Rock State Park in the form of a conservation easement to the Deschutes Land Trust. Besides the property's wildlife and habitat value, the donation ensured no additional development abutting the park.[23] The Ranch at the Canyons precedent served as a reminder that destination resorts were not a foregone conclusion, and in their place, a "more appropriate" rural residential development might result.

While the Ranch at the Canyons project started as a destination resort proposal and ended as a residential community, at least one rural planned unit development, Aspen Lakes Golf Estates, went the other direction. The developers, a local farm family, sought permission for code exemptions that would allow conversion of the existing gated community to a destination resort. With 117 lots for sale and numerous homes and the associated golf course already constructed, the destination resort proposal would have meant that additional resort homes and associated overnight units would be constructed on a nearby and minimally adjacent parcel.

For opponents, the first problem with Aspen Lakes was that the developers were asking for a code exemption. But for many in the area, the more important problem was that the proposed development site would, in their view, ruin the area's rural character. The parcel also abuts portions of Whychus Creek, a tributary to the Deschutes River and the site of efforts to reintroduce steelhead trout. It is also an area where groups such as the Deschutes Land Trust have invested time and effort in conserving and enhancing habitats. In county planning commission meetings, these and other concerns were raised. Together, these were enough for the county to reject the code change. Environmental opponents have used this case to argue for the firm application of existing land development laws. The failure of Aspen Lakes' resort proposal, like the success of seeing the Ranch at the Canyons built as a "preservation ranch" instead of a resort, demonstrates some of the political struggles over destination resorts in Deschutes County.

Beyond Deschutes: Crook County gets into the game

Until recently, destination resorts were entirely a Deschutes County phenomenon. That changed in the early 2000s when Crook County embraced this economic development strategy. Since 2002, when the county finished its process of mapping 35,000 acres in the western part of the county as eligible for destination resorts, officials have reviewed four resort proposals. As of 2009, all four of these were in some stage of construction. Brasada Ranch, a resort featuring 600 homes and 300 overnight units, was the first resort in the county. It was approved and broke ground in 2004. The second project of the Jeld-Wen company in the region, it is located near Powell Butte in the western portion of the county on a former 1,800-acre cattle ranch. Brasada has only one golf course, which it markets as a private course that features "striking views of dramatic snowcapped mountains."[24] Before construction began, neighboring Powell Butte residents appealed the county's approval of the project to LUBA but lost.

Remington Ranch, proposed in 2006 and now under construction, was the second destination resort approved by the county. This 2,079-acre property, located just 25 miles from Bend, has been transformed into a golf community with three golf courses, 800 homesites, and 400 overnight rooms by Winchester Development, a company with prior experience in Arizona, New Mexico, and Montana. Once approved, the developers of Remington Ranch also faced a LUBA challenge from area residents and, this time, Central Oregon Landwatch.[25]

The third resort in Crook County will be constructed by Bend homebuilder Dennis Pahlisch, who purchased 3,250 acres of high desert from a semiretired dentist in Deschutes who raised cattle on the land.[26] Teaming up with RMG Development (a Bend-based development, real estate, and building partnership) in 2006, the developers proposed Hidden Canyon. When built, the project will include 2,450 homes and 1,225 overnight units. As of late 2009, due to a sluggish housing market, Hidden Canyon had not begun construction.

Not long after the Hidden Canyon property was purchased, a fourth project to be called Crossing Trails was proposed for construction on land southwest of Powell Butte—a low rising butte outside of Prineville—and adjacent to the county's irrigated agricultural lands. Developers known as "818 Powell" proposed 490 homes and an undetermined number of overnight units on just 580 acres. The resort would include a golf course and swimming complex.

If (or when) fully built out, these four proposals would increase the overall number of houses found in the county in 2000 by 50%, providing construction jobs while increasing concern about the potential public infrastructure costs.[27]

As the legal challenges discussed above suggest, not everyone has welcomed the boom in destination resorts, including both environmental and land use watch dog groups (statewide and regional), as well as many county residents and voters. For regional environmental groups, there are a number of key concerns. The Sierra Club's Eastern Oregon "Juniper Group" argues that "there are no areas left in Deschutes County that are appropriate for resorts" and the resorts that "have been approved and built under Goal 8 guidelines have proved to be damaging to natural resources, have not resulted in no net loss of wildlife or habitat, and will strain water sources (groundwater, rivers, streams) beyond their carrying capacity." These groups further argue that resorts are actually "resulting in sprawl development."[28] Indeed, this is a concern expressed by many in Central Oregon, namely, that destination resorts are no longer about growing the economy through tourism; instead, destination resorts have become the preferred way to bypass the state planning system's restrictions on nonagricultural, large-scale development in rural areas while developing real estate that features prime amenity opportunities.

Debate about the future of destination resorts has been a feature of Deschutes County planning processes for years. More recently, opposition in Crook County was led by ranchers and resort neighbors in the Powell Butte area,[29] who responded to the rapid spurt of destination resort approvals by the county's leadership and its embrace of this economic engine by mobilizing to stop new resorts through a citizen's ballot initiative. In the 2008 election, 66 percent of Crook County voters endorsed a measure that advised the county's elected officials to withdraw the existing destination resort map. This action effectively banned the county from considering any new resorts for another three years, the minimum time period allowed before any changes to a map of resort lands can be revisited.[30]

Late to the party: Jefferson County

Unlike Deschutes and Crook counties, Jefferson County has no real experience with post-1984 destination resorts inside its boundaries, but like Crook County, until the early 2000s the county had not even prepared an inventory of lands eligible for destination resort development. That changed in 2006 when county officials completed the technical process of identifying lands that would meet Goal 8 criteria and its associated DLCD rules. In doing so, county commissioners signaled their willingness to travel a now well-worn road in Deschutes County, and to a lesser extent in Crook County. Planning staff identified lands in the western end of the county better known for timber harvests and, to a lesser extent, cattle grazing as meeting the eligibility criteria for destination resorts. In a county where the agricultural base had long been a key economic driver, the decision marked an important departure from the past.

A partial exception to the limited history of resorts in Jefferson County is the Crooked River Ranch, which began development in 1971 as a resort but became a residential community with 3,710 residents by 2007[31]— suggesting that fears that "resort" can become merely another word for rural sprawl may not be entirely misplaced.

Indeed, while conflict about destination resorts became a part of life in Deschutes and Crook counties, by far the most contentious and bitter political fight in the region emerged around two very different proposed resort projects for the Metolius River basin in western Jefferson County: the Ponderosa, a large-scale project that fell partially within the basin, and the Metolian, a much smaller project located entirely within the basin.

For the Ponderosa, the Ponderosa Land and Cattle Company, a subsidiary of the Colson & Colson/Holiday Retirement Company, purchased 10,000 acres of forest-zoned land from Weyerhaeuser in 1999. For the Metolian, Shane Lundgren and coinvestor James Kean, under the corporate name Dutch Pacific Resources, bought 627 acres of land from an individual who had purchased the thoroughly cutover land from Weyerhaeuser in 2005. By early 2007, Dutch Pacific Resources began applying for a new development on the site, and Lundgren proposed and extensively researched an "eco-resort" concept. Unlike the Ponderosa Land and Cattle Company and the many other resorts in the region, there was no discussion of a golf course. Indeed, from the beginning the Metolian, with its proposal for a "natural capital fund" (or self-imposed resort tax) to support ecological restoration projects in the community, did not fit the conventional Central Oregon resort model. Both properties would ultimately become key features of the areas mapped as eligible for destination resorts in Jefferson County's official inventory of lands (Figure 12).

Figure 12   Shane Lundgren, on the site of his proposed Metolian resort, raised intriguing questions about "eco-development" that went unanswered (P. Walker 2009)

Derailing the Train Once It's Left the Station

> [T]hey had their marching orders. . . . They knew where they needed to get;
> the governor was very clear about where he wanted to go. . . . He threw the
> bill down and said this is what I want, and then you had some heavy hitters
> in the legislature who care about the area.
> —Rick Allen, lobbyist for Ponderosa[32]

By mapping the two properties owned by Dutch Pacific Resources and the Ponderosa Land and Cattle Company lands as eligible for resorts, Jefferson County signaled the potential for a dramatic transformation of land uses—from forestry to residential—in the Metolius Basin. For the developers, the designation meant that it was safe to begin investing time and money in the planning and design phase. In the view of an emerging opposition, however, the county's decision represented a dangerous threat to the basin and its prized landscapes. *Bend (OR) Bulletin* journalist Nancy Pasternak described it this way: "Local groups [are] wringing their hands over Jefferson County's mapping of two destination resort areas [and] believe it [has] momentum they will be battling in coming years."[33] Sensing the importance of this new momentum, opponents knew the fight to stop the Metolian and Ponderosa destination resorts would mean a battle to derail, as a resident of Camp Sherman in the basin put it, the train that was "leav[ing] the station."[34]

Over the next two-plus years, a small number of active groups and powerful individuals would become the faces of local and regional resistance, working to challenge the county's process and the on-the-ground realization of the resorts. In particular, these included Betsy Johnson, a well-placed and powerful state senator representing Scappoose (outside Portland) in the Oregon legislature; the Central Oregon Landwatch, a regional land use watchdog group; the Friends of the Metolius, composed of residents from Camp Sherman (the only area of any concentrated human settlement within the basin); and the Confederate Tribes of Warm Springs, who have cultural, historical, and spiritual ties to sites in the basin. The three groups received support from 1000 Friends of Oregon, as well as much popular support from citizens at public meetings and through letters to the editor. To assist those efforts, Central Oregon Landwatch maintained a "model letter" on the organization's Web site.

Opposition would focus on concerns about the impacts these resorts would have on the basin's hydrology and water, the impacts traffic would have on area roads and taxpayers, threats to wildlife and wildlife migrations, and the claim that this was clearly just another example of subdivisions landing in the rural countryside outside Central Oregon's UGBs. Above all, perhaps, there was a pervading sense that the Metolius Basin was a *special* place. Destinations resorts? Maybe. But not *there*. The Metolius Basin was too special to entrust to the existing, routine operations of the state's land use planning system. Past experience with the proliferation of destination resorts under the state planning system suggested a new approach was needed.

Beginning in 2007, opponents of resorts in the Metolius embarked on a new, two-pronged strategy. First, they engaged the traditional route of opposition by submitting a series of appeals to LUBA in which they challenged procedural elements by Jefferson County and argued that the county effectively erred during its mapping or inventorying process. In other words, they did not challenge the validity of having resorts in the Metolius Basin. At least at first, this was their only option. Nothing in county code or state law said destination resorts could not be built in the "special" Metolius Basin. In the end, LUBA concluded that the county had acted appropriately, except where the approval related to how the county had evaluated the relationship of the resorts to big game habitat (e.g., deer, elk). And this was not enough to block the county from approving a proposal by either the Metolian or Ponderosa development groups.

Opponents began looking beyond LUBA appeals for a second strategy. If there was nothing in existing law that said resorts were not allowed in the Metolius Basin, then the law would need to be changed. The proposals and any ultimate project approvals had to be derailed, and the best way was to ramp up the scale of their political strategy, asserting that the importance of the issue extended beyond local jurisdiction and required the intervention of the state. As Camp Sherman resident Dick Kellogg put it in a guest column for the *Bend Bulletin*, titled "Legislature should step in and protect the Metolius Basin," "Jefferson County [had] used poor judgment in designating two properties in and adjacent to the basin as eligible for major destination resorts," because among other things, the

Metolius is home to "incomparable scenery and flourishes with wildlife and pristine fish habitat."[35] He further described the basin as "world renowned and . . . one of the crown jewels of the state of Oregon." Anticipating the likely question from opponents, Kellogg concluded, "Yes, it is appropriate and timely that the state legislature step in and override this irresponsible county action."

Thus, opponents began asking the state legislature and state officials to intervene, demonstrating a willingness to abandon, or at least challenge, a long-held understanding among the state's advocates of good land use planning — namely, that land use decisions were best decided *within the established system.*

Supporters of the Metolius resorts seized upon this appeal to the state for help and began explicitly questioning the appropriateness of state intervention, arguing that the will of the local government should be respected. For them, this was a clear-cut case of the state ignoring the will of Jefferson County and the prerogative of the county's commissioners to work within the state's land use laws to create a new economic engine. Put another way, for proponents of the resorts this was another example of a power-hungry state government run amok.

Opponents of the resorts countered with the argument that an apparent majority of Camp Sherman residents believed that *their* opinions had been ignored by the county (or so the Friends of the Metolius said). However, this argument proved problematic for several reasons. First, proponents of resorts responded with the claim that this small unincorporated area of approximately 350 people (only about 50 percent of whom live in the community year-round) was engaging in classic NIMBY (not-in-my-back-yard) politics. After all, the state planning system existed, in no small part, precisely to ensure regularity and predictability in land use decisions and to avoid making land use choices through ad hoc local power struggles.

Above all, however, the claim by opponents of the proposed Metolius Basin resorts that their voices had been ignored proved problematic because of *who* some of these NIMBY neighbors were. Proponents of the resorts focused particular attention on Betsy Johnson, a powerful state senator, heir to a wealthy timber family, president of her family's philanthropic organization, *and* owner of 160 acres of "pristine" land near the headwaters of the Metolius River. The family of another powerful state senator, Ginny Burdick, owned one of a small number of riverfront cabins on land leased from the U.S. Forest Service. The fact that these "local" opponents of the proposed Metolius resorts were also among the key legislators leading the push to change existing land use systems to preserve the Metolius Basin allowed proponents to use the news media and Internet to pull the emergency handle signaling a four-alarm fire of power politics and hypocrisy.

For the *Bend Bulletin*, the efforts to protect the Metolius were "an attempt to create a private reserve for the fortunate few, including a couple of powerful legislators, and to block a new resort so that the few could enjoy the homes and cabins they now own or have access to in that river basin." On the other hand, what the *Bend Bulletin* believed was "far more dangerous, and goes far beyond the Metolius, [was] the opponents' Machiavellian usurpation of the state's land law to short-circuit resort development simply because they [had] the votes to do it."[36] In an interview with the *Portland Oregonian*, even Senator Burdick acknowledged that "I'm a very rational person. I have a land use background. But when it comes to the Metolius, the principles that I know are important sort of go out the window."

Nevertheless, initially it looked as if the efforts of Johnson, Burdick, Central Oregon Landwatch, Friends of the Metolius, and others would pay off. Early in the 2007 legislature, while the LUBA appeal process was under way, a bill to ban destination resorts, Senate Bill 30 (SB 30), was proposed for consideration. In its original form, the draft bill included language that would specifically amend the state statutes governing resort development by implementing a prohibition on the siting of any "destination resort in or within three miles of [the] Metolius River Basin," unless Jefferson County could prove that the siting of a resort would not have adverse impacts on the "invaluable and highly significant natural area."[37] Besides recognizing the Metolius as a "significant natural area," the bill made the case for the basin's importance based on the arguments that it contained a Wild and Scenic river; it featured unique hydrology and geology; the main stem and its tributaries supported sensitive and threatened trout species, included sensitive elk and deer winter range; it was recognized for its cultural and historic values as well as outstanding scenic views; it contained lands in the Deschutes National Forest subject to special management; and it should be protected because it "is a matter of utmost importance and concern to the State of Oregon."

But in the weeks during which first the senate and later the house would consider SB 30, the contents of the bill and the fate of the two projects proposed for the Metolius took a series of unanticipated twists. At one point, the bill was amended to allow the resorts to proceed, passing through the Senate Committee on Education and General Government for consideration by the full senate. Just four days later, the bill was redirected to the senate's rules committee, where the ban on destination resorts was reinstated. The final version, with the ban intact, passed the senate by a vote of 18–11 on May 22, 2007.

In the meantime, new questions about legislator and legislative integrity were emerging. The news media reported that Senator Vicki Walker (D-Eugene) accepted a plane ride from fellow senator Betsy Johnson (an accomplished pilot). While entirely within the ethics rules of the legislature and the state's laws, the fact that Johnson offered to fly this key committee leader from Salem to the Bend-Redmond airport, with a flight path crossing the Metolius Basin, raised eyebrows. It also reinforced questions about the bill and whether Johnson's efforts to pass it were about protecting her own self-interests.

Debate over the bill focused on several key issues of contention, including what Senator Rick Metsger (D-Welches), one of the few Democrats who opposed the bill, described as a "drawbridge mentality. [Metolius residents] have a place near the river, but want to stop others from doing the same." Even a key proponent of SB 30, Senator Ben Westlund (D-Tumalo), conceded, "The proposed law would impede a land use choice made in Jefferson County." But playing to the scalar politics of the day, Westlund clearly saw this as a *state* decision, imploring: "Let's keep Oregon Oregon. Without unspoiled places like the Metolius River, Oregon wouldn't be Oregon. At least not the Oregon we know and love. SB 30 is fair and just, it is badly needed, and it deserves our full support."[38]

The importance of the river, the basin, and all they contain seemed to win the day when a version of the bill that banned resorts from the basin passed in both houses of the legislature. However, in the end a promised veto by Governor Kulongoski killed the legislation. At first, the governor's veto promise appeared based on concerns about the effect its provisions would have on the planning system and the message that this type of state political interference in local land use decision making might send. In a letter to the House Rules Committee chair Diane Rosenbaum, Governor Kulongoski indicated that Jefferson County's destination resort mapping effort "should be assessed on the basis of its compliance with the legal standards and procedures set forth in state and local law." He further acknowledged the presence of challenges to the process with LUBA and stated that he "support[ed] following the established processes for resolving those challenges."[39]

But the governor's desire to uphold the established planning *process* was tempered by concern about the potential *outcome* in the Metolius. In the same letter to Rosenbaum, Kulongoski indicated that he believed "the Metolius Basin is a special place that deserves protection," signaling his concerns about "the future of the Metolius" and "the impact of large-scale destinations on this unique state treasure." Yet, perhaps remembering the case of Dorothy English (see chapter 4) and his own efforts to keep the legislature from setting what he argued would be an "unwise precedent," he came down on the side of avoiding a "site-specific legislative fix." Kulongoski's stated support for the existing planning process kept alive the hopes of developers that they would be able to build their resorts in the basin, and they continued to invest in their projects. But the stage was set for a political showdown in the Metolius. It would just take two more years for the fight to play out.

Political currents in the state legislature demonstrated that protection for the Metolius had powerful allies. Some legislators spoke in uncompromising terms. Senate Bill 30's main sponsor, Senator Westlund, recalled in an interview after the session that "I was incredulous that it would be permissible to site a destination resort in the Metolius Basin. What the mapping of the Metolius Basin demonstrated was that some of Oregon's most special and pristine ecological systems could be vulnerable to commercialization."[40]

If anyone had doubts about where the governor actually stood, these were soon answered. Following the 2007 legislative session, Kulongoski asked several state agencies to consider how *existing* state laws might be used to protect the basin from the impending resort development. When the answer came back, it seemed as if there was nothing in state law that would prevent the Metolian and Ponderosa projects from being approved and built. Yet, by May 2008 the Department of Land Conservation and Development (DLCD) would begin publicly discussing a number of options to address the proliferation of destination resorts in the state, particularly in Central Oregon, making sure they are clearly tourist enclaves and not rural subdivisions.[41] In October 2008, reports emerged from Salem that DLCD was considering putting forward a proposal to the legislature to remove Goal 8 rules from the state code, thereby handing greater control over the issue of destination resorts back to the agency during plan reviews (see chapter 2).[42] Then, in December the governor announced that he was calling for broad protections of the Metolius.

But how did 2008 start out with the governor being told that there was nothing in state law that would allow government officials to prevent resorts from being built in the Metolius and end with the governor calling for broad protections of the Metolius? And why was the governor indicating a new willingness to move forward with legislation that was similar to the legislation (SB 30) he had killed through a promised veto almost two years earlier? Why did the governor shift course and choose state intervention seemingly over the procedural integrity of the process?

The answer lay in the (re)discovery of long-forgotten provisions of the original 1973 Senate Bill 100 authorizing designation of Areas of Critical State Concern (ACSC), and earlier writings by Tom McCall that expressed a desire that the Metolius, *specifically*, be considered for this designation. The suddenness of this new direction, and the political bombshell it represented, left some observers in disbelief. The *Portland Oregonian*, in an article detailing the development early in 2009, described the ACSC as "a never-before-used designation." To opponents of a resort ban and many observers alike, it certainly felt like this was the case, or at the very least that the designation had been "pulled out of a hat."[43]

The ACSC designation was neither pulled out of a hat, nor was it new. The ACSC provisions are part of the original 1973 SB 100 legislation that created the planning system (ORS 197.405). In 1977, DLCD requested that Yaquina Head on the coast receive the ACSC designation. However, before the coastal request could be considered by the legislature, the Bureau of Land Management acquired the site.[44] It seems, however, that during the intervening years the statute had been forgotten. The path to rediscovery of the statute is not entirely clear, but a widely circulated story among some observers ties the reemergence of the idea to a public meeting held by DLCD, in which a citizen participant commented on the "forgotten statute" and asked why the state was not pursuing this option. For supporters of protecting the basin, this was the answer to their prayers: the Land Conservation and Development Commission (LCDC) and the state legislature could take action to protect the basin, *and* that action would not override existing law or procedure. After all, it was a provision specifically spelled out in SB 100—something akin to a sacred text for the state's planning community.

Ultimately Governor Kulongoski, the LCDC, and Oregon state legislators used the newly rediscovered ACSC process to seal the fate of the proposed Metolian and Ponderosa destination resorts in the Metolius River Basin. As the 2009 legislative session got under way, Kulongoski asked DLCD to begin the process to designate the Metolius River Basin as an Area of Critical Statewide Concern. As the *Portland Oregonian* reported, "What followed was a rushed, two-month process in which the Oregon Department of Land Conservation and Development drew up the plan and held four public hearings."[45] During the process, DLCD would attempt to find possible alternate sites to accommodate the Ponderosa, given that part of the land area technically was located outside the Metolius Basin, and some degree of accommodation for the Metolian. Finally, on Friday, March 13, LCDC voted to recommend that the legislature designate the Metolius River Basin an Area of Statewide Critical Concern.

But once again, the fight in the legislature proved tough going and full of political maneuvering inside and outside the legislature. Within two weeks of the LCDC recommendation, Jefferson County's three commissioners voted unanimously to sue the state over the ACSC designation. Later, the same Jefferson County officials offered to withdraw their court case in exchange for approval for the Metolian alone and approval for a golf course elsewhere in the county. But legislative machinations continued; no bill moved very far, and in the final weeks of the session things heated up.

House Bill 3298 designating the Metolius River Basin as an Area of Critical State Concern, including a ban on destination resorts in the basin, passed the senate by a vote of 16–12 (two Democrats crossed party lines). In the house, the bill initially failed on a 30–29 vote, with five Democrats voting nay. Within just one week, and following a phone call from the governor, Representative Larry Galizio (D-Tigard) reversed his vote on the bill, ensuring HB 3298's passage. Critics would later make much of Galizio's subsequent appointment to an attractive job in the Oregon University System, adding to the public appearance that the fight to kill the Metolius resorts was all about bare-knuckle politics and dubious ethics.

Yet, in the new post–Measure 37/Measure 49 era, the legislature passed laws to provide the owners of both the Metolian and the Ponderosa properties a measure of compensation for their out-of-pocket losses.[46] The legislature provided approval for the Metolian developers to build one unit in the Metolius Basin and a 35-unit "eco-resort" in a less sensitive area, even though the owners complained they had no other suitable property for such a project. On the portion of the Ponderosa land that falls outside the actual basin, owners were given rights to build 100 homesites and a lodge with 20 overnight units. For proponents of the developments, these entitlements were a mere consolation prize, while opponents called them "windfalls" for developers.[47] No common ground was achieved—indeed, developers and environmentalists each felt they had literally lost ground.

However, all parties agreed on one thing: the Metolius Basin *is* a special place. Those who fought against the resorts made that clear from the start, but investors and Jefferson County, too, were counting on it. The question that the saga of the first-of-its-kind Metolius ACSC designation exposed, however, was this: For whom are certain places special? In what ways do we observe the specialness of such places? And, *who decides?* To some extent, these questions reflect ambiguities built into Oregon's planning system. At one level the fight over the Metolius was a fight over competing visions of a special place. More fundamentally, the fight over the Metolius quickly became a struggle to control ideas about *which public*, at *what scale*, exactly, the state planning system serves. And the overarching political question of the day was this: in an era of Measure 37 and Measure 49 turmoil, when tensions about fairness and a heavy-handed state role in land use planning were still high, should the state dare to intervene?

Remember the Metolius

In the eyes of critics and even some supporters of the ACSC designation, the state crossed a dangerous threshold, overriding (or at least applying in a new way) the state's *own* system of local autonomy guided by statewide goals to achieve a specific land use outcome desired by certain powerful people against the will of a local government working within the law. With a sense of righteous victimhood, some property rights supporters in Oregon now see the Metolius ACSC designation as the epitome of cruel, distant, almost imperial power—Oregon's Alamo.

LCDC chair John VanLandingham stated to us that he supported the outcome of preserving the Metolius, but he regretted the way that outcome was achieved: "Jefferson County feels that we've [the LCDC] been unfair to them and I understand that. If I were God and I could go back in time, I would not have had Jefferson County go through that huge process to map destination resorts, pick those two, and then block them."[48] One can argue that the intervention by the Oregon state government through the use of the ACSC designation fit within the existing planning system and possibly even fulfilled the wishes of Tom McCall. At the same time, the role that hardball politics played in producing this particular land use outcome raises important concerns. By invoking the ACSC, the state legislature decided to directly intervene in a local decision-making process. It did so in a way that narrowed Jefferson County's development options, despite the fact that, like previous resort decisions in the region, the process had been affirmed by LUBA as conforming to the statutes that regulate the destination resort review process. Seemingly lacking options within the established planning law, opponents of the Metolius resorts took the necessary means. They did not choose the path of Crook County resort opponents and its citizens, using the initiative process to demand a long-term reexamination of land use policy. Instead, they took hold of the levers of power in the legislature and governor's office for an immediate solution. And they found powerful allies who could successfully derail the train as it was leaving the station.

When one considers that fairness is a key question surrounding the ongoing initiative battles (i.e., Measures 37 and 49) and that the Oregon Task Force on Land Use Planning (the "Big Look") recommended that local governments be given *greater* deference in making planning decisions, the case of the Metolius ACSC portends stormy weather ahead. Some observers called the ACSC designation a "nuclear option." This manner of exercising state power to decide the outcome of a particular local land use issue called into question the state land use planning system's *own* commitment to honoring the established principle of local decision making within a framework of statewide goals. The placement of decision-making authority at the county level in SB 100 was no accident — and it contributed to decades of relative stability in the state's planning system. In the years after the passage of Measure 37 — a political earthquake motivated at least in part by genuine concerns about unfairness and insensitivity to local needs — the *timing* (if nothing else) of the Metolius ACSC designation certainly threatened to reopen still-fresh wounds and inject still greater antipathy and instability into the state's ongoing land use battles.

Our next case study, of the Greater Bear Creek Valley Regional Problem Solving planning process in southern Oregon's Rogue Valley, illustrates the intriguing consequences when the state of Oregon pursued a nearly opposite path — giving *greater* planning autonomy to local governments in one of Oregon's most politically turbulent regions.

8 Southern Discomforts

Jackson County—oh yes! Southern Oregon. I made lots of trips to southern Oregon. But I didn't really convince anybody.

—Hector Macpherson Jr. on his efforts in 1972–1973 to build support for SB 100[1]

I voted "no" on Senate Bill 100 not because I do not believe in the concept of land-use planning but because I believe this bill transfers unwarranted legislative powers to an appointive board, granting that board rule-making authority which thwarts the people's right to referendum in matters of land-use planning.

—L.W. Newbry, Jackson County state senator, 1973[2]

It's awkward and it hasn't been done before. But we are perched—sometimes uncomfortably—on the cutting edge of urban growth planning.

—John Eads, founder of Bear Creek Valley RPS, 2002[3]

The current [Bear Creek Valley RPS] plan . . . fails to provide a path by which the Rogue Valley can both grow in population and preserve what is special about this unique place.

—Don Moore, vintner, and Porter Lombard, vineyard consultant, 2008[4]

I have to tell you, I've been tearing my hair out about the Bear Creek Valley RPS.

—Richard Whitman, DLCD director, 2008[5]

When Oregon's statewide planning system was created in 1973, southern Oregon[6] was immediately vocal in its discomfort with this system. In the ensuing decades the relationship between southern Oregon and planners in Salem did not improve greatly (locally, "Salem" is often a "four-letter" word for centralized state power). In the early 1990s, Jackson County—the most populous county in southern Oregon—was accused of systematic violations of state land use laws,[7] and as a result county planning was monitored by the state for six years.[8] In the mid-2000s, Jackson County offered unique interpretations of Measure 37 (see chapter 4)—including ideas that Measure 37 claims were transferable and that approval of Measure 37 claims by the state land use authority was not required (both of these views were struck down by the state). It is probably fair to say that of all regions in the state, southern Oregon has had the most discomfort with the statewide land use planning system. Yet, seemingly paradoxically, today southern Oregon could justifiably lay claim to being at the "cutting edge" of urban growth planning. This is a distinction, however, that looks more complex and less certain upon close examination. Such an examination reveals much about the politics of promoting "flexibility" in the state's land use planning system in Oregon.

To begin any discussion of southern Oregon, it is important to note what the region is not: it is *not* the heavily populated, urbanized, and politically left-leaning Willamette Valley (see chapter 1, Figure 2). In this chapter, we focus our attention mainly on southern Oregon's Rogue Valley, which follows the Rogue River and its tributaries through the most populous areas of Jackson and Josephine counties, including the cities of Medford and Grants Pass (Figure 13).

The most important tributary to the Rogue River for the purposes of our study is the Bear Creek—site of the Greater Bear Creek Valley Regional Problem Solving (RPS) planning process that is the main focus in this chapter. In the Rogue Valley, the Bear Creek runs parallel to Interstate 5, through the cities of Ashland, Medford, and Central Point (Figure 14)—an area that has grown rapidly in recent decades, forming by far the most concentrated population center in southern Oregon. Yet the Rogue and Bear Creek valleys are tightly contained by the high Cascade Mountains to the east, the rugged Siskiyou and Klamath mountains to the south and west, and many lower but still substantial mountain passes through Douglas and Lane counties to the north. Visitors driving into Oregon from California (15 miles south of Ashland) are often surprised that in southern Oregon Interstate 5 (the main West Coast artery run-

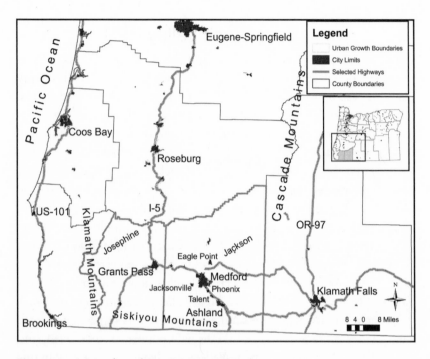

Figure 13 Map of southern Oregon (P. Hurley 2010)

ning from Canada to Mexico) becomes a difficult high-elevation, windy, snowy, and (in winter months) sometimes impassable mountain road. As we discuss below, the rugged isolation of the region is matched by the area's cultural and political sense of independence and difference.

Euro-American settlement in the Rogue Valley began in earnest in the mid-nineteenth century with the discovery of gold near Jacksonville, the completion of roads to California and the Willamette Valley, and the building of the Oregon & California Railroad. After southern Oregon's Gold Rush diminished, agriculture (especially pears and other fruit) and timber production dominated the region's economy for many decades. Today's economy is more diverse. In Jackson and Josephine counties in 2008, employment comprised mostly (in descending order) retail trade, transportation, and utilities (23 percent); health services and education (17 percent); government (15 percent); leisure and hospitality (11 percent); manufacturing (8 percent); professional and business services (8 percent);

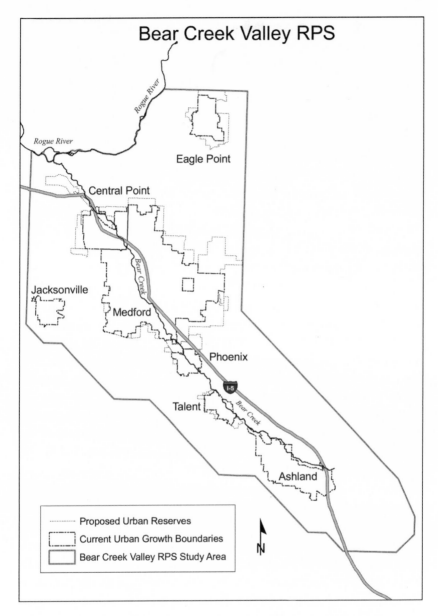

Figure 14   The Greater Bear Creek Valley Regional Problem Solving planning process area, part of southern Oregon's Rouge River Valley (I. McKinnon 2010)

financial services (5 percent); construction (4 percent); and natural resources and mining (3 percent).[9] In recent decades most economic growth
in the region has come from the service, trade, and information sectors
rather than the traditional resource trades. In particular, recreational
trade and services have grown greatly in importance. The agricultural
sector, while still strong, has suffered from changing market conditions
and development pressures, making it difficult for some farmers to survive in the region's traditional pear and other fruit production. However,
new opportunities in agriculture have also opened up, particularly in
wine grapes and organic produce farming, reflecting wider market demand and serving the region's growing trade in tourism and recreation.

Overall, however, the region is relatively poor—with a 2007 median
household income of $44,344 in Jackson County and $37,209 in Josephine County. The number of persons in Jackson and Josephine counties
living below poverty in 2008 were, respectively, 16.0 and 19.4 percent.[10]
In the Great Recession of the late 2000s, the region was hit particularly
hard, with unemployment levels at 12.4 percent in Jackson County and
14.2 percent in Josephine County (as of October 2009).[11] While the employment and income statistics for southern Oregon were particularly
grim at the end of the 2000s owing to global recession of the time, the
region suffers underemployment and low wages even in relatively good
times.

In this context, it seems understandable that many in the region consider
population growth an opportunity for economic advancement—particularly in the real estate, construction, retail, and service sectors. And few
regions in Oregon have matched the rates of population growth in the
Rogue Valley in recent decades. Surrounded by striking natural beauty in
every direction, abundant recreational opportunities, a relatively dry and
warm climate (with usually less than 20 inches of rain and mild winters),
and low real estate prices compared to neighboring California (or urban
areas of Washington State), the Rogue Valley emerged by the latter half
of the twentieth century as a growth magnet for the state. In particular,
Jackson County's population grew 26 percent in the 1950s, 28 percent in
the 1960s, 40 percent in the 1970s, 11 percent in the recession-plagued
1980s, and 24 percent in the 1990s. From 2000 to 2009, Jackson County's estimated population grew another 11 percent.[12] Much of this growth

came from a single source: transplanted Californians, who (remembering the paving over of the own native places) are now often among the leaders seeking to contain further growth.

The State of Oregon predicts a doubling of the Rogue Valley's population sometime in the next several decades. Notwithstanding the severe recession of the late 2000s, the region's astonishing rates of growth in the past suggest that these long-term projections are not unrealistic. While there is debate in the Rogue Valley as to whether this growth should be seen as a beacon of economic hope or as a threat to special landscapes and a way of life, few deny that adapting intelligently to growth of anywhere near this scale is a preeminent challenge for the region.

To understand the particular (or perhaps "peculiar," to Oregonians in other areas) ways the Rogue Valley has chosen to respond to this challenge, one must know something about the distinctive political and cultural traditions of southern Oregon.

An Ornery Tradition

Southern Oregon is *different*, and proud of it. Oregon as a whole relishes a political identity of independent-mindedness, often either of a certain brand of populist conservatism (e.g., the recent property rights movements in the state) or progressive liberalism (e.g., Portland's earned reputation for "green" politics). But southern Oregon possesses its own brand of independence *within* this state of proudly independent-minded political thinkers. As southern Oregon political historian Jeff LaLande describes it, southern Oregon is proud of its "ornery tradition":

> Southern Oregon's voters and politicians have often marched to the beat of their very own drummer, one with a different beat than the rest of the state. This difference has often been one of more volatile politics, an electorate more prone to extremes, and those tendencies have typically manifested themselves as movements that we, today, consider to be "conservative" and/or "populist." Southern Oregon has been a distinctive region, politically and in other ways, since even before 1859 [when Oregon gained statehood]—a region that was even then viewed by residents of the Willamette Valley (i.e., the earlier-settled and more

"connected to the outside world") as a much wilder place, one populated by somewhat less "cultured" and less even-tempered people. Currently, for many people living in the Willamette Valley and Portland, southern Oregon is that benighted, unenlightened place . . . the place where "they close down libraries," it's where "teachers bring handguns to school," it's where in the 1990s loggers feasted on spotted owls "deep-fried, stewed, or baked." So, it's a real reputation that we have. Sometimes it's been justly earned, sometimes it's been exaggerated. But it's ours nevertheless—a reputation in which Oregonians living outside of our area tend to hold the view that in political matters, southern Oregonians are somehow notably different.[13]

While a populist conservative streak runs strong throughout the state (even including parts of the greater Portland metropolitan area), this tradition is arguably most concentrated (or at least most noticeable) in southern Oregon. Little documentation or research is available explaining this distinctive tradition. LaLande, who earned his doctorate in history at the University of Oregon and teaches part time at Southern Oregon University in Ashland, emphasizes that his is only one person's educated opinion. He describes this region's distinctive political culture as a product of a number of geographical and historical forces. Among these, the region has always been and remains geographically isolated—surrounded by rough coastline, thick forests, and inhospitable mountains. The largest city in the region is Medford with an estimated 2009 population of 77,240.[14] The nearest larger cities are the greater Eugene-Springfield metropolitan area (population 351,109 in 2009) 168 miles north and Redding, California (population 90,898), 150 miles south. In satellite imagery, the most populous part of the region, the Rogue River Valley at the confluence with Bear Creek, appears almost lost between dense forests and rugged mountains. This is also the only region of the state to have had a gold rush (though there were also minor discoveries in Baker City and Sumpter in eastern Oregon)—an extension of California's, with a similar rough-and-tumble culture. It was also the only region of Oregon to witness active and bitter, large-scale conflict with Native populations.

Perhaps most important, the region was mainly settled by whites from the border states and lower Midwest/Ohio Valley (e.g., Missouri, Kentucky) with a more "southern" political culture, including fierce anti-government and often racist views. (Settlers in the Willamette Valley and Portland had similar origins, but with an important and powerful New England overlay—see Bowen [1978].) Although (contrary to local legend) there is no direct connection to the Confederacy, some of this "southern" political culture has morphed into myths of Confederate links—visibly expressed on many modern-day pickup trucks today waving the "Stars and Bars." Southern Oregon and northern California maintain a marginal but active secessionist subculture that calls the region the State of Jefferson, after Thomas Jefferson—though the name is sometimes (inaccurately) said to be a tribute to Confederate President Jefferson Davis.[15]

When this political culture mixes with a statewide land use planning system that has been described by critics as "Soviet style," the result is not difficult to predict. Michael Cavallaro, executive director of the Rogue Valley Council of Governments, describes the region as "bad boys" in the eyes of state planners.[16] When a local group known as the Jackson County Citizens League complained that the county was systematically violating state planning rules to favor development, the county responded that they were justified in issuing building permits in agricultural-zoned areas because, in their view, the state had zoned these areas incorrectly (prompting then-staff attorney for 1000 Friends of Oregon Robert Liberty to quip, "That's like driving 100 mph on the freeway because you don't agree that 55 miles an hour should be the speed limit").[17] More recently, Jackson County was taken to court for approving Measure 37 applications without requiring claimants to also obtain necessary approval from the state and for allowing transfer of Measure 37 rights in contradiction to state interpretations of the law. Circuit court judge Phil Arnold replied sternly that "[Jackson] County does not have the authority to sanction wholesale disregard for compliance with state statutes."[18] Jackson County is also the only county in which property owners, supported by an opinion by a U.S. district judge, claimed that Ballot Measure 49 could not undo waivers of land use rules they obtained under Measure 37 (based on the theory that Measure 37 established binding contracts).

However, while politics in the region remain indisputably rough-and-tumble in nature, the modern political culture of the region is far from homogeneous. Particularly with the large waves of Californians and other in-migrants in the 1960s, 1970s, and 1980s, "counterculture" migrants brought very different worldviews that spurred intense local cultural clashes (Brown 1995). But these in-migrations since the 1960s permanently altered the cultural and political landscape. Ashland, for example, is something of a haven for upscale, educated cultural and political liberals and "elites" (and hosts an internationally renowned annual Shakespeare Festival).

Predictably, these cultural extremes often produce volatile politics. Far less predictably, as we show in this chapter, the result can also be unsurpassed intraregional cooperation in land use planning. What that might imply for Oregon's statewide planning system is worth examining.

Regional Problem Solving

John Kitzhaber had his own point of view, but he understood southern Oregon. The Democratic governor (1995–2003, and elected for an unprecedented third term in 2010) began practice as a medical doctor in Roseburg, Oregon, in the same year that Oregon's landmark land use legislation, Senate Bill 100, was passed. In his first two terms as governor, Kitzhaber became an ardent defender of the state's land use planning system, vetoing bill after bill from the then Republican-controlled state legislature aimed at weakening the planning system. However, as a resident and physician in Roseburg (an hour and a half north of Medford—but a next door neighbor in culture and politics), Kitzhaber knew the region's "ornery tradition" well. And Kitzhaber had something else in common with his neighbors to the south—an independent streak (particularly in natural resource management) that renewed the state's claim to possessing a special "Oregon way" of doing politics (Collette 1998). Kitzhaber had lived near ground-zero during southern Oregon's "spotted owl wars" in the 1980s and 1990s (Brown 1995), and the trademark of his "Oregon way" was to "hunker down" and find consensus between otherwise seemingly irreconcilable, entrenched political positions, a trait he displayed as governor in his support of the Oregon Plan for Salmon and Watersheds.

As a candidate for governor in 1994, Kitzhaber was aware of the growing desires of the cities in Bear Creek Valley to do things their own way—a position Kitzhaber could understand. Once Kitzhaber's term began, he dispatched the then-director of the Oregon Department of Land Conservation and Development (DLCD), Richard Benner, to a two-day series of meetings in Bear Creek Valley to "brainstorm." Ultimately, the product of these meetings was the regional problem solving (RPS) statute, written by Benner. The bill was passed in 1995 as part of a legislative package that was later invalidated on constitutional grounds. The bill was reintroduced and passed in 1996, with generous funding. As Benner explained to us in 2009, "Although the [Bear Creek Valley] can fairly be said to have inspired what became RPS, there was more going on. Both houses of the legislature were controlled by opponents of the statewide planning program. Legislators, including some in southern Oregon, were pushing for amendments to SB 100 to devolve authority from the state to local governments under the banner of 'local control.' New Governor 'Kitz' wanted to respond in some way, a positive way, if possible, to deflect the attack on the land use program."[19] Kitzhaber's concern was well founded. By the mid-1990s, Oregon's planning community recognized that they faced significant challenges that threatened the effectiveness and political stability of the statewide planning program. In regard to effectiveness, there was a widespread perception that "top-down" control by the state worked against effective planning in certain matters, particularly in complex regional problems involving multiple local jurisdictions. Also, by the mid-1990s property rights activists had become organized and active through groups such as Oregonians in Action. By the late 1990s, DLCD was officially promoting "less regulation," "greater flexibility," and "*regional* solutions" (emphasis added).[20]

The RPS statute (House Bill 3482) was a centerpiece of these broader political efforts to politically stabilize the state planning system. According to DLCD, the new law "calls for local governments, state agencies, citizens, and affected organizations to work together to address land-use problems that transcend city or county boundaries . . . it calls for solutions 'outside the box.' If all participants agree on a solution to the land-use problems, LCDC [Land Conservation and Development Commission] can approve it even if it does not conform in every respect to LCDC rules (the solution must conform to the purposes of the goals)."[21] RPS was touted as a way to bring greater "vision," "voluntarism," and "consensus" to the state's "top-down" regulatory system.[22]

The planning advocacy group 1000 Friends of Oregon was concerned that RPS could undermine statewide planning.[23] The group complained that the legislature heard no testimony explaining precisely what sort of problems a regional approach could solve that the existing state system could not. In the statement from the DLCD biennial report cited above, for example, it was unclear what it meant to say a plan approved under RPS might fail to fully comply with state land use rules but could still "conform to the purposes of the goals." The answer would not come for many years later. It appeared it would come from where RPS started—Bear Creek Valley.

Bear Creek Valley RPS

Officially known as the Greater Bear Creek Valley Regional Problem Solving planning process, this 10-year effort by communities to work together to plan their region's future is now widely acknowledged as being by far the most ambitious and advanced RPS in Oregon. Other areas made similar efforts and virtually all failed. Thus, despite its notably inelegant acronym (GBCVRPSP—hereafter "Bear Creek Valley RPS"), to the extent that giving greater autonomy and flexibility within the statewide planning system is considered the future of the program, this collective community effort probably earned the claim by former coordinator John Eads that the project is on the cutting edge (or at least *a* cutting edge) of urban growth planning. For those less familiar with Oregon's cultural and political geography, it is worth pausing to connect these unlikely "dots": a home-grown, community-based, collaborative project that can plausibly claim to be at the cutting edge of urban planning emerged in the "ornery," anti-authoritarian Rogue Valley of southern Oregon of *all* places. How could this have happened?

The region's geography played a role. With rapid population growth in a valley tightly contained by rugged mountains, over recent decades of rapid growth the cities of Bear Creek Valley inevitably grew closer together. Already, two of the biggest cities in the valley (Medford and Central Point) are actually contiguous. As the cities grew closer together, practical matters such as transportation, infrastructure, emergency services, and so on, became more interdependent.

Yet, until the creation of the RPS law in 1996, Oregon's statewide planning system was largely geared for planning by *individual*, independent cities (with the exception of special provisions for Portland Metro—see chapter 6). Specifically, Oregon planning law requires each city to undergo periodic review to ensure that its urban growth boundaries (UGBs) are adequate to allow for 20 years of growth, and to designate "urban reserves" that identify longer term areas designated for future expansion of UGBs over a 50-year time frame (see chapter 2). With the very rapid growth experienced in the past and anticipated in the future in the Rogue Valley, designating areas for future expansion is a pressing matter.

With very little area remaining between the cities of Bear Creek Valley, coordination became necessary to avoid conflicts. (For example, the cities of Medford and Phoenix wanted to designate urban reserves on the same unincorporated land.) Thus, the RPS law addressed an important practical need for cities to coordinate their planning to avoid this kind of potential conflict (and take advantage of opportunities for cooperation) in ways that would not typically happen if each city created growth plans independently in coordination only with the state planning agencies. In 1999, DLCD invited the cities of Bear Creek Valley to apply for an RPS, and they did.

However, Bear Creek Valley's successful application for state authorization to conduct an RPS could be said to have merely codified a process that started considerably earlier, with a genuinely local, grassroots effort by local citizens and farmers to address the pressing need for coordinated planning in the region. According to local participants in the current Bear Creek Valley RPS, in the early and mid-1990s when population growth in the region was accelerating (but before the RPS statute was created), local land use attorney John Eads initiated a series of informal meetings of local leaders over morning coffee, culminating in the creation of two reports called "Our Region" that identified likely scenarios and options for growth in the region over a 50-year period. The Our Region project was carried out independently and on a voluntary basis by local leaders over three years. By the time the cities of Bear Creek Valley applied for official RPS status, the communities of the valley had already laid much of the groundwork for regional cooperation.

By all accounts, the level of cooperation and coordination among the participants in the Bear Creek Valley RPS was a major accomplishment. Local jurisdictions had a history of antagonism not only toward the state government but in some cases between each other as well. To have overcome much initial skepticism about collaborative planning and to have built personal and institutional bridges of trust between jurisdictions in historically "ornery" Jackson County was no small feat. Ironically, local antipathy toward the state planning system may have played a role: participants stated that they saw the RPS as their only way to get "Salem" off their backs. If that meant having to cooperate with the neighbors—well, so be it. (In the end, however, a single notable defection from this remarkable consensus proved potentially fatal to the Bear Creek Valley RPS—a story we return to later in this chapter.)

The desire to escape the rule of "Salem bureaucracy" was by no means limited to crusty Jackson County "old-timers." Ex-Californian Kate Jackson, an Ashland resident who chairs the governing Bear Creek Valley RPS Policy Committee (and a self-described "environmentalist"), explained to us why she supported the RPS process: "We took up the Regional Problem Solving statute as a possible way for our jurisdictions to deal with the state land use program that was so hard for us to deal with otherwise. We were unsuccessful and unhappy with the interactions between the state-level bureaucracy and the local cities' and county's planning departments. Over the decades the state regulations just kept getting longer and more complicated. . . . This [RPS] statute gives us flexibility. It allows us to look at our specific situation and make some tradeoffs and compromises."[24] Thus, there appeared to be nearly unanimous perception by long-time residents and newcomers, conservatives and liberals, that state land use regulations had become onerous and inflexible and that the RPS (itself a state policy, to be clear) represented the "only way out" for Bear Creek Valley. However, it is one thing to concur that some degree of local control is better than (at least perceived) near-total control by a distant, allegedly unresponsive authority; it is quite another thing to agree on what, exactly, local control should aim to achieve, and for whose benefit. Trade-offs and compromises toward *what*, precisely, and for *whom*? It is over these questions that the Bear Creek Valley RPS appeared poised at the end of 2009 to potentially stumble and fall.

Whose Flexibility?

By Christmas 2009, virtually everyone involved hoped the Bear Creek Valley RPS was near the end of its marathon effort to create a viable regional plan for the valley's future. A series of local meetings was scheduled for January 2010 to elicit public comments on the completed draft plan before it would go to the state land use authority, the LCDC, for approval. However, depending in part on what, if any, changes emerged in the final plan, some critics were considering taking the Bear Creek Valley RPS plan to court—potentially invalidating or suspending the 10-year effort for what might be indefinite additional months or years.

Any challenge to the plan would likely be based on the withdrawal of the City of Jacksonville from the RPS process. On January 6, 2009, following many months of tension between the city and the RPS, the Jacksonville City Council (backed by groups such as the local League of Women Voters) unanimously decided against signing a participants' agreement that would pledge the city to adhere to the final RPS plan, on the grounds that the exact form of the final plan had not yet been determined and had not received comments in public hearings.

However, Jacksonville's discomfort with the RPS had at least as much to do with the *outcome* toward which the RPS seemed headed as it did with the RPS process. The 2009 Jacksonville City Council vote was taken by an "anti-growth" leadership who had voiced increasing concerns that the RPS had taken a pro-growth turn. Councilor John Dodero was among the most outspoken, complaining that the RPS plan proposed to develop too much high-value farmland and that the RPS process had "flipped from regional planning to an end run around Oregon land laws," thwarting efforts by his city to create buffer areas with nearby Medford and protect farmland around the city's boundaries.[25]

However, Jacksonville's withdrawal from the RPS had far greater potential significance than simply removing one of the seven Bear Creek Valley cities from the table: in the view of some critics, legally speaking the absence of Jacksonville ended the RPS altogether. The Bear Creek Valley RPS, like other RPS efforts in the state, followed a policy of consensus-based decision making: all participants had to agree to each step in the process. Jacksonville maintained that it did not remove itself from the process but was ejected from the RPS because it could not agree to sign the participants' agreement without more public input. The language of the RPS statute itself included phrases such as requirements that "all local governments within the region affected by the problems that are subject to the problem-solving process" must participate.[26] In other RPS processes where a city stopped participating, the RPS was declared dead. In Bear Creek Valley, the RPS leaders and the local DLCD representative maintained that because Jacksonville is a small city, its absence did not invalidate the overall RPS. Much would hinge on this argument. Critics of RPS acknowledged that this issue offered a legal "hook" to upend the RPS to anyone who might choose to use it. As Greg Holmes, the southern Oregon representative of 1000 Friends of Oregon, explained to us in late 2009,

> The Jacksonville [withdrawal from the RPS] and the [bending of the administrative rules]—I think that's a huge chink in their armor. I think that hook is available to any party who wants to appeal their final decision for any reason. [The RPS leaders] keep looking at us [1000 Friends of Oregon] like we're the ones who'll end up bringing the lawsuit. Well, that's possible. Don't know, because we haven't seen what they're going to end up with. But it doesn't have to be us. [The RPS leaders] should be worried about what *they're* doing, and doing it *right*. A property owner who wanted [to be included in the urban reserve] that testifies at any one of these hearings on the record can appeal this, and use that reason. Or an owner who is in the urban reserve and wants out. Or the next door neighbor, or anybody . . . it just has to be somebody who doesn't like what the RPS did, and they've got that hook.[27]

The crux of the concerns by Jacksonville and other critics of the RPS centered on the decision of the RPS leadership to include substantial areas of high-value farmland in its urban reserves—the areas designated for long-term urban growth—rather than pushing more aggressively for greater urban density and "infill" within existing urban boundaries. The validity of this choice to expand into certain areas of high-value farmland, in turn, hinged on critical legal and political questions—namely, precisely how much "flexibility" would the RPS statute allow with respect to state land use rules, and *whose vision or interests* would this flexibility serve?

As described in chapter 2, "Thou shalt grow onto prime farmland only as a last resort" might be considered the First Commandment of Oregon state planning regulations. The state RPS statute, however, allows RPS projects to propose plans that "do not fully comply with the rules" under certain specified conditions.[28] In true Jackson County fashion, the Bear Creek Valley RPS possibly took the idea of "not fully complying" with the rules further than most. In a public information insert in the *Medford (OR) Mail Tribune* in December 2002, the RPS promoted itself literally under the banner of "Making Our Own Rules":

> [The] state rule designed to protect farmland could have the opposite effect here. The rule says residential land in a rural area has a high priority to be developed into urban land. This rule protects farms in a place like the Willamette Valley, with large tracts of uninterrupted farmland. In Jackson County, however, we have a lot of residential land sprinkled out among some of our best and most productive farms and orchards. Strictly applying the state rule here in some cases would force cities to grow into farmland simply because there were concentrations of rural housing nearby. Meanwhile, less valuable resource land would have to remain undeveloped. Regional Problem Solving allows us to say "No" to this kind of decision making, and devise rules that make sense here.[29]

In Oregon as a whole and Jackson County in particular, saying "no" to state land use rules has an irresistible appeal to many people. The RPS statute requires that plans must "conform, on the whole, with the purposes of the statewide planning goals."[30] This language leaves much room for interpretation. Thus, to what extent a plan prioritizing development on farmland is legal or desirable, even under the RPS, is very much at the nub of tensions about the Bear Creek Valley RPS, and would be decided by the state land use agency, or possibly in a court of law.

No one disputes, however, that the Bear Creek Valley RPS did interpret the law loosely (or "innovatively," depending on one's perspective). Under the 2009 draft plan, approximately 8,800 acres would be designated as urban reserves for future development, of which about 75 percent was zoned for farm use, including about 1,200 acres of "high-value" farmland. Ordinarily, state rules prioritize expansion onto so-called exceptions lands (mixed-rural residential areas that were "grandfathered" into the land use zoning system). Michael Cavallaro, executive director of the Rogue Valley Council of Governments (which played a central role in organizing the RPS), acknowledges that the Bear Creek Valley RPS reordered state priorities, but for good reasons:

> The system for designating [farmland] when the state land use system took effect and zoning decisions were made—a lot of it wasn't that scientific. So, there are a lot of pretty marginal [farmlands]. And the trouble with relying on exceptions land, especially in this area, is that some of the exceptions land is pretty densely populated, so there isn't really a lot of buildable capacity in those exceptions lands. So, to accommodate, say, 1,000 people, if you can only fit another household, or say two households, on an acre, and there's another piece of [undeveloped] rural land where you could fit six households on, then you need about three times as much exceptions lands to provide the buildable land. So you're markedly increasing the footprint of the urban area.[31]

The arguments for and against the strategy pursued by the RPS quickly become technical and open to differing, but valid, points of views. The deeper problem, at least from the perspective of critics of the RPS, is the *vision* that guides the overall process, as well as choices on critical technical matters. Critics said that while the RPS began with one type of guiding vision, it was later guided by a very different one, serving quite different individuals and social interests. In a 2009 op-ed in the *Medford Mail Tribune*, Jacksonville city councilor Linda Meyers, former representative of Jacksonville on the RPS, drew attention to these shifting visions:

> On Jan. 31, 2000, [local governments] applied to Oregon's Department of Land Conservation and Development for a grant to form the Greater Bear Creek Valley Regional Problem Solving Project. According to the application, the project's primary purpose was to work regionally to protect agricultural lands from urban sprawl while planning for a doubled population. The application for creating the RPS project stated that it would first identify specific lands—prime agricultural and open space lands, buffering areas between cities, and land considered nonbuildable for environmental or logistical reasons—to be removed from

"consideration for future conversion to urban levels of development." The lands not identified would remain "available for future urban development." The project soon deviated from its original purpose. One participant asked at the December 2001 Technical Committee meeting, "I thought we were supposed to be deciding where not to grow first. What happened to that?" . . . the RPS project interprets the "flexibility" allowed by the ambiguous RPS statute to mean that participating cities can, when determining their proposed urban reserves, overlook the potential of efficient urbanization within their existing UGBs. As a result, far more agricultural acres are proposed for urban reserves than are needed.[32]

Similarly, Greg Holmes, the southern Oregon representative for 1000 Friends of Oregon, draws very important links among guiding visions, process, and *outcomes*:

One of the things that is really telling to me is that the group that started the conversations [about regional planning in Bear Creek Valley in the mid-1990s] weren't government folks. They were mostly agriculturalists. They started coming together over coffee in the mornings and chatting about things, and a concern was brought up that we're losing our best farmland as the cities are growing. So, they started an effort where their priority was, "let's figure out what the most important agricultural land we have is, identify it, and figure out how to grow *around* it, rather than over it." And somewhere between that and what we have now, that idea was lost. Now it's not "let's figure out where the good stuff is and not grow over it," but "let's figure out how to grow our cities, and if we need to take some of this good [farmland] that our committee of experts told us is the best of the best we have left, well, then let's figure out a way to justify that." It's a very different approach, and it brings you to a very different place in the end."[33]

Some believe that bringing the Bear Creek Valley RPS to a very different place in the end was no accident—that while the RPS began with a conservationist vision, it ended up "captured" by interests that realized they might benefit economically from the RPS. Innisfree McKinnon, a doctoral student at the University of Oregon who has conducted the most

in-depth research on the Bear Creek Valley RPS to date, described to us
the perceptions of some local RPS critics:

> What I've been told is that originally developers were really nervous
> about this [RPS] process, and that there was a lot of opposition to the
> idea of this regional process, and that gradually certain developers—
> the larger developers that were in a better position to take advantage
> of this [RPS]—have come around and are now supportive. So, you'll
> hear people say stuff like, "This is a land grab," and, "this [RPS] has
> been taken over by the developers." I don't know how much of that's
> true. But it's true there are developers who have had representatives
> at these [RPS] meetings long-term, and are definitely investing in this
> process.[34]

Michael Cavallaro made similar observations, referring to influential
long-time landowners as well as speculators who recognized the long-
term economic importance of a process that would decide which lands
would be identified for future development:

> At the point at which some of these [urban reserve] areas were being
> identified, then you started getting support from the people who had
> land in those areas—or who went in and took a chance and bought
> land in these areas, took options. So [the RPS] built a support network
> of those who would benefit from the outcome of it [the RPS]. There
> were indeed some of those [areas of land] that were already owned by
> influential people who got their areas in [to the urban reserve] because
> they're influential, because they know people. But on the other hand,
> again, those are people who are very knowledgeable about what makes
> good urbanizable land. In all likelihood the vast majority of those lands
> would have come [into the urban reserves] anyway under any dispas-
> sionate look at what's appropriate, so that's not necessarily a bad thing.
> And then, other people took a chance and started buying up some of
> this land when it looked likely that certain areas would be in [the urban
> reserve]. Now, these people have something to lose, so they became
> staunch supporters of the process and want to see it done.[35]

The strong involvement in the RPS by the development community and
other interests should come as no surprise. By making planning more

"local," the RPS in effect offered more opportunities for engagement of the planning process by local interests than the state-level planning process would have offered. These interests included those whose concerns were primarily economic, but also included aesthetic and ideological interests. For example, from as early as 2001, when the "Greater Bear Creek Valley Regional Problem Solving: Phase One Status Report" was issued, developers, real estate brokers, and individual property owners came forward requesting that their properties be included in the proposed urban reserve.[36] At the same time, other property owners came forward insisting that their properties be *excluded* from the urban reserve to preserve their picturesque views and the tranquility of their surroundings.[37] Other interests were more ideological, or perhaps environmental, in nature—for example, the active participation and leadership role in the RPS by "anti-growth" Ashland leaders, who engaged the process to promote a nearly zero-expansion vision for their city's future.

These "local" interests may all have had valid concerns. However, it is important to observe that by making land use planning more "local," the Bear Creek Valley RPS process appeared to allow a more parochial sort of planning politics to emerge—one that could be said in certain ways to contradict the very purpose for which the statewide planning system was created and more characteristic of development in states where no statewide approach exists. For example, in the 1960s when former Republican governor Mark Hatfield caustically referred to strip development along Highway 101 in coastal Lincoln City as "twenty miserable miles," he was responding to the failure of leaders to resist local pressures from "opportunistic" developers who had created "helter-skelter development out of control."[38] To be very clear, the landscape toward which the Bear Creek Valley RPS plan would lead would almost certainly look nothing like Lincoln City (which, in rhetorical one-upmanship with his Republican colleague, governor Tom McCall referred to as "a model of strip-city grotesque"). Still, in a limited fashion the Bear Creek Valley RPS allowed back into the planning process certain elements of local politics that arguably had not been seen in Oregon in nearly four decades.

Although RPS leaders acknowledge that some "influential people" may have gotten their way "because they know people," this kind of influence may have had less impact on the outcome of the RPS than a kind of live-

and-let-live ethic between local participants. For example, when we asked RPS Policy Committee chair Kate Jackson how the RPS resolved differences between "liberal" cities (Ashland, Jacksonville) and "conservative" cities (Central Point, Eagle Point) on "big vision" questions such as when to expand UGBs and when to promote urban "infill," she replied:

> It didn't come in that much, because this is such a long-range plan that we weren't talking about infill inside each others' urban growth boundaries. We were looking outside [the UGBs]. . . . One of the goals [of the governing RPS Policy Committee] is not to step on each others' toes, to recognize the individuality of each individual city in the RPS, and housing is one of those issues where, you know . . . within the policy committee we were respecting the individual choices and individuality of the cities. So, the fact that Jacksonville, for example, wants to cap its population and the fact that [housing in] Ashland is so much more expensive than other cities is just accepted as the variations among us all. When looking at the urban reserves we were not going to say, "well, Medford, you really ought to do a lot more infill." We weren't going to talk about each others' infill inside the city limits because that was touchy.[39]

Whether this mutual "respect" and unwillingness to address "touchy" issues is good, bad, or indifferent is not our point. Rather, this history illustrates that by shifting some autonomy from the state to the local level in land use planning, a different political dynamic is likely to emerge. To some extent Oregon's state-level planning system exists in response to exactly the kinds of interest group politics and unwillingness or inability to address big-picture, difficult issues that appeared to emerge in the Bear Creek Valley RPS. "Big brother" (the state) was *supposed* to take the flak for imposing a vision for the claimed benefit of society that surely not all Oregonians would cooperate with on their own, even if they agreed that the outcome was beneficial (the classic "tragedy of the commons" argument—Hardin 1968). At the same time, if the state receives so much flak that the entire state-level planning system becomes politically destabilized, a plausible argument could be made that those who advocate state-level planning should recognize the value of a strategic retreat. These questions, in turn, seem to depend greatly on who, precisely, is able to "participate" in local decision making, and whose "visions" are represented.

Whose Participation?

There was a lot of citizen participation in all of this [RPS]. Don't let anybody tell you there wasn't.
—Michael Cavallaro, Rogue Valley Council of Governments, 2009[40]

To sign the [RPS] agreement before [holding] public hearings would render public input irrelevant.
—Linda Meyers, Jacksonville city councilor, 2009[41]

I mean, you have ten years of 7:30 a.m. meetings like this [RPS] Policy Committee has, people who don't have a direct discernable interest are not going to be able to stick with it that long—if they're not being paid, or not standing to gain something. That's one thing, the duration. Another thing is the complexity of [the RPS draft plan]. This isn't something simple. You look at the report and its many hundreds of pages. If somebody picks that up, where do they start? . . . it's overwhelming. So [the public participation process] does present a bias toward a certain outcome. . . . But, how do you keep people involved in something this complex that lasts this long? It's a tough one.
—Greg Holmes, 1000 Friends of Oregon, 2009[42]

The Bear Creek Valley RPS is far from alone in its participatory approach. With the 1980s and 1990s Reagan/Thatcher conservative revolution, an emerging activist property rights movement, and a general anti-regulatory mood, there emerged a major shift among planners and resource managers at home and abroad toward more collaborative approaches that allowed greater "local control" (e.g., see Wondolleck and Yaffee 2000; Freeman 1997). However, this push for greater local participation proved to be far from a panacea. One problem that has been widely observed is the difficulty of determining appropriate levels of local control amid weaknesses of *both* centralized and local government (e.g., see Berkes 2004; Barrett et al. 2001). Also, the democratic intent of "participation" may be undermined in various ways. In some cases, central governments may "devolve" control in name only, highly "containing" local, participatory processes (Few 2001). A more widespread concern, however, has emerged about the tendency of "local control" to be "captured" by local elites, as powerful groups and individuals come to control and direct the "participatory" process for their narrow interests (Mansuri and Rao 2004; Platteau 2004), especially where there is no single, homogeneous "local" point of view (Agrawal and Gibson 1999). To an extent, all of these problems described in the academic literature were present in the Bear Creek Valley RPS.

The question of precisely how much local autonomy the state had granted to local governments in the RPS statute dogged the Bear Creek Valley RPS from beginning to end. Early in the process, some members of the community were wary of participating in the process at all, based on deeply held suspicions that the state land use authorities would ultimately pull back on any significant "flexibility" the RPS chose to build into the final plan. And indeed, several key leaders informed us that as the Bear Creek Valley RPS moved closer to completion, the level of scrutiny and restrictions they received from DLCD headquarters in Salem began to tighten. Since no other RPS of anywhere near the same level of complexity had reached such an advanced stage in the planning process, there was no precedent and no clear guidance in the RPS statute to suggest precisely what level of "not fully in compliance" with state rules the state would accept. If the Bear Creek Valley RPS were approved by the county and sent to LCDC for approval, the precedent set by LCDC's decisions about acceptable levels of flexibility would be profound.

However, as described in previous sections of this chapter, in 2010 the fate of the Bear Creek Valley RPS appeared likely to hang on the question of whether the absence of Jacksonville from the participatory process would legally block the RPS from advancing. In turn, the choices made by Jacksonville that removed it from the RPS were motivated in part by concerns about the appropriate time and place for public participation.

It is demonstrably true that there was a great deal of public participation in the RPS from the very beginning. However, it also appeared true that few substantive changes seemed likely to emerge from the first-ever county-level public hearings about the *completed* draft plan (held in January 2010), given that the participating jurisdictions had already signed pledges to support the plan. As Jacksonville mayor Bruce Garrett complained, "If everyone signs agreeing to whatever the final document is, the fact there is a public hearing down the road is really a moot point."[43] RPS leaders, however, argued that signing the participants' agreement in advance was necessary to encourage participants to "invest" in the process, being assured that a single jurisdiction would not "torpedo" the whole process at the last minute for some reason. Regardless of the merits of these arguments, this dispute illustrates the broader question of what level of public participation is appropriate in a local "collaborative" process, and at which stages in the planning process.

In regard to the question of local "elite capture" of the RPS, it appeared both true and logically unavoidable that those members of the public with both a strong and clearly defined interest in the outcome of the RPS *and* the ability to invest time (usually at 7:30 a.m. on Tuesdays) to attend key policy committee and other meetings over a period of 10 years would have the most opportunity to be "heard" during the creation of the plan (vs. the opportunity to respond to the completed plan in public meetings at the end of the process). However, there seem to be few clear ways to avoid this. Greg Holmes, the representative of 1000 Friends of Oregon and one of the strongest critics of the public participation element of the Bear Creek Valley RPS, acknowledged, "I don't know what they could have done differently." Holmes added, "If I wasn't being paid to be there, *I* wouldn't have been at all those meetings."[44] Moreover, the subject matter itself poses challenges. Kate Jackson, the Bear Creek Valley RPS chair, noted that she and her colleagues on the policy committee were not professional planners and that over the years "we all learned a huge amount," because as the plan moved closer to completion, "the more we had to recognize the detailed numbers the planning profession uses."[45] To expect meaningful public involvement throughout such a long, demanding, and sometimes arcane process seems at best optimistic. In the *absence* of such public involvement, however, it is difficult to see how it could be avoided that those who have relatively narrow interests and adequate time, resources, and knowledge will dominate the public participation process.

Under such circumstances, the likelihood that certain visions, voices, and outcomes will prevail over others seems high—possibly aggravating, at the *local* level, the very kinds of political turmoil that the RPS statute was intended to reduce.

Between a Rock and Hard Place

The lessons of the Bear Creek Valley RPS are difficult. On the one hand, the need for regional problem solving is not in dispute. As cities grow together, becoming more interdependent and facing new challenges and opportunities (e.g., finding new transportation options), the need for coordinated planning among local jurisdictions seems beyond question. The absence of a well-functioning regional coordination system for most of Oregon's cities and counties (apart from Portland Metro) is a major challenge for Oregon's planning system. Moreover, truly engaging local knowledge and innovation in land use planning represents a much-needed opportunity to release pent-up frustrations among local communities that perceive the state planning system as insensitive to (or, worse, uninterested in) local conditions, needs, and opportunities. Effective local engagement could go far to defuse the powder keg of hostility toward statewide planning that built up over many years and—in our view—remains a serious threat to the long-term stability of Oregon's land use planning system. To those steadfastly unwilling to depart from strict "top-down" models of the past, we say good luck with that.

On the other hand, one of the important lessons from the Bear Creek Valley RPS is that engagement of local communities with the statewide planning system is *hard*. The Bear Creek Valley RPS and its precursors under different names stretched over 15 years—a time frame that might have made John Eads, sitting with local farmers over coffee in the mid-1990s to envision the valley's future, shudder. Michael Cavallaro, the Rogue Valley Council of Governments director and coordinator of the Bear Creek Valley RPS, estimates that each jurisdiction in the RPS added about one year to the length of time it took to reach agreement on a plan, and that at each critical step at least one jurisdiction in this consensus-based process "dragged its heels," making progress painfully slow.[46] At least three of the founding organizers of the Bear Creek Valley RPS died before its completion. The task of educating all-volunteer, nonplanner RPS committees was also enormous. And overcoming old animosities and mistrust between certain jurisdictions within Bear Creek Valley took time and commitment. It is a testament to the determination and dedication of the Bear Creek Valley RPS participants that they overcame these obstacle over so many years, and—by near-universal agreement—achieved a remarkable degree of trust and coordination among the cities and the county that did not exist previously, which will serve participants well as the region faces interdependent problems in the future (with or without an RPS). A close study of the Bear Creek Valley RPS could nearly "write the book" on what to do and not do in regional land use planning.[47]

Perhaps the most important observation about the Bear Creek Valley RPS, however, is the question left unanswered through most of the years that the project operated: what is an acceptable level of "flexibility" in the state's land use rules? Despite the obstacles we have described, the RPS succeeded in giving local jurisdictions in Bear Creek Valley a greater sense of ownership and empowerment in the planning process. By the beginning of 2010, all cities of significant size in the valley, with the exception of Jacksonville, supported the final draft plan. Even the two (out of three) staunch pro-property rights Jackson County commissioners were eager to see the plan enacted. Everyone involved agreed that achieving this level of local support required significant bending of the state rules. As we have described, to critics this amounted to a reversal of visions—from how to preserve farmland to who would get which chunks. Some called it a land grab. We would call it a virtually inevitable outcome of devolving decision-making power to this conservative, economically struggling region. Past *in*flexibility is what upheld the state's vision. Any notion that the state could expect local people to voluntarily do the hard work of strictly enacting a vision created by others is a nonstarter. Geographer Jesse Ribot has described this illusory proposition as "participation without representation" (see Ribot 1996).

When the state chose to defuse political tension by authorizing local governments to not fully comply with state rules, it kicked the question of *how much* noncompliance was acceptable down the road. To nearly everyone's surprise, Bear Creek Valley produced a plan (where other less ambitious RPS efforts had failed). The plan would force the state to decide how much flexibility in the state's vision for growth could be accepted, putting the state between a rock and hard place. Deciding against the Bear Creek Valley plan could be politically explosive. Deciding in favor would sanction quite a different vision for growth in Oregon. It was a choice the state did not want to make. It seemed to assure southern Oregon's "ornery" reputation would live on.

9   Paradise Lost?

[P]ersons with the longer view are not at all certain that the debate over Oregon's land use planning system has been laid to rest. . . . [Measure 49] does not address many of the underlying discontents with the system.

—Ellen Bassett, "Framing the Oregon Land Use Debate," 2009

In fact it is actually very hard to predict the long term consequences of Measure 37 as amended by Measure 49. . . . My take on the recent success of property rights advocates in Oregon is that it is largely attributable to the sclerotic, unimaginative character of the Oregon land use advocacy community.

—John D. Echeverria, land use law scholar, 2009[1]

Americans have often pursued environmental quality at the expense of social justice. One would like to imagine that the two goals are complementary and that the only way to achieve a healthy environment is through a truly democratic society. But for now, these two objectives remain separate guiding stars in a dark night sky, and we can only wonder if they will lead us to the same hoped-for destination.

—Karl Jacoby, *Crimes against Nature*, 2001

I'm very glad finally we can talk without treating Senate Bill 100 as sacred.

—Jon Chandler, Oregon Home Builders Association, 2009[2]

Much American social theory can be found on bumper stickers (and much silliness, of course). Or, if you happen to live in Africa or Asia, similar expressions can be found painted on the cabs or tailgates of trucks. One particularly profound automotive-philosophical statement is popular in

Ghana: "No condition is permanent" (Berry 1993). As social scientists, we are accustomed to thinking of all conditions being fluid. Economics, politics, culture—*everything* changes. The natural state of the world is change. Yet, in the course of our examination of the history and politics of land use planning in Oregon, we were struck by the degree to which neither Oregon's planning system nor the well-intentioned people who legislate and administer it have grappled adequately with change. We are even struck by an element of resistance to change among Oregon's planning community. If Oregon's land use planning system is to thrive another three or four decades, learning to adapt will be essential. Few in Oregon's planning community seem to remember how close they came to losing the whole program in 2000 with Measure 7. And the long-term effects of Measure 37 and its reworked form in Measure 49 cannot yet be fully known. But certainly big changes *have* happened, and planning advocates were often left playing a defensive game. We submit that if Oregon's planners want more big surprises and more big losses, all they need to do is hold on tight to the system they have.

No Condition Is Permanent

If the quality of an idea or policy can be roughly measured by its durability, it is worth noting that Oregon's statewide planning system as set forth by Senate Bill 100 in 1973 had a very good run. Despite multiple political efforts to undo the statewide planning system in the 1970s, 1980s, and 1990s, the core of the SB 100 model remained intact. But no condition is permanent. In 2000, when statewide Ballot Measure 7 was approved by Oregon voters by a substantial majority, Oregon's planning system looked vulnerable. As we have described in this book, Measure 7 should have been seen as a hard shot across the bow, yet the planning community failed to adequately heed the warning. In 2002, the planning system was rescued from Measure 7 by a fluke of legal procedure. However, when Ballot Measure 37 passed by an even larger majority in 2004 and was upheld by the Oregon Supreme Court in 2006, the basic SB 100 framework for land use planning in Oregon was fundamentally undermined for the first time. Measure 49, which was passed by voters in 2007, imposed limits on the scope of Measure 37 claims, but it did not undo the fundamental conceptual and policy shift established by Measure 37: as described in chapter 5, Measure 49 actually reinforced the core idea in Measure 37 that private property owners must be granted waivers or compensation for proven reductions in property values resulting from new land use regulations. How this shift will play out over time remains to be seen. Regardless, Measure 37 was a huge departure from the SB 100 model, which was not crafted with mechanisms to address questions of equity. Measure 37 and Measure 49 forced a fundamentally new reality onto Oregon's planning system. We submit that fundamentally new kinds of responses are needed.

To be clear, Oregon's planning system has never been static. As Oregon historian William Robbins reminds us (chapter 5), no legislative session since 1973 has ever left Oregon's land use laws untouched—it is always changing, and has been from its beginning. New statewide planning goals have been adopted, and existing ones have been amended; a new regional planning authority (Metro) has been created; reforms of the "exceptions" process have been adopted; inches-thick binders of new administrative rules have been adopted—many specifically for the purpose of allowing more flexibility while upholding the basic planning structure; a new urban and rural "reserve" system has been added to provide greater long-term certainty about where and when urban growth boundary (UGB) expansions will occur; and, not least, Measure 49 (and Measures 7 and 37 earlier) generated a higher degree of sensitivity within the planning system to equity questions—that is, how fairly the costs and benefits of the planning system are distributed. Such changes have made the system better. Our question and concern is not whether Oregon's planning system has the ability to change—it clearly has and does. Our question is whether Oregon's planning system can and will change *enough* to survive in an era that is in so many ways fundamentally different than the time of its birth in the 1970s.

Small-bore fixes that smooth over the most immediate points of tension are unlikely to resolve the Oregon planning system's recent instability. For example, on February 25, 2010, a special session of the Oregon legislature overwhelmingly passed (with a combined house and senate vote of 82–4) the aptly titled SB 1049, which addressed both 1973 SB 100 and 2007 Ballot Measure 49 by granting waivers of land use regulations to up to 1,600 Oregon property owners whose Measure 49 claims had been denied earlier due to various procedural errors. SB 1049 demonstrated flexibility in the bureaucracy. It also responded to concerns about equity by granting waivers to some landowners who stated they were unjustly denied the right to use their property as they intended when they bought it. After the political turmoil that began in 2000 with the victory of Measure 7, two subsequent major statewide ballot initiatives on land use, and seesaw Oregon Supreme Court reversals of these ballot initiatives, in 2010 some were eager to declare that SB 1049 would bring the political instability of the previous decade to an end. However, state senator Floyd Prozanski, who sponsored SB 1049, stated on Oregon Public Radio[3] that his bill would bring to a close "this chapter" of Oregon's tumultuous land use politics. Prozanski did *not* claim that more than a "chapter" had been closed. We agree. New leaks in the dam will come. Political turmoil will transform, reconfigure, and emerge anew until fundamental destabilizing forces in the current system are addressed.

To understand this claim, it is important to recall that Oregon's statewide planning system, created by SB 100 in 1973, was born from roughly equal measures of idealistic landscape visions (framed as "quality-of-life" concerns) emanating largely from urban constituencies and economic pragmatism by Oregon's farmers. As described in chapter 3, land use planning advocates outside Oregon (and many inside Oregon) often incorrectly perceive that Oregon's planning system was a product of environmentalism (even though scholars have conclusively refuted this view—see Abbott, Adler, and Howe 2003). This perception misses the seminal role of Oregon's agricultural community, including dairy farmer and state senator Hector Macpherson, who conceived of statewide planning in the late 1960s and early 1970s as a way to protect farmers from conflicts with rural-residential land uses and upward pressure on land prices and taxation. More generally, this view misses the crucial point that Oregon's planning system was first and foremost conceived from hard-nosed economics and practical self-interests among certain state constituencies. At the same time, such an ambitious idea as SB 100 could not have become law without the tremendous political persuasion provided by the environmental and quality-of-life visions offered by then-governor Tom McCall and others. (What legislator, after all, wanted to appear in favor of, in

McCall's words, the "grasping wastrels of the land"?) In 1973, a firm economic base of support aligned with a powerful public environmental vision. SB 100 worked politically because it got both the economics and the vision right.

Yet, it is easy—and *dangerous*—to focus on the "visionary" aspects of SB 100 and its political leaders while ignoring the economics and politics. As noted in the early chapters of this book, many planning advocates in Oregon today attribute the political weakness of the Oregon planning system today to an absence of leadership comparable to the early 1970s Tom McCall era. All indicators in our historical analysis suggest this diagnosis is simply wrong and will lead the planning community toward the wrong remedies. The leaders we interviewed who were most directly involved in the creation of SB 100—including Hector Macpherson, the author of SB 100; Mike Thorne, member of the 1973 Senate Committee on Environment and Land Use; and Nancie Fadeley, chair of the 1973 House Committee on Environment and Land Use—all insist that without the political and economic support of the key constituencies of the time behind SB 100, Tom McCall, Ted Hallock, and other charismatic leaders could *not* have passed the bill. In other words, *even in 1973*, without getting the most important economic and political constituencies on board with SB 100, Tom McCall could not have gotten the legislative votes to pass the bill. The near-cultlike status of Tom McCall among many in Oregon's planning advocacy community appears to have blinded some to this essential reality.

And, by the first decade of the 2000s, this is precisely the predicament that the SB 100 planning system was in. Poignantly, Bob Stacey, the executive director of 1000 Friends of Oregon at the time that Measure 37 passed in 2004, told us that his pollsters tried every conceivable public relations angle against the initiative, and nothing worked. Simply put, the message or the messenger was simply not enough. The SB 100 model itself had lost too much of its economic and political base of support, at least relative to the Measure 37 property rights model. When planning advocates celebrated the 2007 victory of Measure 49 (which limited the development potential under Measure 37), what they almost universally failed to note was that Measure 49 did not repeal Measure 37; it only limited the effects of Measure 37—and it retained the core principle in

Measure 37 of requiring compensation for future land use regulations. When we asked the political leaders behind Measure 49 why they did not simply draft the initiative to repeal Measure 37, they were unambiguous in their response: they did not attempt a repeal of Measure 37 because they *knew* they would fail. The economic and political base of support behind the property rights message was too strong; the economic and political base behind the SB 100 model of planning was, in relation, too weak. A lot had changed since 1973.

Seen from this historical political-economic perspective, it is little wonder that, by the first decade of the 2000s, Oregon's celebrated planning system faltered and appeared vulnerable. By that time, the economics of land use had changed dramatically, and the public visions of "quality of life" and protecting rural landscapes—though still strong—faced stiff new competition from the visions offered by the ascendant property rights and populist conservative movements, not to mention a renewed and growing demand for housing in the rural countryside. Neither the by-then large bureaucratic and political institutional structure born of SB 100 nor the community of ardent supporters of the state planning system seemed to fully absorb the significance of these new realities.

As evidence of this claim, even today most land use planning advocates in Oregon fail to recognize that they were outfoxed by Dorothy English (chapter 3) not once but *twice*: not only was the Dorothy English story a political masterstroke that gave the property rights community the moral high ground in the state's land use battles, but it also provided land use planning advocates with an all-too-easy, superficial explanation for their political defeats with Measure 7 and Measure 37. In the two years of research we conducted for this book, we found that even today planning advocates consistently blame their election defeats on clever political tactics by opponents—mainly, Dorothy English and wickedly brilliant selection of ballot titles.

The possibility that the state's planning system had become politically vulnerable because of more fundamental shifts in the state's economic, ideological, and political terrain was almost never mentioned. A notable exception is Bob Stacey, who described his own failure, as executive director of 1000 Friends of Oregon, to think deeply and proactively about the meaning of the planning system's near-death experience following

Figure 15 Dorothy English offers important lessons for planning advocates—if they will listen (Ross William Hamilton, *Portland Oregonian*, 2003, reproduced with permission)

the passage of Measure 7 (which was overturned on a technicality in 2002) as probably the worst political mistake of his career. In blaming the stooped, wispy-haired, raspy-voiced Dorothy English (Figure 15) and her presumed nefarious political choreographers, the planning community let itself off the hook too easily. The planning community has yet to fully absorb the real lessons of their defeats in the 2000s. If Dorothy English (and the associated "clever" politics by the property rights community) beat the planning community, she did so in a more profound way than most people recognize. Ultimately, her greatest victory may be in providing an emotionally satisfying scapegoat that distracted the planning community from their own failure to recognize the fundamental shifts occurring under their feet. In this chapter we summarize some of the most important changes, including population increase and new pressure on UGBs, changing markets and increased pressures to develop rural land, evidence of a more ideologically conflicted electorate than the planning community had understood, changes in the farm economy, and increasingly vocal and legitimate concerns about unfairness in the distribution of costs and benefits of the statewide planning system.

Oregon's planners once set the standard for innovative problem solving. In today's changed economic, social, and cultural environment, Oregon's planners need to learn to be innovative again. Clinging to the old ways will surely bring the planning community more losses. We also suggest that all of these challenges indicate an urgent need for revitalized public engagement to help recalibrate the planning system to contemporary conditions and reestablish a public sense of ownership, trust, and even pride in the planning system.

An obvious and important example of major changes in underlying conditions since 1973 is the growing pressure on UGBs. When state planning Goal 14 (which created the requirement for local jurisdictions to establish UGBs) was created in 1974, it required governments to draw these boundaries in such a way as to accommodate 20 years of growth. Most jurisdictions took several years to establish these boundaries. Portland Metro, for example, established its UGB in 1979. In doing so, the state planning system in effect built into place a 20-year period of relative political calm. By design, the 20-year rule meant that at first there was enough land for development within the UGBs, and therefore relatively little to fight about. Or, putting it another way, the 20-year rule could be seen as having set the timer on a 20-year political time bomb. In fact, with remarkable precision, by the late 1990s when many jurisdictions were facing the task of updating their UGBs, economic and political pressures in urban housing markets had built up greatly.

It is almost certainly no coincidence that major political turmoil began to rock Oregon's planning system at just the time when many cities were pressing up against their UGBs. As we discussed in the case of Portland Metro (chapter 6), for example, the original 20-year UGB period expired in 1999, and in 2000 Measure 7 passed—including in two of the three Portland Metro counties (the exception being Multnomah County). In Central Oregon (chapter 7), population pressures and changing rural land markets contributed to threats to the Metolius Basin—a kind of sacred landscape for many Oregonians. In southern Oregon (chapter 8), population growth, booming rural land markets, and a changing agricultural economy forced reexamination of rural and urban land use planning methods. The links between such changes and the political turmoil we have described in the statewide planning system as a whole were sometimes indirect, but certainly new demographic and market pressures (including the emerging housing bubble) made for fundamentally different planning politics in the early 2000s than in the early 1970s.

Pressure has been growing outside the UGBs as well as inside. As described in chapters 6 and 8 (Portland Metro and southern Oregon), pressure on farmers and farmland is greater than ever. Nearly 60 percent of Oregon farmers are 55 or more years of age, and the single largest age cohort (at 17.5 percent) is farmers 70 and above.[4] Many wonder about the ability and willingness of a new generation to take up the family farm. Pressure to sell off portions of family farms likely will only intensify. At the same time, the crops that are showing greatest promise in Oregon, such as greenhouse and nursery products (now Oregon's top-value agricultural commodities), as well as wine grapes, are produced mostly in areas of Oregon where there is also the highest population growth, particularly in the Willamette Valley and the Interstate 5 corridor. And, as described in chapter 6, new niche markets such as specialty produce for urban consumers *require* close proximity to the densest urban areas. In an interview with us in 2009,[5] Oregon Farm Bureau spokesperson Shawn Cleave noted that while the farm community remains divided in its support for the planning system (much as it was in 1973), overall the farm community in Oregon maintains support for the statewide planning system that has protected many of its members from sprawl and rising property taxes for decades. And in Central Oregon (chapter 7), destination resorts threatened to become, in effect, rural subdivisions—doing an end-run around Oregon's SB 100 model for protecting rural land. Serious questions have been raised about whether in twenty-first-century Oregon's urban-rural divide is adequate, or even appropriate, to support farmers and rural landscapes.[6]

With regard to support from the general public, there is little evidence that attitudes toward land use planning have changed substantially since 1973. However, enough experience has now accumulated that should signal to the planning community that they may be on shakier ground in terms of public support than they think. On the one hand, when asked about the general principle of controlling growth and protecting natural areas, Oregonians continue to strongly support planning, at least in concept. SB 100 itself—which created a structure for planning without proposing specific regulations—is an example of a vote on planning as a *concept*. It passed in 1973 with a bipartisan combined house and senate vote of 58–30. In voting on ballot initiative efforts to repeal statewide planning, the public voted in 1970, 1976, 1978, and 1982 to uphold statewide planning—each time with substantial, if not overwhelming, margins. More recently, in statewide polling taken for the Oregon Task Force on Land Use Planning (the "Big Look"), 60 percent of survey respondents said they support using public funds to "protect" farms and forests, and 65 percent support "additional protections" for natural areas.[7]

Such figures have long provided comfort to advocates of Oregon's statewide land use planning system. However, Oregon's planning advocates need to be clear that there are many regulatory and *non*regulatory ways to "protect" rural lands (as in our discussion of approaches to statewide planning in other parts of the United States—see chapter 2) and that such survey responses cannot be assumed to be an endorsement of existing or additional regulations in Oregon. Even more fundamental, perhaps, land use planning advocates do not appear to have fully absorbed the meaning of a now large accumulation of indicators that this public support, though broad, is also shallow and conflicted—and therefore politically unreliable. A statewide public opinion survey conducted in 2005, shortly after the passage of anti-planning Measure 37, showed strong support for "protecting" farms, forests, and natural areas. However, even greater numbers in the *same* survey showed, for example, that 67 percent of Oregonians believe that "protecting the rights of property owners" is "very important."[8]

Oregonians display seemingly contradictory values: they do value regulations that protect farms, forests, and natural areas (particularly if those regulations affect someone *else*), and yet populist anti-"government" attitudes run deep. Lane Shetterly, a former Republican legislator and the director of the Oregon Department of Land Conservation and Development (DLCD) at the time Measure 37 was passed in 2004, commented to us that "even urban people, who don't have a dog in the rural lands fight, are going to respond to that issue of government intrusion into their lives. They may not have a land use issue, but they know they don't want government telling them what to do. So, they were easy pickings, easy to attract as supporters for Ballot Measure 37."[9]

Oregon's planning community has had a surprisingly difficult time absorbing the fact that Oregonians can say they support planning and still vote for policies that undermine planning. This slow learning has had grim consequences for the planning system. In 2009, Bob Stacey, executive director of 1000 Friends of Oregon, explained to us that, in the vote for Measure 37,

> we got our heads handed to us in that election. As it [the election loss] sank in, there was a belief that Oregonians had changed their minds about land use planning. What we were able to do through a lot of public opinion research was to demonstrate that Oregonians haven't changed their minds; they really had two opinions about [planning]. They really want to see Oregon protected from unplanned development, *and* they really don't want government impinging on people's property rights. . . . The media were calling up our pollsters for weeks saying, "Are you sure that's right? They said both that they support land use planning and we think Measure 37 was right? How does that make sense?"[10]

A brief conversation with any of the key participants in the creation of SB 100 and the DLCD (many of whom are still alive) would have revealed that this should have come as no surprise. Deep and widespread suspicion of "big government" was a powerful source of resistance against the statewide planning concept from the very beginning. That it took planning advocates more than three decades to absorb this lesson might be interpreted as indicating that planning advocates are indeed slow learners.

A kinder and probably more accurate interpretation is that deep dedication to the long-successful model of planning that Oregon's planners created in the 1970s has made the community perhaps overly conservative and resistant to change. As Oregon's planning system approaches its 40th birthday, the need to rethink some of the fundamental principles has become increasingly apparent. In chapter 6, for example, we described the struggles of the new City of Damascus to address the legal requirements to accommodate growth from the Portland Metro core using a planning model that fits awkwardly with modern conditions on the ground. The state's planning institutions have demonstrated slowness to accept the need for change. City of Damascus community planning director Anita Yap observed to us, "The state planning program has 30 years of success containing growth and protecting farmland and forest land. But I think . . . there need to be new conversations based on the [conditions of the] economy, peak oil, climate change, and infrastructure costs on the state planning program. I'd love to see it. But I think people who have been in it [the planning system] since Senate Bill 100 are still there, and they're kind of the gatekeepers. They're afraid to open it up to that discussion."[11]

As the one-time firebrands and planning revolutionaries of Oregon's idealistic and vibrant decade of the Bottle Bill, the Beach Bill, and SB 100 became "the establishment," their ideas arguably became hardened and defensive rather than creative and idealistic. Oregon's governor at the time when Measure 37 passed, Ted Kulongoski, lamented that Oregon's planning system had lost sight of its goals.[12] Oregon's planning community would do well to take heed of critics who complain that SB 100 has become almost sacred, inviolable, and sclerotic.

Oregon's planning advocates would do well to think of Oregon's system as goals and visions rather than rules and institutions. As much as SB 100 has achieved, clinging too tightly to the particular mechanisms for planning that it created in the 1970s puts the broader goals at risk. Rigidly defending old and often unpopular rules and institutions rather than creatively seeking new ways to achieve the system's widely supported goals makes the system vulnerable. Henry Richmond, founder of 1000 Friends of Oregon, has warned that the Oregon public has no particular "fealty" to the institutions of state planning in their own right.[13] If these institutions work against things that Oregonians value—*including* property rights—Oregonians may sweep that system aside again in the future, with potentially disastrous results for the state's planning system. Once again, we stress that the decade beginning in 2000 with Measure 7 should be seen as a stark warning. As Portland Metro president David Bragdon explained to us,

In the 1970s, the [land use planning] system really was arranged to enable people to continue making a living [in agriculture]. It's a different situation today in terms of the economics. Now, in many cases the planning system is preventing people from cashing in, in a way they might like to cash in. That definitely changes the political dynamic. Over time, what was seen as a system that only created winners—in that it enabled people to do what they wanted to do [continue farming, or live a high quality of life]—changed from a system that enabled people to do what they wanted to do into a system that prevents them from doing things they want to do. Or prevents their descendents, in many cases, from doing what they want to do. That's a huge change. That's the major unspoken issue. The [planning] system was basically set up to keep things the way they were in the 1970s. So, to the extent that the gap between the conditions at that time and market conditions today grows, the political pressure grows with it.[14]

As described at the beginning of this chapter, by early 2010, with the passage of SB 1049 and the processing of the final Measure 37 claims (relabeled as Measure 49 claims) for waivers of land use regulations, some land use planning advocates hoped that the lull in the land use battles of the previous decade would extend into a lasting peace. It is far more likely that any relative political calm resulted not from legislative or administrative actions but from the near-collapse of new construction in the housing market following the collapse of the housing bubble and the subsequent Great Recession at the end of the first decade of the 2000s. And any student of economic history knows that in economics a kind of reverse gravitational law applies—what goes down far enough will, eventually, come back up. The heat may have been turned down, but the lid on the pressure cooker is still in place. When the heat turns back on, a potentially explosive situation is virtually inevitable.

In the meantime, with new construction still nearly dead at the beginning of the 2010s, land use planning advocates had some breathing space and time to regroup and think about the fundamental lessons of the first decade of the 2000s. In 2002, after the Oregon Supreme Court overturned Measure 7 on a technicality, Oregon's planning advocates had a similar window of opportunity, but they squandered it. By the time the planning advocates realized their mistake, it was too late—and Measure 37 (and its modified form as Measure 49) forever changed land use planning in Oregon. In 2010, there was no clear indication that Oregon's planning advocates had learned the lesson of 2002: windows close, and the time for proactive policies can be fleeting.

If, however, Oregon's planning advocates take heed of the lessons of the early and mid-2000s, a proactive new land use planning approach will almost certainly require steps to more effectively address questions of fairness, in both planning choices and processes. Whether real or perceived, concerns about fairness (think Dorothy English) unquestionably became the battering ram that opponents of Oregon's statewide planning system used to knock the first large holes in Oregon's SB 100 planning structure. The perception of unfairness is, in turn, tied to changing economic conditions: in the 1970s, as David Bragdon observed above, Oregon's planning system mostly made winners, and the costs of the system were relatively minor. As economic conditions changed—in particular, as opportunities to sell land at high prices for development increased and as some types of farming became less viable through forces such as global market competition— the opportunity costs of land use regulation increased as well.

But, in the view of many, these increased burdens were not distributed fairly. For example, in the 1990s and 2000s, as growth pressed up against UGBs in many Oregon cities, the differential in property values and options inside and outside the UGBs grew dramatically. If farmer Smith and farmer Jones happen to live across the road from each other on opposite sides of the UGB, the differential in opportunities and burdens associated with the UGB have grown proportionally with the dramatic increases in land values since the 1970s. If farmer Smith lived inside the UGB and became wealthy selling land for development, but farmer Jones can only sell at farm value prices *and* gets the burden of increased traffic and conflicts with new residents on the other side of the UGB, Jones might understandably feel the system is unfair. Moreover, if an urban dweller enjoys nearby rural landscapes (e.g., farmer Jones's land) but does not bear any cost of land use regulations to preserve this landscape, then questions of equity inevitably arise. At a statewide level this kind of uneven distribution of the costs and benefits of the system creates enormous pressure, especially when real estate markets heat up. As the stakes grow (land values, recreational and aesthetic values, etc.), the role of the planning system in distributing costs and benefits to different individuals and groups becomes more pronounced as well.

Yet, there were no mechanisms built into the original SB 100 land use planning structure to enable the state to address these issues. The following extended excerpt from our 2009 interview with Oregon DLCD director Richard Whitman illustrates both the limitations of the existing system and recent efforts to address equity issues:

> Almost the most important [cause for the political vulnerability in the land use system in the 2000s was] a lack of attention on the part of regulators to equity and fairness concerns. The focus of regulation at the state level has been, "How can we make this program be the most effective it can be in terms of protecting the things it's supposed to protect? Or accomplish the things it's supposed to accomplish?" Equity was not on the list. Compare that to the local land use level, where you have a political system with planning directors and planning commissions and city councils and boards of commission that provide a safety valve, frankly, to deal with some of the equity issues. This [observation] is very much from the nonlawyerly side: from the political side, those local systems are much better at addressing equity and fairness issues than the state-level system. . . . That's how we got to where we were in 2000 [when Measure 7 passed]. There were some very [politically potent] stories about unfairness. When your average citizen is told those stories about unfairness, they resonate. They have a lot of force behind them. I don't think the state had good answers to counter that. . . . The equity and fairness issues do need to be more consciously considered at the state level. That's not to say we let local politics dictate land use results, but I think at the state level we do need to care about whether there are individuals or groups of individuals who have really gotten an unfair burden as a result of the system. . . .
>
> [And] we [state regulators] do pay much more attention now as a result of the ballot measures [Measures 7, 37, and 49] to the effects of proposals on particular groups than we used to. Equity is now being put in place, as an effect of the "Big Look" process, as one of the four guiding principles for the land use system. I think that's a good thing. I think that's healthy and removes some political instability. . . . [Measure 49] is the continuation of a discussion about equity and about the impacts of regulation. I view it as a marker, a serious marker, that is

going to require the legislature, this agency [DLCD], and government generally to consider the burdens created by new regulation. . . . I think that makes it less susceptible to political attack.[15]

While it is unquestionably true that Oregon's land use laws and institutions have begun to respond to the need to integrate equity concerns into the planning process, it is far less clear that the broader political culture of planning in Oregon has changed. How Measure 49 compensation requirements will play out in practice, for example, may depend in part on whether the broader political culture of planning in Oregon changes as a result of the hard lessons of Measure 7 and Measure 37. Some recent events seem to indicate that Oregon's planning community has not accepted these lessons about the importance of equity to the stability of the planning system. As described in chapter 7, the designation of the Metolius River Basin Area of Critical State Concern was done in an old-fashioned, bare-knuckles style of politics that, in the eyes of the affected landowners and local government, displayed the very worst of heavy-handed exertion of state power. Whether accurate or not, the sincere perception in the affected community was that ideologues from Portland and Salem were willing to use any means necessary to achieve their desired ends—making the state's recent efforts to include equity concerns in the planning process (through innovative compromises, e.g., transferrable development rights) look like mere window dressing. The old culture of Oregon's land use wars still lives. Such eminent planning advocates as former 1000 Friends of Oregon attorney and Portland Metro councilor Robert Liberty have almost proudly described land use planning in Oregon as a "blood sport."[16]

Indeed, there is little clear indication from *either* side that the culture of Oregon's planning community or property rights community has moved away from a take-no-prisoners approach. Property rights advocates, for example, probably could have gotten a more palatable outcome from their perspective than Measure 49 had they been willing to offer serious compromises after their all-out victory with Measure 37. If the only outcomes acceptable to advocates of either side cannot include significant compromises, the prospects for a less turbulent future for Oregon's land use system might seem bleak.

Fortunately, at least one path seems to offer hope for achieving compromise and a more stable future for Oregon's planning system. This path can be found by looking to the historical roots of the Oregon planning system's original successes in the 1970s and finding ways to revitalize public engagement in the state's planning system. Meaningful engagement by ordinary citizens in Oregon's planning system is literally Goal 1 for good reasons. In the youthful days of Oregon's planning system, Tom McCall and others offered powerful visions for why ordinary Oregonians should *care* about effective land use planning. After that time, however, the system seemed to slip more toward Robert Michels, Eden Paul, and Cedar Paul's (1915) model of a so-called iron law of oligarchy: a system dominated by a handful of leaders on each side fighting for control of the system to serve relatively narrow interests, while the public becomes more disengaged and disenchanted. In a democracy, public support for such a system becomes volatile, if not inevitably unsustainable.

Yet, in our observation, some planning advocates have lost faith in the capacity of the public to meaningfully engage planning. Some planning leaders seem to believe that ordinary citizens are simply too volatile, too uninformed. Such an attitude ignores the fact that, with coordination from the first DLCD staff, ordinary citizens literally wrote the state's planning goals.[17] Early leaders of the Oregon planning system understood the critical importance of reaching out and building a political constituency for planning. If current and future generations of Oregon planning leaders want the public to trust them, they might need to remember that any enduring trust is always a two-way street. If the private consultants who dominate the implementation of the planning system's public engagement efforts today cannot evoke a sense of genuinely listening to and caring about public opinion, they should be replaced.

If some in Oregon's planning community consider this merely romantic and unrealistic wishful thinking, they should note that evidence from modern social science shows that truly effective public participation in land use planning *makes* informed, engaged, and thoughtful citizens who are far more likely to support sound planning. A plethora of modern research from other regions of the United States and overseas strongly indicates that the *practice* of public engagement creates a sense of ownership and commitment to making planning and environmental policies that are effective, fair, and practical (Agrawal 2005). This is actually old—if somewhat lost—knowledge in Oregon. As Arnold Cogan, the first director of DLCD, recalls, "In order to get these [statewide planning] goals written, instead of doing the usual—appointing a task force, or several task forces, and giving them a few months and having them report back . . . that was rejected. I really wanted us to go out to the communities throughout the state, from the smallest to the biggest [communities]. We knew it was important *to develop a constituency* for the land use program, and to build the kind of energy that was going to be required to implement these goals."[18]

For example, as described in chapter 8, a sense of personal "ownership" of the planning process inspired many dyed-in-the-wool conservatives (along with some of their more liberal neighbors) in southern Oregon's Bear Creek Valley to commit to more than 10 years of intensive efforts to creating a comprehensive regional plan for growth that satisfies state rules as well as the interests of most, if not all, local participants. It is worth noting that Bear Creek Valley is a region where far-right political commentators dominate the radio airwaves and "U.S. out of the U.N." signs adorn the highways. Whatever one might think of its land use plan, advocates and critics of the Greater Bear Creek Valley Regional Problem Solving planning process agree that it has greatly enhanced community cohesion and the ability of local governments to work together. There is even agreement that communities collaborating is a *good* thing! Some former adversaries and skeptics of collaborative planning are now among the strongest supporters of the Bear Creek Valley collaborative process. This is no trivial matter considering that, to fellow conservatives from other parts of the United States, such efforts might seem socialist.

Perhaps above all, Oregon's planning community needs, rather urgently in our view, to learn once again to be positive and creative rather than defensive and conservative in its vision for Oregon planning. As Ellen Bassett (2009) has observed,

> Those advocating for the land use planning system and arguing for the legitimacy of public interests in private land were on the defensive— they were not casting the terms of the debate. Planners need to be proactive—not reactive—here. We need to effectively communicate what

it is we do, why we do it, and why it is valuable. Drawing from Lakoff (2004), we need to be able to speak to multiple audiences with various moral perspectives and conceptual frames. Most specifically, we need to move from the fact-filled technocratic language with which planners are most comfortable and acknowledge that planning as an enterprise is an expression of community values and a means for achieving those values.

Oregon's planning community should take courage from the fact that they have "framed" the debate in the past, and there is no reason they cannot do so again. In the 1960s and 1970s, Oregon's planning community was all about protecting livelihoods (e.g., farmers) and quality of life (e.g., rural landscapes), and generally about keeping Oregon special. To an extent Oregon's planning politics may have become a victim of its own success: with the passage of SB 100, the creation of DLCD, and the establishment of the state's planning goals, the task at hand was to work on the technical side, making the established institutions achieve their goals. The dreams and visions that made Oregon's planning system politically successful in the 1970s had won—but then took a back seat to the bureaucracy they had helped to create. By the time Measure 7 and Measure 37 became law, the power of Oregon's planning vision had clearly dissipated. With Measure 49, however, advocates successfully invoked the vision of quality of life once again. But the lesson is obvious: complacency and allowing others to capture the public's imagination can be extremely hazardous. Thus, in addition to addressing the underlying economic and political changes that we have discussed, keeping the vision and public engagement in Oregon's planning fresh, vibrant, and more politically stable is essential.

The Country *Is* the City

Making Oregon's planning vision more equitable and politically stable will, in turn, require greater recognition of the political interdependency of rural and urban landscapes under Oregon's comprehensive statewide planning law. It is common to hear Oregonians speak of the "urban-rural divide," and the "bright line" between country and city. Physically, this divide is very real. However, as noted in chapter 6, while Oregon's farms and cities may be geographically separated, they are functionally inter-dependent: cities are compact because rural areas have been protected, and rural land is intact because cities have contained sprawl. We would add that under Oregon's unique statewide planning law, farms and cities are also profoundly *politically* interdependent—with important implications that Oregon's planning community may not fully grasp.

Oregon's planners would do well to consider Raymond Williams's classic book *The Country and the City* (they might also note the book's fitting year of publication—1973). In it, Williams notes that from the sixteenth century and, even more so, from the eighteenth century, English landlords "learned new ways of looking at landscape" and sought to create such landscapes "as prospects from their own houses" (1973: 122). The landscape ideal to which these English landlords aspired can be traced to images of a Persian walled garden, described in Milton's *Paradise Lost* (1669) as "a happy rural seat of various view" (cited in Williams 1973: 123). However, this new relationship between landlord and landscape did not emerge on a geographically or socially blank slate—it emerged in rural places (*not* wilderness) occupied by people. Thus, the ideal of a rural landscape as a place of leisure was always a political ideal, in that, according to Williams (1973: 124–125), it created the necessity of concealing or erasing the already-existing rural landscape shaped by the work of peasants:

> In the one case the land is being organized for production, where ten-ants and laborers will work, while in the other case it is being orga-nized for consumption—the view, the ordered proprietary repose, the prospect. . . . a rural landscape emptied of rural labor and laborers; a sylvan and watery prospect, with a hundred analogies in neo-pastoral painting and poetry, from which the facts of production had been ban-ished: the road and approaches artfully concealed by trees, so that the very fact of communication could be visually suppressed; inconvenient barns and mills cleared out of sight.

In other words, in a world with few (if any) "empty" places to be oc-cupied, the physical creation or preservation of particular landscapes is an inherently political act. As demonstrated in chapter 7, in many rural places the politics consist of the imposition of urban ideals on existing rural landscapes, cultures, and economies. In Oregon, as in eighteenth-century England, this rural landscape ideal has tended to center on scenic qualities that emanate largely from the city and are advocated mainly by urban dwellers, or by "exurbanites" who move from the city bringing their ideas of how the landscape should look (ideas described as "environmental imaginaries" by Peet and Watts 1996; see also Walker and Fortmann 2003; Hurley and Walker 2004).

The consequences can appear unjust in the eyes of some rural people if mainly urban-based visions of rural places shape policies that largely, if not primarily, benefit urban (or exurban) people. For example, in 2008 one Oregon woman from rural Columbia County complained,

> Land-use laws are anti-family because if you own 70 acres and you got four kids and you want to give each one of them a couple acres to have your family live all together, so when the kids get off the school bus they can all stay at grandma's house till mom and dad get home from work, you can't do that in Oregon. And that's not right. . . . I'm tired of the urban recreationalist wanting to lock up what they see on their drive out to the beach or whatever. You know, the whole state isn't your park. Don't dictate to rural property owners what they can do with their land.[19]

What is almost unique about Oregon's statewide land use planning system is that it has formalized and institutionalized state-level visioning of the *entire* state—rural and urban areas—all together. In a democracy with a population that lives primarily in cities (including most government leaders), it seems almost inevitable that in this statewide planning process urban-based values will tend to "dictate" to rural people. It could be argued that by formalizing and institutionalizing the process of visioning rural and urban areas, Oregon's planning institutions systematically submerge, or makes less visible, the exertion of the visions and values of some—mostly, urban dwellers—over others. Buried within the minutia and technical language of planning is a very political act of choosing whose visions and whose values will decide how landscapes "should" look across the state. Or, as we describe in the case of the designation of the

Metolius River Basin Area of Critical State Concern (chapter 7), central-ized state-level power can legitimate the dismissal of local resistance.

In the time and social context described by Williams, the raw exertion of power by urban-based landlords over the rural peasant or proletariat classes to create what Williams describes as "pleasing rural prospects" was plain to see. If, as we argue, Oregon's planning system has become a conduit for a similar exertion of largely urban power over rural land-scapes and people, the politics of this form of control becomes legitimated by ideas of progressive, foresighted, and technical processes of institu-tionalized land use regulation.

To be clear, from the standpoint of many urbanites—*as well as* some rural dwellers, especially multigenerational farmers—in Oregon, the de-sire to limit sprawl is entirely understandable—and, in our view, laudable. Even the most astute scholars of socially just urban and rural land use pol-icy strongly advocate policies to limit sprawl (see, e.g., Walker 2007). We nevertheless suggest that too often it is utterly forgotten that containing sprawl has *costs*, and that these costs are not borne equally between city and country. As in Williams's eighteenth-century England, rural places become, to an extent, "parks" for urban people. In a sense, the country *is* the city—its vision, its values, its ideals. Yet it is rural people who arguably pay the largest portion of the cost for achieving aesthetic, recreational, or other values that they do not themselves necessarily share.

At the same time, ironically, the success of Oregon's planning system in encouraging compact development almost certainly has made rural spaces even more attractive—and valuable—to certain kinds of pro-spective property buyers who are willing to pay for "elbow room" and other rural qualities (and, as we show for the Metolius Basin and the City of Damascus, may vigorously defend these "rural" qualities). To be sure, these aesthetic qualities and potentially high property values might not have been possible without a planning system that protects rural qualities. But, politically, such arguments are likely to gain little traction. Rural owners will often see only the economic opportunity denied. And, as the economy heats up again in the future, new economic opportunities for development in rural areas will make this apparently unequal distribution of the costs and benefits of urban and rural land policy more acute, positioning the state land use system for yet more political instability.

If the conceptual paradigm for land use planning in the new millennium is "sustainability," we suggest that Oregon's planning community should consider whether Oregon's planning system needs to be not only environmentally, economically, and aesthetically sound, but also more politically stable—politically "sustainable." For the planning system's own sake, if for no other reason, greater attentiveness to such political instabilities may be not only fair but necessary. As Henry Richmond, founder of 1000 Friends of Oregon, told us, the system is eminently losable.

Planning Paradise

In our research for this book, we drove a lot of miles. We observed Oregon intensively and extensively. Former Governor Tom McCall once called Oregon "a state of excitement." Now we know something about what he meant. While driving through the Columbia Gorge, it is hard for us to not become excited by the bumper crop of homegrown power-generating windmills that seem to pop up in greater numbers each year like spring flowers. It is hard to not get excited seeing sea lions waiting at the gates of Bonneville Dam for unlucky salmon. It is hard not to get excited watching the rebounding population of bald eagles diving out of the sky for fish in the chilled waters of the upper Willamette River, merely feet from our children's playground. It is hard not to get excited when the wind of the Oregon Coast pulls open patches of sky, letting in rays of sun that glisten on fog so thick you can almost hold it in your hand. We are aware of no other state where rest stops along major highways adjoin thundering, cascading waterfalls and hiking trails along salmon streams (Figure 16).

It is also hard not to get excited when we hear the passionate voices of Oregonians of all walks of life so dedicated to the places they live, working to make these places even better. In the new City of Damascus, where there is no money for infrastructure, local planners explore ecologically based alternatives to store water and protect against flooding. In Central Oregon, the idea of sustainable destination resorts, if not yet achieved, sets a lofty goal. In southern Oregon, communities that once would barely talk to each other discover that, when done right (including years

Figure 16 University of Oregon students at a rest stop on Oregon's Highway 126 (P. Walker 2008)

of effort), talking to one's neighbors can produce win-win outcomes. As social science researchers, we could not avoid becoming excited watching literally thousands of ordinary citizens turning out in every corner of the state for land use planning meetings that might have induced the uninitiated into a catatonic state, but kept Oregonians literally on the edges of their seats. Passions often run high, but we see this as a measure of how much Oregon's citizens care about the special place in which they live. Even those who feel disenfranchised from the planning system often do so precisely because they feel so strongly about their special places.

Supporters and opponents of Oregon's planning deserve to be passionate. Oregonians did indeed find a special place. But that which is found can be lost. No other state has protected public access to its stunning beaches as Oregon has. No other state has been more innovative in cleaning up litter and protecting its family farms and forests. Few other states have a metropolitan center as vibrant, creative, and enchantingly off-beat as Portland. But these and other exceptional qualities of Oregon are no accident. As we state at the beginning of this book, if Oregon is a kind of paradise, it is very much a *planned* paradise. Oregon remains special today to no small degree because it was clear to a handful of visionaries in the 1970s that the specialness of the place could be lost—and they came up with a bold plan to save it.

But times have changed. When Hector Macpherson and Tom McCall (and others) created SB 100, they created one of the most innovative and effective planning systems in the country. Today, however, this system appears to us more vulnerable than most of its proponents seem to believe. The land use conflicts of the first decade of the 2000s showed that tensions are high, and we find no indication that the underlying factors that contributed to these tensions, which we have outlined in this chapter, will go away without innovative *new* ways of thinking about what has worked, and what needs to be changed. In this book we deliberately sought to understand the weaknesses of a system we admire. We conclude that Oregon's planning system has stuck too closely to the old and familiar. The vulnerability of the system that was revealed in 2000 and 2004 remains. The system can and probably will be lost if bolder reforms are not made.

We offer this critique as admirers and beneficiaries of the boldness of previous generations who did remarkable things to help make Oregon the special place it is. We have done so because we wish Oregon's special qualities to endure for our own children. History tells us that in the past Oregon dared to do what no one else had done—what few believed even *could* be done. It succeeded. And it can again. Now is no time to lose our creativity and our boldness.

With a hard eye to the realities around us, a willingness to think and dream big, and the boldness to make it happen, we will keep alive the ideal of Oregon as a landscape of promise (Robbins 1997). It is indeed a kind of paradise, if we can keep it.

Notes

Chapter 1: Introduction

1. See *New York Times*, May 19, 2008, p. A15.

2. The Oregon Country was a larger area than the present-day State of Oregon, encompassing all of what is today Oregon, Washington, Idaho, and parts of British Columbia, Montana, and Wyoming.

3. Oregon Blue Book, "Oregon History: World War II." Online: http://bluebook .state.or.us/cultural/history/history26.htm. Last accessed March 27, 2009.

4. U.S. Bureau of the Census, "1990 Census of Population and Housing: Population and Housing Unit Counts: Oregon." CPH-2-39. U.S. Department of Commerce, 1992. Online: http://www.census.gov/prod/cen1990/cph2/cph-2-39.pdf. Last accessed November 4, 2010.

5. George C. Hough, Jr., "Oregon's Changing Demographics 2000," Population Research Center, College of Urban and Public Affairs, Portland State University, July 2000.

6. Tom McCall, Governor's Legislative Address, Oregon State Archives, 1973.

7. McCall, Legislative Address.

8. Quoted by William Robbins in his 2006 essay "The place we call home: A history of land use planning in Oregon." *Oregon Humanities*, Spring/Summer 2006. Online: http://www.oregonhum.org/place-we-call-home.php. Last accessed March 13, 2009.

9. Another approximately 600–700 claims were filed with county and city governments, according to widely circulated media accounts, for a total of more than 7,500 claims—though no precise total is available.

10. Oregon Department of Land Conservation and Development, "Measure 37 summary of claims." Online: http://www.oregon.gov/LCD/MEASURE37/summaries _of_claims.shtml. Last accessed November 1, 2009.

11. Oregon State University, Institute for Natural Resources, "The Oregon Land Use Program: An Assessment of Selected Goals." Oregon Department of Land Conservation and Development, August 2008.

12. In late 2010 several online news sources reported that Gosnell et al. (2010) had shown that the Oregon land use system was "not working as planned"—an interpretation Gosnell vehemently disputed. Hannah Gosnell, personal communication, September 21, 2010.

13. Measure 37 neighbor letters received by the Department of Land Conservation and Development, reviewed by P. Walker, May 2008.

14. Reader comment to Jonathan Maus, "Obama in Portland: Props to our 'bicycle lanes' and bikes as far as the eye can see." May 19, 2008. Online: http://bikeportland .org/2008/05/19/obamas-bicycle-lanes-remark-and-the-rising-profile-of-bicycles-in -american-politics/. Last accessed April 3, 2009.

Chapter 2: Planning for Growth

1. John Echeverria, Professor of Law, Vermont Law School, e-mail to P. Walker, December 16, 2009.

2. Mike Burton, Portland Metro executive officer, as quoted in Mitchell (2001).

3. This project benefits from earlier analyses, such as the extended discussion of Oregon's planning system at the twentieth anniversary of its inception (see Abbott, Howe, and Adler 1994), and specifically builds on key observations about land use politics within that work by Gerrit Knaap (1994). Our analysis differs in two key ways from Knaap's discussion of land use politics in Oregon. First, Knaap focuses primarily on diagnosing and characterizing the diverse actors (e.g., citizens, legislature, state interest groups, agencies, local interest groups, local governments, landowners) within the planning process from a functionalist perspective. Thus, he focuses on which actors are involved at different states of the process: adoptions, policy formulation, acknowledgment, planning, and implementation. Viewed from this perspective, the system is largely divorced from the political economic changes that produce particular types of politics and political engagement at multiple scales, ranging from the local to the national. Support for, or opposition to, the system as well as distinct issues here are largely taken as part of a static landscape of interest groups. Second, our analysis covers the more than 15-year period of land use decision making, including major planning and citizen initiatives, that has characterized the Oregon system in its third and fourth decade. Thus, we attempt to both expand discussion of "local networks" that seek to influence planning and address the efforts of the property rights movement, helping to demonstrate the ways that new links are forming among the disparate actors identified by Knaap.

4. For more extensive discussions of the emergence of state land use controls, see the works of Bosselman and Callies (1972), Popper (1981), and Mason (2008).

5. 1000 Friends of Oregon, *The Battle to Keep Oregon Lovable and Livable* (audio recording), 1998.

6. For a deeper history of land use controls and their evolution in Oregon specifically, see Knaap and Nelson (1992).

7. North Carolina Division of Coastal Management, "CAMA rules and policies: The Coastal Area Management Act." 2009. Online: http://dcm2.enr.state.nc.us/rules/ cama.htm. Last accessed September 14, 2010.

8. Washington State Legislature, "Revised Code of Washington (RCW) 36.70A. 020. Planning Goals." 2002. Online: http://apps.leg.wa.gov/RCW/default.aspx?cite=36 .70A.020. Last accessed December 28, 2009.

9. Washington State Legislature, RCW 36.70A.020.

10. For a fuller discussion of these regional programs, see Mason (2008).

11. State of Colorado, "2009 real estate manual." Online: http://www.dora.state .co.us/real-estate/manual/manual.htm. Last accessed December 29, 2009; M. Apel, "Arizona's changing rural landscapes: Fundamentals of land use planning." Arizona Cooperative Extension, 2008. Online: http://ag.arizona.edu/rurallandscape/node/40. Last accessed December 30, 2009.

12. Colorado Revised Statutes, "Title 29, Local government." 2009. Online: http://www.michie.com/colorado/lpext.dll?f=templates&fn=main-h.htm&cp=. Last accessed December 28, 2009.

13. Montana Environmental Information Center, "Land use policy." 2009. Online: http://www.meic.org/montanas_land/land_use. Last accessed December 29, 2009.

14. For a fuller description, see Knaap and Nelson (1992) and Abbott, Howe, and Adler (1994).

15. OAR 660-015-0000(1) identifies the corresponding chapter within the Oregon Administrative Rules that spell out a specific planning goal.

16. Oregon Department of Land Conservation and Development (DLCD), "Oregon's Statewide Planning Goals and Guidelines, Goal 1: Citizen Involvement." 2009. Online: http://www.lcd.state.or.us/LCD/docs/goals/goal1.pdf. Last accessed December 28, 2009.

17. DLCD, Goal 1, p. 1.

18. DLCD, "Oregon's Statewide Planning Goals and Guidelines, Goal 2: Land Use Planning," p. 1. Online: http://www.lcd.state.or.us/LCD/docs/goals/goal2.pdf. Last accessed December 28, 2009.

19. DLCD, Goal 2, p. 2.

20. DLCD, Goal 2, p. 2.

21. DLCD, "Oregon's Statewide Planning Goals and Guidelines, Goal 3: Agricultural Lands," p. 1. Online: http://www.lcd.state.or.us/LCD/docs/goals/goal3.pdf. Last accessed December 28, 2009.

22. DLCD, "Oregon's Statewide Planning Goals and Guidelines, Goal 4: Forest Lands," p. 1. Online: http://www.lcd.state.or.us/LCD/docs/goals/goal4.pdf. Last accessed December 28, 2009.

23. DLCD, "Oregon's Statewide Planning Goals and Guidelines, Goal 5: Natural Resources, Scenic and Historic Areas, and Open Spaces." Online: http://www.lcd .state.or.us/LCD/docs/goals/goal5.pdf. Last accessed December 28, 2009.

24. DLCD, "Oregon's Statewide Planning Goals and Guidelines, Goal 6: Air, Water and Land Resources Quality." Online: http://www.lcd.state.or.us/LCD/docs/ goals/goal6.pdf. Last accessed December 28, 2009.

25. DLCD, "Oregon's Statewide Planning Goals and Guidelines, Goal 7: Areas Subject to Natural Hazards." Online: http://www.lcd.state.or.us/LCD/docs/goals/goal7.pdf. Last accessed December 28, 2009.

26. DLCD, Goal 5, p. 1.

27. DLCD, "Oregon's Statewide Planning Goals and Guidelines, Goal 8: Recreational Needs." Online: http://www.lcd.state.or.us/LCD/docs/goals/goal8.pdf. Last accessed December 28, 2009.

28. DLCD, Goal 8.

29. DLCD, "Oregon's Statewide Planning Goals and Guidelines, Goal 10: Housing." Online: http://www.oregon.gov/LCD/docs/goals/goal10.pdf. Last accessed December 28, 2009.

30. DLCD, "Oregon's Statewide Planning Goals and Guidelines, Goal 11: Public Facilities and Services," p. 1. Online: http://www.lcd.state.or.us/LCD/docs/goals/goal11.pdf. Last accessed December 28, 2009.

31. DLCD, "Oregon's Statewide Planning Goals and Guidelines, Goal 14: Urbanization," p. 1. Online: http://www.lcd.state.or.us/LCD/docs/goals/goal14.pdf. Last accessed December 28, 2009.

32. DLCD, Goal 14, p. 1.

33. DLCD, Goal 14, p. 1.

34. Oregon Revised Statutes, "195.137. Urban and Rural Reserves." 2009. Online: http://www.leg.state.or.us/ors/195.html. Last accessed December 28, 2009.

35. Oregon State Legislature, House Bill 3482, 68th Oregon Legislative Assembly—1996 Special Session. 1996. Online: http://www.leg.state.or.us/96ss/measures/hb3482.int.html. Last accessed December 28, 2009.

36. DLCD, Land Conservation and Development Commission." 2009. Online: http://www.lcd.state.or.us/LCD/lcdc.shtml. Last accessed December 28, 2009.

37. DLCD, Agency Summary. 2009. Online: http://www.lcd.state.or.us/LCD/docs/budget/arb_09-11/AR_09_11_3_Agency_Summary.pdf. Last accessed December 28, 2009.

38. Oregon State Archives, "Oregon Administrative Rules 660-025-0010-0250. Land Conservation and Development Department, Division 25, Periodic review." 2009. Online: http://arcweb.sos.state.or.us/rules/OARS_600/OAR_660/660_025.html. Last accessed December 28, 2009.

39. Land Use Board of Appeals, Home page. 2009. Online: http://www.oregon.gov/LUBA/index.shtml. Last accessed December 28, 2009.

40. Land Use Board of Appeals, Home page.

41. State Archives, "Oregon Administrative Rules: Land Conservation and Development Department." 2009. Online: http://www.oregonmetro.gov/index.cfm/go/by.web/id=24270. Last accessed December 28, 2009.

42. The U.S. Census Bureau distinguishes between metropolitan areas, which "contain at least one urbanized area of 50,000 or more" people, and micropolitan areas, which "contain at least one urban cluster of 10,000 and less than 50,000" people.

Chapter 3: A Star Is Born

1. Hector Macpherson Jr., interview by Peter Walker, June 9, 2009.
2. Excerpts from Macpherson (2010).
3. William Robbins, interview by Peter Walker, May 14, 2009.
4. While some key Democrats did play key roles, the movement toward statewide land use planning was clearly a Republican-led effort at the time.
5. Henry Richmond, interview by Peter Walker, March 13, 2009.
6. Macpherson interview.
7. Quoted by Russ Beaton, Willamette University economist and former adviser to Senator Hector Macpherson, at the SB 100 Roundtable: Oregon's Pioneering Land Use Law, Salem, Oregon, September 9, 2006, video recording by the Oregon State Capitol Foundation, 2007.
8. Macpherson interview.
9. Oregon Legislative Assembly—, 1973 Regular Session, Senate Bill 101.
10. Mike Thorne, interview by Peter Walker, May 8, 2009.
11. Macpherson interview.
12. Robbins interview.
13. Macpherson interview.
14. 1000 Friends of Oregon, *The Battle to Keep Oregon Lovable and Livable* (audio recording), 1998.
15. John Kitzhaber, Joseph [Ted] Hallock's obituary, *Portland Oregonian*, March 11, 2007.
16. Kitzhaber, Hallock's obituary.
17. Fred VanNatta, interview by Peter Walker, August 15, 2009.
18. Nancie Fadeley, interview by Peter Walker, May 22, 2009.
19. 1000 Friends of Oregon, *The Battle to Keep Oregon Lovable and Livable.*
20. Fadeley interview.
21. Fadeley interview.
22. Fadeley interview.
23. Robbins interview.
24. Nadine Jelsing, producer, *Oregon experience: The Beach Bill* (video). Oregon Public Broadcasting, 2007.
25. Walt Daggett, a key aide to Senator Ted Hallock (cosponsor of SB 100), suggests that Hallock was enthusiastic about SB 100 largely because he was enthusiastic about *everything* he did. Although Hallock represented the interests of an environmentally minded Portland constituency, Hallock was not himself a particularly ideological environmentalist. Interview by Peter Walker, August 6, 2009.
26. Thorne interview.
27. Robbins interview.
28. Daggett interview.

29. Fifty-Seventh Legislative Assembly of the State of Oregon, *Journal and Calendar of the Senate and House*, 1973, p. J-101.

30. Fifty-Seventh Legislative Assembly.

31. The origins of the term "Californication" are unclear. Curiously, the term became popular again in 2007 when the Showtime network began a television series by that name. The rock band Red Hot Chili Peppers sued Showtime, claiming they had created the term, and it was the title of a successful album by the group. In fact, the term unambiguously long predates its use by either litigants: abundant documentation and eye witness accounts indicate that at least as early as 1973 it was commonly used in Oregon and appeared on many bumper stickers.

32. Rebecca Clarren, "Planning's poster child grows up." *High Country News*, November 25, 2002.

33. Loren Dodge, Associated Press, "Oregon's anti-California sentiment still strong." *Seattle Post-Intelligencer*, April 5, 1999.

34. Linda England, "Oregon suffers from an inferiority complex." *Los Angeles Times*, April 14, 1979, p. C4.

35. Then-governor of Oregon Oswald West passed a law declaring the entire Oregon coast a "public highway," which gave the state the power to block private development. Legal loopholes in West's law were discovered and exploited by some coastal landowners in 1966, leading to an epic battle for the Oregon Beach Bill in 1967.

36. Art Seidenbaum, "Oregon—land of enough." *Los Angeles Times*, January 18, 1978, pp. F1, F7.

37. Macpherson interview.

38. As quoted in Clarren, "Planning's poster child grows up."

39. Clarren, "Planning's poster child grows up."

40. Steven Smith, "Land-use watchdogs enter their fourth year." *Eugene (OR) Register-Guard, March 5, 1978*, pp. C1, C3.

41. Henry Richmond, on 1000 Friends of Oregon, *The Battle to Keep Oregon Lovable and Livable* (audio recording), 1998.

42. In 2005, 1000 Friends of Washington changed its name to Futurewise.

43. Steve Law, "Land-use guru finds developers adding to Oregon's 1000 Friends." *Portland Business Journal*, January 6, 1992, p. 12.

44. Art Seidenbaum, "Oregon—land of enough." *Los Angeles Times*, January 18, 1978, p. F1.

45. Seidenbaum, "Oregon—land of enough."

46. Law, "Land-use guru."

47. Law, "Land-use guru."

48. Law, "Land-use guru."

49. Richmond interview.

50. Art Seidenbaum, "Master plan for a state." *Los Angeles Times*, January 16, 1978, pp. E1, E5.

51. U.S. Department of Agriculture, Census of Agriculture, County Data, 1950, 1974, as cited in Richmond and Houchen (2007: 3).

52. U.S. Department of Agriculture, Census of Agriculture, 1974, 2007.

53. Ward Armstrong, interview by Peter Walker, August 3, 2009. Armstrong also noted that there were important dissenting voices within the industry, most notably the conservative timber giant Georgia-Pacific Corporation.

54. Richmond interview.

55. Ray Wilkeson, Oregon Forest Industries Council, interview by Peter Walker, June 4, 2009.

56. Associated Press, "Hewlett Packard official urges defeat of Measure 6." *Eugene (OR) Register-Guard*, October 12, 1982.

57. VanNatta interview.

58. VanNatta interview.

59. Richmond interview.

60. VanNatta interview.

Chapter 4: Falling Star

1. English said she disliked the term "poster girl," but it was used explicitly by property rights advocates.

2. Oregon Governor Theodore Kulongoski, letter to House Speaker Karen Minnis, August 18, 2003. Online: http://ecfd.oregon.gov/Gov/pdf/letters/letter_081803.pdf. Last accessed October 31, 2010.

3. Laura Oppenheimer, "Lines drawn on land use put victory within reach." *Portland Oregonian*, November 7, 2004, p. A01.

4. Portland-based talk show host Lars Larson, on NW Republican Blogspot. Online: http://nwrepublican.blogspot.com/2006/12/paul-jacob-on-dorothy-english .html. Last accessed May 24, 2009.

5. Eric Mortenson, "Court orders Multnomah County to pay $1.15 million to Dorothy English estate." *Portland Oregonian*, April 16, 2009. Online: http://www .oregonlive.com/environment/index.ssf/2009/04/court_reverses_multnomah_count .html. Last accessed May 24, 2009.

6. Reader comments to "Dorothy English, face of Measure 37 campaign, dies." *Portland Tribune*, April 11, 2008. Online: http://www.portlandtribune.com/news/ story.php?story_id=120793534141965700. Last accessed September 6, 2009.

7. Oregon Secretary of State, Oregon State Archives. Online: http://arcweb.sos .state.or.us/. Last accessed October 31, 2010.

8. The most ambitious effort to address property rights in the 1990s was the 1995 "ecotake" bill (SB 600), which would have required state compensation for future environmental regulations that reduced property value. The bill passed both chambers of the state legislature, but then-governor John Kitzhaber vetoed the bill in a very

public ceremony in the Portland Rose Garden that property rights activists remember even today with anger.

9. For an excellent history of Measure 7, see Abbott, Alder, and Howe (2003).

10. Gregory Nokes, "Study sees billions in boundary costs if measure passes." *Portland Oregonian*, October 17, 2000, p. A01.

11. *Portland Oregonian*, October 22, 2000, p. G05.

12. Gregory Nokes, "Judge blocks property measure." *Portland Oregonian*, December 7, 2000, p. A01.

13. Gregory Nokes, "Property measure battles lie ahead." *Portland Oregonian*, November 11, 2000, p. C01.

14. Editorial, *Portland Oregonian*, November, 26, 2000, p. E04.

15. As cited in Dave Hogan, "Court rejects property rights measure." *Portland Oregonian*, October 5, 2002, p. E01.

16. Population Research Center, "*2009 Oregon Population Report*," p. 9. Portland State University, 2010. Online: http://www.pdx.edu/sites/www.pdx.edu.prc/files/media_assets/PopRpt09b.pdf. Last accessed October 31, 2010.

17. In 1968, McCall's mother, Dorothy, published a book about their days on their Central Oregon ranch titled *Ranch under the Rimrock* (Hillsboro, OR: Binford and Mort).

18. Rachael Scarborough King, "Prineville pair files second M37 claim." *Bend (OR) Bulletin*, November 29, 2006. Online: http://www.bendbulletin.com/apps/pbcs.dll/article?AID=/20061129/NEWS01/611290332. Last accessed October 31, 2010.

19. Erin Golden, "Prineville will pay $180,000 M37 claim." *Bend Bulletin*, September 12, 2007.

20. Laura Oppenheimer, "Land use laws on turf that is uncharted." *Portland Oregonian*, November 2004, p. A01.

21. John Taylor, "Make 37's beneficiaries pay." *Portland Oregonian*, November 7, 2004, p. F05

22. ORS 197.352.

23. Oregon Department of Land Conservation and Development, "Measure 37 summary of claims." Online: http://www.oregon.gov/LCD/MEASURE37/summaries _of_claims.shtml. Last accessed November 1, 2009.

24. Laura Oppenheimer, "Governor: Set aside big claims." *Portland Oregonian*, February, 6, 2007, p. B01.

25. 1000 Friends of Oregon, *And fairness for none: The impacts of Measure 37 on Oregonians and Oregon's landscape* (video). Online: http://www.youtube.com/watch?v=EGVaVS6U91A. Last accessed October 21, 2010.

26. Laura Oppenheimer, "Yamhill County gingerly treads new ground." *Portland Oregonian*, February, 1, 2005, p. A01.

27. Pseudonym.

28. Judge James's decision spurred an angry backlash. A campaign to recall Judge

James was initiated, although some angry citizens pronounced that they would rather shoot her than recall her. Julie Sullivan, "Firestorm over Measure 37 clouds judge's long-held dream," *Portland Oregonian*, December, 4, 2005, p. B01.

29. Laura Oppenheimer and James Mayer, "Poll: Balance rights, land use." *Portland Oregonian*, April 21, 2005, p. C01.

30. Rick Bella, "Measure 37 a bait and switch." *Portland Oregonian*, April 25, 2007, p. B01.

31. "California North: Influx worries Oregonians" (letters to the editor). *Portland Oregonian*, March 6, 2006, p. B05.

32. Greg Macpherson, interview by Peter Walker, June 12, 2009.

33. See Oregon Department of Agriculture, Natural Resources Division, "Land Use—Measure 37." Online: http://www.oregon.gov/ODA/NRD/m37.shtml. Last accessed September 22, 2010.

34. Lane Shetterly, interview by Peter Walker, September 29, 2009.

35. Laura Oppenheimer, "Measure 37 stuck in circle of chambers." *Portland Oregonian*, June, 21, 2005, p. B04.

36. Macpherson interview.

37. Floyd Prozanski, interview by Peter Walker, June 11, 2009.

38. Laura Oppenheimer, "Land-use hearing is a hot ticket." *Portland Oregonian*, January 11, 2006, p. A01.

39. Laura Oppenheimer, "Re-write of land use law heads to voters." *Portland Oregonian*, April 27, 2007, p. B01.

40. Dave Hunnicutt, interview by Peter Walker, May 15, 2009.

41. Macpherson interview.

42. 1000 Friends of Oregon founder Henry Richmond, as quoted in Eric Mortenson, "Report lauds new land use idea." *Portland Oregonian*, September 25, 2007, p. B01.

43. Eric Mortenson, "Trying to beat the system?" *Portland Oregonian*, May 28, 2008, p. A01.

44. Study by Portland Metro attorney Richard Benner and researcher Carol Hall, as cited in Eric Mortenson, "Measure 49 study finds big cutback." *Portland Oregonian*, October 17, 2007, p. A01.

45. Mortenson, "Measure 49."

46. Bob Emmons and Nena Lovinger, Lane County Landwatch, interview by Peter Walker, December 30, 2008.

47. Hunnicutt interview.

48. Richard Benner, interview by Peter Walker, September 4, 2009.

49. Bob Stacey, interview by Peter Walker, June 2, 2009.

50. Richard Whitman, interview by Peter Walker, October 5, 2009.

51. Dave Hunnicutt, Editorial, *Portland Oregonian*, November 13, 2007, p. D09.

52. Stacey interview.

Chapter 5: "What Were People Thinking?"

1. As quoted in Andy Parker, "Wake-up call on land use went unheeded." *Portland Oregonian*, November 15, 2004, p. Co1.

2. Bob Stacey, interview by Peter Walker, June 2, 2009.

3. Dave Hogan, "Land use battles warming up." *Portland Oregonian*, November 12, 2002, p. Co1.

4. Dave Hunnicutt, interview by Peter Walker, May 15, 2009.

5. Hunnicutt interview.

6. Henry Richmond, interview by Peter Walker, March 13, 2009.

7. Reflecting these internal divisions, the Oregon Farm Bureau remained neutral on Measure 37 in 2004, but its members voted to support Measure 49 in 2007.

8. Fred VanNatta, interview by Peter Walker, August 15, 2009.

9. Richmond interview.

10. In particular, Stimson Lumber of Portland and Seneca Jones Timber of Eugene.

11. Ward Armstrong, interview by Peter Walker, August 3, 2009.

12. Ray Wilkeson, interview by Peter Walker, June 4, 2009.

13. Dave Hogan, "2 measures attract more cash than all 10 raised a year ago." *Portland Oregonian*, October 18, 2007, p. Do2.

14. Robert J. Shiller, *Irrational exuberance*, 2nd ed., updated data. Online: http://www.irrationalexuberance.com/. Last accessed November 22, 2009.

15. Mike Thorne, interview by Peter Walker, May 8, 2009.

16. Hunnicutt interview.

17. Thorne interview.

18. Richmond interview.

19. John Renz, interview by Peter Walker, September 18, 2009.

20. See Robin Franzen and Brent Hunsberger, "Have we outgrown our approach to growth? . . . Legacy on the line" (part 1 of 5). *Portland Oregonian*, December 13, 1998, p. Ao1.

21. Stacey interview.

22. Randy Gragg, "Two pillars of urban planning fall." *Portland Oregonian*, December 26, 2004, p. Mo1.

23. Stacey interview.

24. Although Washington State's 1990 Growth Management Act was intended to create a "flexible, bottom-up" system, there is "no agreement" that the Act has achieved this objective. State of Washington Department of Commerce, "Flexible application of the GMA." Issue Paper No. 8. Online: http://www.commerce.wa.gov/landuse/issue_papers/issue083.html. Last accessed September 13, 2010.

25. Robbins interview.

26. Lane Shetterly, interview by Peter Walker, September 29, 2009.

27. Oregon Blue Book. Online: http://bluebook.state.or.us/local/cities/sy/shadycove.htm. Last accessed November 23, 2009.

28. Renz interview.

29. As quoted in Abbott and Howe (1993: 27).

30. Andy Parker, "On land use, the problem is the process." *Portland Oregonian*, October 24, 2005, p. D01.

31. Robert Liberty, interview by Peter Walker, June 18.

32. Initiative and Referendum Institute, "A brief history of the initiative and referendum process in the United States," p. 7. Online: http://www.iandrinstitute.org/New%20IRI%20Website%20Info/Drop%20Down%20Boxes/Quick%20Facts/History%20of%20I&R.pdf. Last accessed October 31, 2010.

33. "Supreme court confirms Bill Sizemore as racketeer." *Hillsboro Argus*, July 8, 2008, p. A1.

34. Jeff Mapes, "Conservatives aim to restore initiative clout." *Portland Oregonian*, August 2, 2009, p. A01.

35. Damian Mann, "Looser rules for private land." *Medford Mail Tribune*, November 14, 2004. Online: http://archive.mailtribune.com/archive/2004/1114/local/stories/01local.htm. Last accessed November 1, 2010.

36. Michael Cavallaro, interview by Peter Walker, November 20, 2009.

37. Healthy Democracy Oregon, "The Citizens' Initiative Review: Restoring trust and accountability in our initiative process." Online: http://www.healthydemocracyoregon.org/about_us. Last accessed November 25, 2009.

38. Nancie Fadeley, interview by Peter Walker, May 22, 2009.

39. Hector Macpherson Jr., interview by Peter Walker, June 9, 2009.

40. William Robbins, personal communication, June 15, 2009.

41. U.S. Census, "Oregon: 2000—Census 2000 Profile." C2KPROF/00-OR. U.S. Department of Commerce, August 2002. Online: http://www.census.gov/prod/2002pubs/c2kprof00-or.pdf. Last accessed October 31, 2010.

42. Macpherson interview.

43. Bill Moshofsky, interview by Peter Walker, May 20, 2009.

44. Oregonians in Action, "About us." Online: http://www.oia.org/index.php/about-us. Last accessed November 26, 2009.

45. Dave Hunnicutt, personal communication, November 30, 2009.

46. "Oregonians need 'The Big Look'" (editorial). *Portland Oregonian*, June 27, 2005, p. D08.

47. Thorne interview.

48. Oregon Senate Bill 82 (2005).

49. There was only one exception—a follow-up meeting in the city of Medford to accommodate an overcapacity audience at the first Medford meeting several weeks earlier. This relatively unscripted meeting was in our view the most substantively productive and harmonious of all the Big Look town hall meetings.

50. Oregon State Bar, "The 'Big Look' at land use." *Capitol Insider*, October 20, 2006, pp. 3–4. Online: http://www.osbar.org/_docs/lawimprove/capinsider/ci_061020.pdf. Last accessed November 1, 2010.

51. Thorne interview.

52. Stacey interview.

53. As quoted in Rodger Nichols, "Big Look task force draws big local crowd." *Dalles Chronicle*, September 30, 2008. Online: http://www.thedalleschronicle.com/news/2008/09/news09-30-08-01.shtml. Last accessed November 1, 2010.

54. Oregon Task Force on Land Use Planning "Town Hall" meeting in The Dalles, Oregon, September 29, 2008. From audio recordings and notes by Peter Walker.

55. To their credit, organizers scheduled a second Medford meeting several weeks later. Nevertheless, for many would-be participants, especially those who had traveled long distances for the first meeting, the damage was done.

56. On, June 17, 2009, the Oregon Legislature gave final passage to House Bill 2229, which was signed into law by Governor Ted Kulongoski on August 4, 2009. The bill incorporates many of the recommendations of the Big Look task force, most prominently, allowing counties more opportunity to rezone rural land for development subject to protections of farms, forests, and natural areas and state approval.

57. Richmond interview.

58. No official tally of the number of approved Measure 37 claims that became actual building construction is available from the state at the time of this writing.

59. William A. Van Vactor, "Successes and failures of Oregon's Big Look task force." November 9, 2009. Online: http://naturalresourcereport.com/2009/11/successes-and-failures-of-oregons-big-look-task-force/. Last accessed November 27, 2009.

Chapter 6: Metro Visions

1. Steven Smith, "Land-use watchdogs enter their fourth year." *Eugene (OR) Register-Guard*, March 5, 1978, pp. 1C, 3C.

2. As quoted in Robin Franzen, "Attacks grow on Oregon land-use laws." *Portland Oregonian*, February, 22, p. A01.

3. Dee Wescott, first mayor of the City of Damascus, Oregon, a designated growth area for the Portland Metropolitan Region, testifying to the Metro Regional Council in 2002. Oregon Public Broadcasting radio news, "Former Damascus mayor dies at 81." January 30, 2009. Online: http://news.opb.org/article/4162-former-damascus-mayor-dies-81/. Last accessed October 31, 2010.

4. Rallying cry of more than 500 residents, organized in 2006 by the Damascus Community Coalition in opposition to a controversial land use "concept plan" for Portland's expansion into the Damascus area. Dennis McCarthy, "Landowners band together to fight Damascus plan." *Portland Oregonian*, March 16, 2006, p. 15.

5. U.S. Census Bureau, "United States and Puerto Rico—Metropolitan Area GCT-PH1-R. Population, housing units, area, and density (geographies ranked by total population): 2000." Online: http://factfinder.census.gov/servlet/GCTTable?_bm=y&-geo_id=%200%201000US&-_box_head_nbr=GCT-PH1-R&-ds_name=DEC_2000_SF1_U&-format=US-10S/. Last accessed October 31, 2010.

6. David Laskin, "36 hours in Portland, Ore." *New York Times*, April 15, 2007. Online: http://travel.nytimes.com/2007/04/15/travel/15hours.html?scp=1&sq=36%20 hours%20in%20portland&st=cse. Last accessed December 28, 2009.

7. Don Hamilton, "More polish for the Pearl." *Portland Tribune*, April 29, 2005 (updated October 30, 2009). Online: http://www.portlandtribune.com/news/story .php?story_id=29660. Last accessed December 28, 2009.

8. Eric Mortenson, "Growing without pushing into the country irks cities on the edge." OregonLive.com, September 19, 2009. Online: http://www.oregonlive.com/ environment/index.ssf/2009/09/expanding_by_a_million_people.html. Last accessed December 29, 2009.

9. For example, *Popular Science*, the Natural Resources Defense Council, and Grist.org.

10. SustainLane.com, "About SustainLane.com." Online: http://www.sustainlane .com/about/. Last accessed December 27, 2009.

11. Andrew Revkin, "Portland again tops a sustainable cities list." *New York Times*, September 22, 2008. Online: http://dotearth.blogs.nytimes.com/2008/09/22/ portland-again-tops-a-sustainable-cities-list/?scp=1&sq=SustainLane&st=cse. Last accessed December 27, 2009.

12. SustainLane.Com, "1. Portland Oregon: A role model for the nation." Online: http://www.sustainlane.com/us-city-rankings/cities/portland. Last accessed January 17, 2010.

13. Walt Daggett (Hallock's former chief of staff), interview by Peter Walker, August 6, 2009. Hallock passed away in 2007.

14. U.S. Census, "State and county quickfacts." Estimates for 2008. Online: http:// quickfacts.census.gov/qfd/states/00000.html. Last accessed October 31, 2010.

15. Oregon Secretary of State, Elections Division, "November 6, 2007, special election." Online: http://www.sos.state.or.us/elections/nov62007/. Last accessed December 28, 2009.

16. Oregon Public Broadcasting Radio, "Up or out?" *Think Out Loud*. December 15, 2009. Online: http://www.opb.org/thinkoutloud/shows/or-out/. Last accessed November 1, 2010.

17. Homebuilders Association of Metropolitan Portland president Tom Skaar, as quoted in Eric Mortenson, "Land plan: Anger on west side, amity east." *Portland Oregonian*, September 20, 2009. Online: http://www.allbusiness.com/legal/property -law-real-property-zoning-land-use/13006809-1.html. Last accessed December 28, 2009.

18. No kidding—these are real names, not pseudonyms.

19. U.S. Department of Agriculture, National Resources Conservation Service, "Web soil survey." Online: http://websoilsurvey.nrcs.usda.gov/app/HomePage.htm. Last accessed December 29, 2009.

20. Gordon Oliver, "Architect presents dream plan for neighborhoods." *Portland Oregonian*, May 12, 1994, p. B02.

21. Gordon Oliver, "Damascus, Stafford face the future." *Portland Oregonian*, August 7, 1994, p. E04.

22. R. Gregory Nokes, "Officials lighten map's hues to lessen growth cost fear." *Portland Oregonian*, August 24, 1995, p. B02.

23. Gregory Nokes and Gail Kinsey Hill, "The faster the growth, the faster the tab mounts." *Portland Oregonian*, October 24, 1995, p. B01.

24. R. Gregory Nokes, "Metro council grapples with boundary expansion." *Portland Oregonian*, November 1, 1995, p. A01.

25. R. Gregory Nokes, "Burton says expand urban growth limit." *Portland Oregonian*, September 8, 1995, p. C01.

26. David Bragdon, interview by Peter Walker, December 14, 2009.

27. Peter Farrell, "Damascus tries to control development." *Portland Oregonian*, October 29, 2001, p. C02.

28. Steve Mayes, "Coalition will design an urban Damascus." *Portland Oregonian*, January 31, 2002, p. D02.

29. Laura Oppenheimer, "Damascus groups display design concept for a new city." *Portland Oregonian*, June 6, 2002, p. C03.

30. Dennis McCarthy, "Decisions divisive in Damascus." *Portland Oregonian*, January 5, 2006, p. 01.

31. Dan Phegley, interview by Peter Walker, December 14, 2009.

32. Dan Phegley, personal communication, December 14, 2009.

33. This initiative was related to the 2005 U.S. Supreme Court decision *Kelo v. City of New London* upholding the right of the City of New London to use eminent domain to transfer land from one private owner to another as part of a comprehensive redevelopment plan.

34. Amy Reifenrath, "Road to bigger, better Damascus leads to dead end." *Portland Oregonian*, January 16, 2009.

35. Anita Yap, interview by Peter Walker, December 14, 2009.

36. Larry Thompson, interview by Emily Harris, *Think Out Loud*, Oregon Public Broadcasting Radio, October 2, 2009. Online: http://www.opb.org/thinkoutloud/shows/rurban-living/. Last accessed November 1, 2010.

37. Comment in response to "Rurban living," *Think Out Loud*, Oregon Public Broadcasting Radio, October 2, 2009. Online: http://www.opb.org/thinkoutloud/shows/rurban-living/newest-first#rurbanistia-10-03-09-15-04. Last accessed December 13, 2009.

38. Yap interview.

39. Eric Mortenson "Is the urban-rural divide outdated?" *Portland Oregonian*, August 9, 2009.

40. John VanLandingham, interview by Peter Walker, December 10, 2009.

41. Bragdon interview.

42. Ozawa (2008) notes that surveys showed that 60 percent of local residents

were opposed to the UGB expansion into their community—a matter on which they were not consulted and had no say whatsoever. In this regard, the opposition's war chant that "They didn't ask us in Damascus!" was accurate. Ozawa concentrated her analysis on the "Conversations with Damascus program" sponsored by Clackamas County. She found that residents came into this public involvement process already angry and suspicious because they felt no one had asked or cared about their point of view on the most contentious issue of all—the UGB expansion itself. To ask local residents *after* the UGB expansion to trust "government" to listen to them in the formation of the concept plan was possibly steep uphill struggle. Rather than facing this public resentment head-on from the beginning, Ozawa noted "the retreat of the process and project staff into the bowels of the expert agencies" (2008: 10), only to emerge a year later with a set of development options on which the public could comment but that they had not created. Moreover, in public meetings facilitators permitted no dialog, commanded audience members to comply with strict hearing-style protocol, and failed to provide any two-way communication or response to citizen comments. In Ozawa's analysis, it was clear that "the Advisory Committee did not want to speak with the angry public" (13). Ozawa concludes, "Had the planners chosen to engage in consensus building, the events of the following months [and years] might have unfolded quite differently" (14) and that the quality of the citizen involvement effort was in some respects shockingly poor and may have actually contributed to increased rather than reduced public hostility and political resistance.

Chapter 7: Central Destinations

1. Erik Kancler (executive director of Central Oregon Land Watch), "Why resorts, Metolius River don't mix" (editorial). *Bent (OR) Bulletin*, June 6, 2007. Online: http://www.bendbulletin.com/apps/pbcs.dll/article?AID=/20070606/OPIN01/706060320/. Last accessed October 31, 2010.

2. "The legislature's ugly little lesson" (editorial). *Bend Bulletin*, June 6, 2009.

3. Editorial, *Bend Bulletin*, February 20, 2009 (emphasis added).

4. Mike Carrier, natural resource policy adviser to Governor Ted Kulongoski, April 1, 2009, as quoted in Jim Springhett, "Jefferson County, state battle over Metolius River basin development." *Portland Oregonian*, April 1, 2009.

5. As quoted in "How dare Jefferson officials be mad?" (editorial). *Bend Bulletin*, April 3, 2009.

6. We note that, in a number of communities, particularly in parts of the Interior West, resource booms tied to renewed investment in energy extraction have become more prevalent.

7. We focus here on western states, but amenity migration and accompanying rural change are well documented in eastern states as well (e.g., see Hurley and Halfacre 2009).

8. The three counties each score 6 out of a possible 7 on the U.S. Department of Agriculture's natural amenity index. See McGranahan (1999: 11).

9. U.S. Census Bureau. "County population estimates: 100 fastest growing counties." Online: http://www.census.gov/popest/counties/CO-EST2009-08.html. Last accessed October 31, 2010.

10. Interview A, by Patrick Hurley, Deschutes County, June 12, 2006.

11. Interview A.

12. Interview A.

13. Interview D, by Patrick Hurley, Deschutes County, June 9, 2006.

14. Ecoregions are large areas of land or water that contain similar vegetation patterns and characteristic climates and ecological processes (e.g., fire, floods) and are often used by environmental nongovernmental organizations as a planning tool (e.g., see Stein et al. 2000).

15. Including Black Butte, Brasada, Eagle Crest, Kah-Nee-Ta, Pronghorn, Remington, Seventh Mountain, Mt. Bachelor Village, Crooked River Ranch, Sunriver, Caldera Springs, and Thornburg.

16. M. Graves, "Oregon's first wine-country resort nears completion." *Portland Oregonian*, April 17, 2009, business section.

17. Nave Jean, "Black Butte Ranch: A brief history." Sisters County Historical Society, 2002. Online: http://www.blackbutteranch.com/about-us/history/. Last accessed November 24, 2009.

18. Oregon Department of Land Conservation and Development, "Oregon's Statewide Planning Goals and Guidelines, Goal 8: Recreational Needs." OAR 660-015-0000(8). Online: http://www.lcd.state.or.us/LCD/docs/goals/goal8.pdf. Last accessed December 28, 2009.

19. Central Oregon Association of Realtors, "Written statement of the Central Oregon Association of Realtors® on the subject of destination reports before the Deschutes County Planning Commission." October 23, 2008. Online: http://lava5.deschutes.org/cdd/compplan/assets/files/staffmemos/10-23-2008%20COAR%20handout.pdf. Last accessed November 24, 2009.

20. Eben Fodor, "Fiscal and economic impacts of destination resorts in Oregon." Central Oregon Landwatch, March 2009. Online: http://www.centraloregonland watch.org/files/Destination%20Resort%20Impact%20Study%20Revised.pdf. Last accessed December 1, 2009.

21. William Boyd, "Destination resorts destroying the area" (editorial). *Bend Bulletin*, July 27, 2005.

22. Jeff Meyers, "Too many resorts" (letter to the editor). *Bend Bulletin*, August 16, 2005.

23. Kate Ramsayer, "Land north of Smith Rock will remain undeveloped." *Bend Bulletin*, December 28, 2007. Online: http://www.deschuteslandtrust.org/pressroom/press-clips/2009-press-clips/land-north-of-smith-rock-to-remain-undeveloped/. Last accessed October 31, 2010.

24. Brasada Ranch, "Indulge your passion." Jeld-Wen, 2009. Online: http://www .brasada.com/site_Golf/Course-Tour.aspx?page=GF-Course-Tour. Last accessed November 24, 2009.

25. Central Oregon Landwatch is unaffiliated with 1000 Friends of Oregon but serves a similar role in the Central Oregon area.

26. "New Pahlisch parcel could become resort." *Bend Bulletin*, December 22, 2005.

27. James Holman, "Central Oregon resorts face backlash from locals." Oregon Online. Online: http://blog.oregonlive.com/pdxgreen/2008/04/central_oregon_resorts _face_ba.html. Last accessed November 24, 2009.

28. Sierra Club, "Destination resort actions." 2009. Online: http://oregon.sierra club.org/groups/juniper/action/resorts.asp. Last accessed November 24, 2009.

29. Holman, "Central Oregon resorts."

30. "Destination resort map repeal questioned." *Bend Bulletin*, September 18, 2009. The article points out that the initiative led the county to repeal the map before the three-year period was up: between the start of the LUBA process and the ultimate remand, the time period expired, which allowed the county to move forward with repeal of the map.

31. City-data.com, "Crooked River, Oregon." Online: http://www.city-data.com/ city/Crooked-River-Oregon.html. Last accessed December 10, 2009.

32. Rick Allen, former Jefferson County commissioner and lobbyist for the proposed Ponderosa destination resort, interview by Peter Walker, October 21, 2009.

33. Nancy Pasternak, "Metolius Basin braces for change." *Bend Bulletin*, January 2, 2007.

34. Camp Sherman resident and Friends of the Metolius spokesperson Gregory McLarren, as cited in Pasternak, "Metolius Basin braces for change."

35. Dick Kellogg (guest columnist), "Legislature should step in and protect the Metolius Basin." *Bend Bulletin*, March 29, 2007.

36. John Costa, "In our view" (editorial). *Bend Bulletin*, June 21, 2009.

37. Senate Bill 30. 74th Session of the Oregon Legislature, 2007. Online: http:// landru.leg.state.or.us/07reg/measures/sb0001.dir/sb0030.b.html. Last accessed October 31, 2010.

38. As quoted in Erik Kancler, "Why resorts, Metolius river don't mix" (guest column). *Bend Bulletin*, June 6, 2007.

39. Oregon Governor Theodore Kulongoski, letter to House Rules Committee chair Diane Rosenbaum. "Re: Senate Bill 30 and Destination Resorts in the Metolius Basin." June 22, 2007. http://www.oregon.gov/LCD/docs/general/letter_from_governor_062207 .pdf. Last accessed October 31, 2010.

40. Hillary Borrud, "Destination resort rules might see tightening." *Bend Bulletin*, April 4, 2008.

41. James Sinks, "With eye region, state may revisit law on resorts." *Bend Bulletin*, May 17, 2008.

42. Although Goal 8 was adopted in 1984, the legislature passed legislation in

1987 to place the states' destination rules in the state's revised statutes, which effectively limited the power of DLCD to intervene in individual counties' and municipalities' planning processes. Only LUBA would have the authority to do so.

43. Mary Kitch, "Protecting Oregon's beloved places" (editorial). *Portland Oregonian*, June 22, 2009.

44. Department of Land Conservation and Development, "Metolius River Basin ACSC." 2009. Online: http://www.oregon.gov/LCD/metolius_river_basin_acsc.shtml. Last accessed October 31, 2010.

45. Mark Graves, "Land-use battle rages along beautiful river." *Portland Oregonian*, April 2, 2009.

46. For example, the Metolian owners had paid $1.1 million for their property and said they spent $4 million and much time on design plans and application fees.

47. Nick Budnick, "Resort ban may spark 'brawl.'" *Bend Bulletin*, August 21, 2009.

48. John VanLandingham, interview by Peter Walker, December 10, 2009.

Chapter 8: Southern Discomforts

1. Former state senator Hector Macpherson Jr., architect of Oregon's 1973 statewide land use planning law, Senate Bill 100, on his efforts in 1972–1973 to build support for his bill. Interview by Peter Walker, June 9, 2009.

2. Fifty-Seventh Legislative Assembly of the State of Oregon, *Journal and Calendar of the Senate and House*, 1973, p. J-93.

3. John Eads, founder and coordinator of the Greater Bear Creek Valley Regional Problem Solving (RPS) land use planning process in southern Oregon's Rogue Valley, as quoted in Melissa Martin, "A sticky situation." *Medford Mail Tribune*, February 17, 2002.

4. Don Moore and Porter Lombard, "Is the valley going to lose its best farmland?" (editorial). *Medford Mail Tribune*, March 9, 2008. Online: http://www.mailtribune.com/apps/pbcs.dll/article?AID=/20080309/OPINION/803090308. Last December 24, 2009.

5. Richard Whitman, Oregon Department of Land Conservation and Development director, addressing the Oregon Task Force on Land Use Planning (the "Big Look") at a meeting in Prineville, Oregon, October 17, 2008.

6. We use the term "southern Oregon" in the way it is typically used in Oregon—to refer to the counties of south*west* Oregon, mainly Jackson, Josephine, and Douglas counties. Coos, Curry, and Klamath counties have certain political, economic, and cultural similarities but smaller populations and a somewhat lower profile in land use planning politics (with the exception of Klamath County—home to a strong property rights community). Populations in southeast Oregon counties are so small and thinly spread that politics in these counties are often overlooked altogether by the rest of

the state. We apologize to the citizens of Lake, Harney, and Malheur counties for perpetuating this regrettable habit.

7. Roy Scarbrough, "LCDC eyes claims of Jackson County violations." *Portland Oregonian*, May 7, 1992, p. D02; Roy Scarbrough, "Assertions to be eyed by LCDC." *Portland Oregonian*, May 8, 1992, p. D02.

8. Tony Boom, "Regional solutions sought by land-use advocates." *Medford Mail Tribune*, March 27, 2003. Online: http://archive.mailtribune.com/archive/2003/0327/local/stories/16local.htm. Last accessed December 23, 2009.

9. Oregon Labor Market Information System, Region 8 (Jackson and Josephine counties) data, 2008. Online: http://www.qualityinfo.org/olmisj/Regions?area=000008 &page=2. Last accessed December 18, 2009.

10. U.S. Census, "State and county quickfacts: Jackson County, Oregon." Online: http://quickfacts.census.gov/qfd/states/41/41029.html; "State and county quickfacts: Josephine County, Oregon." Online: http://quickfacts.census.gov/qfd/states/41/41033 .html. Both last accessed October 31, 2010.

11. Oregon Labor Market Information System, Region 8 (Jackson and Josephine counties) data.

12. U.S. Census Bureau, "Population Finder: Jackson County, Oregon." Online: http://factfinder.census.gov/servlet/SAFFPopulation?_event=Search&geo_id=01000 US&_geoContext=01000US&_street=&_county=Jackson+County&_cityTown =Jackson+County&_state=04000US41&_zip=&_lang=en&_sse=on&ActiveGeoDiv =geoSelect&_useEV=&pctxt=fph&pgsl=010&_submenuId=population_0&ds _name=null&_ci_nbr=null&qr_name=null&reg=null%3Anull&_keyword=& _industry=/. Last accessed October 31, 2010.

13. Jeffrey LaLande, unpublished speech given to the Southern Oregon Historical Society, February 2009.

14. Population Research Center, "2009 Oregon Population Report." Portland State University, 2010. Online: http://www.pdx.edu/sites/www.pdx.edu.prc/files/media _assets/PopRpt09b.pdf. Last accessed October 31, 2010.

15. All the evidence points to Thomas Jefferson (Declaration of Independence) as the inspiration for the "state" name. The big movement for creating the State of Jefferson was in 1941. Professor Donald Holtgrieve, personal communication, September 21, 2009.

16. Michael Cavallaro, interview by Peter Walker, November 20, 2009.

17. Roy Scarbrough, "Assertions to be eyed by LCDC." *Portland Oregonian*, May 8, 1992, p. D02.

18. Damian Mann, "Court stops Measure 37 transfers: County acted with 'wholesale disregard' for law." *Medford Mail Tribune*, January 20, 2007. Online: http://archive .mailtribune.com/archive/2007/0120/local/stories/m37judgement.htm. Last accessed December 8, 2009.

19. Richard Benner, personal communication, December 23.

20. DLCD, "Message from the director: Building a more responsive land use planning system," introduction. In: *Biennial Report for 1997–1999*. February 1999. Emphasis added.

21. DLCD, *Biennial Report for 1997–1999*, p. 35.

22. Region 2050 (an RPS in the Eugene-Springfield metropolitan area that later collapsed due to bickering between the major cities involved), "Regional growth management strategy timeline and regional problem solving process." Online: http://www.region2050.org/pdf/meetings/062005/R2050TimeRPS2.pdf. Last accessed December 19, 2009.

23. 1000 Friends of Oregon, "Questions and answers about Oregon's land use program." Online: http://www.onethousandfriendsoforegon.org/resources/qanda3.html. Last accessed December 19, 2009.

24. Kate Jackson, interview by Peter Walker, November 20, 2009.

25. Damian Mann, "Jacksonville's hesitation puts regional growth plan at risk." *Medford Mail Tribune*, September 18, 2008. Online: http://www.mailtribune.com/apps/pbcs.dll/article?AID=/20080918/NEWS/809180331. Last accessed December 21, 2009.

26. ORS 197.652–197.658, 1996.

27. Greg Holmes, southern Oregon representative for 1000 Friends of Oregon, interview by Peter Walker, November 10, 2009.

28. ORS 197.656, 1996.

29. Bear Creek Valley RPS, "Now X 2" (newspaper insert). *Medford Mail Tribune*, December 2002, p. 9.

30. ORS 197.656(2)(c), 1996.

31. Michael Cavallaro, interview by Innisfree McKinnon, University of Oregon doctoral student, September 18, 2009, quoted with permission.

32. Linda Meyers, "Regional Problem Solving has gone astray" (editorial). *Medford Mail Tribune*, April 7, 2009. Online: http://www.mailtribune.com/apps/pbcs.dll/article?AID=/20090407/OPINION/904070302. Last accessed December 22, 2009.

33. Greg Holmes interview.

34. Innisfree McKinnon, interview by Peter Walker, October 30, 2009.

35. Michael Cavallaro, interview by Peter Walker, November 20, 2009.

36. Melissa Martin, "Where do we grow from here?" *Medford Mail Tribune*, December 6, 2001. Online: http://archive.mailtribune.com/archive/2001/december/120601n1.htm. Last accessed December 23, 2009.

37. Melissa Martin, "Plan tackles urban growth into the hills." *Medford Mail Tribune*, October 7, 2009. Online: http://archive.mailtribune.com/archive/2001/october/100701n3.htm. Last accessed December 23, 2009.

38. William Robbins, "The place we call home: A history of land use planning in Oregon." *Oregon Humanities*, Spring/Summer 2006. Online: http://www.oregonhum.org/place-we-call-home.php/. Last accessed March 13, 2009.

39. Kate Jackson, interview by Peter Walker, November 11, 2009.

40. Cavallaro interview by McKinnon.

41. Meyers, "Regional Problem Solving has gone astray," explaining why her city could not participate further with the RPS, jeopardizing the whole process.

42. Holmes interview.

43. Tony Boom, "Jacksonville cut from county process." *Medford Mail Tribune*, January 9, 2009. Online: http://www.mailtribune.com/apps/pbcs.dll/article?AID=/20090109/NEWS/901090324. Last accessed December 23, 2009.

44. Holmes interview.

45. Jackson interview, November 20.

46. Cavallaro interview by McKinnon.

47. In 2009, Oregon passed revisions to the RPS statute based largely on assessments of the Bear Creek Valley RPS by the Oregon Task Force on Land Use Planning (the "Big Look"). Local leaders complain that the Big Look did not take the time to study the *successes* as well as the failures of their project, choosing instead to simply tighten controls over RPS.

Chapter 9: Paradise Lost?

1. John D. Echeverria, e-mail to P. Walker, December 16, 2009.

2. Jon Chandler, president of the Oregon Home Builders Association, testifying before the Oregon Senate hearings on House Bill 2229, May 19, 2009.

3. Floyd Prozanski, Oregon Public Radio news, February 22, 2010.

4. Oregon Department of Agriculture, "Oregon agriculture: Facts and figures." June 2010. Online: http://www.nass.usda.gov/Statistics_by_State/Oregon/Publications/facts_and_figures/facts_and_figures.pdf. Last accessed October 31, 2010.

5. Shawn Cleave, interview by Peter Walker, August 3, 2009.

6. Eric Mortenson, "Is the urban-rural divide outdated?" *Portland Oregonian*, August 9, 2009, p. A1.

7. Oregon Task Force on Land Use Planning, "Final Report to the 2009 Oregon Legislature," January 2009, p. 13.

8. Conkling, Fiskum & McCormick for the Oregon Business Association, 2005.

9. Lane Shetterly, interview by Peter Walker, September 29, 2009.

10. Bob Stacey, interview by Peter Walker, June 2, 2009.

11. Anita Yap, interview by Peter Walker, December 14, 2009.

12. As cited in Laura Oppenheimer, "Land-use laws on turf that is uncharted." *Portland Oregonian*, November 4, 2004, p. A01.

13. Henry Richmond, interview by Peter Walker, March 13, 2009.

14. David Bragdon, interview by Peter Walker, December 14, 2009.

15. Richard Whitman, interview by Peter Walker, October 5, 2009.

16. As quoted in Eric Mortenson, "Once firebrands, now the establishment, 1000 Friends of Oregon seeks new footing." *Portland Oregonian*, December 18, 2009.

17. To be precise, the 10 goals of the 1969 SB 10 served as interim goals and

became models for the new statewide planning goals under SB 100. However, these goals were extensively discussed and ultimately endorsed by the public through town hall meetings in every corner of the state. Unlike the 2008 "Big Look" town hall meetings, historical accounts describe the public as positive and in agreement that state leaders had genuinely listened and responded to ordinary citizens.

18. 1000 Friends of Oregon, *The Battle to Keep Oregon Lovable and Livable* (audio recording), 1998.

19. Big Look town hall meeting in Tillamook, September 17, 2008.

Bibliography

Abbott, C. 2002. Planning a sustainable city: The promise and performance of Portland's urban growth boundary. In *Urban sprawl: Causes, consequences, and policy responses*, ed. G. Squires. Baltimore, MD: Urban Institute Press.

Abbott, C., S. Adler, and D. Howe. 2003. A quiet counterrevolution in land use regulation: The origins and impact of Oregon's Measure 7. *Housing Policy Debate* 14(3):383–425.

Abbott, Carl, and Deborah Howe. 1993. The politics of land-use law in Oregon: Senate Bill 100, twenty years after. *Oregon Historical Quarterly* 94:5–35.

Abbott, Carl, Deborah A. Howe, and Sy Adler. 1994. *Planning the Oregon way: A twenty-year evaluation*. Corvallis, OR: Oregon State University Press.

Agrawal, A., and C.C. Gibson. 1999. Enchantment and disenchantment: The role of community in natural resource conservation. *World Development* 27(4):629–649.

Agrawal, Arun. 2005. *Environmentality: Technologies of government and the making of subjects. New ecologies for the twenty-first century*. Durham, NC: Duke University Press.

Apostol, Dean, and Anita Yap. 2009. The Damascus story: A great Oregon experiment. *Oregon Planners' Journal* July/August: 3–9.

Arrieta-Walden, Michael, Randy Rasmussen, and Brian Harrah. 2000. *The Oregon story, 1850–2000*. Portland, OR: Graphic Arts Center Publishing.

Barrett, C.B., K. Brandon, C. Gibson, and H. Gjertsen. 2001. Conserving tropical biodiversity amid weak institutions. *BioScience* 51(6):497–502.

Bassett, Ellen M. 2009. Framing the Oregon land use debate: An exploration of Oregon voters' pamphlets, 1970–2007. *Journal of Planning Education and Research* 29(2):157–172.

Berkes, F. 2004. Rethinking community-based conservation. *Conservation Biology* 18(3):621–630.

Berry, Sara. 1993. *No condition is permanent: The social dynamics of agrarian change in sub-Saharan Africa*. Madison: University of Wisconsin Press.

Bosselman, Fred P., and David L. Callies. 1972. *The quiet revolution in land use control*. Available online: http://www.eric.ed.gov/PDFS/ED067272.pdf. Last accessed October 31, 2010.

Bowen, William A. 1978. *The Willamette Valley: Migration and settlement on the Oregon frontier.* Seattle: University of Washington Press.

Brogden, M.J., and J.B. Greenberg. 2003. The fight for the west: A political ecology of land use conflicts in Arizona. *Human Organization* 62(3):289–298.

Brown, Beverly A. 1995. *In timber country: Working people's stories of environmental conflict and urban flight.* Philadelphia: Temple University Press.

Brown, D., K. Johnson, T. Loveland, and D. Theobald. 2005. Rural land-use trends in the coterminous United States, 1950–2000. *Ecological Applications* 15(6):1851–1863.

Bruegmann, Robert. 2005. *Sprawl: A compact history.* Chicago: University of Chicago Press.

Calbick, K.S., J.C. Day, and T.I. Gunton. 2003. Land use planning implementation: A "best practices" assessment. *Environments* 31(3):69–82.

Callenbach, Ernest. 1975. *Ecotopia: The notebooks and reports of William Weston.* Berkeley, CA: Banyan Tree Books.

Carson, Rachel. 1962. *Silent spring.* Boston: Houghton Mifflin.

Collette, Carlotta. 1998. The Oregon way. *High Country News*, October 26.

Cray, Ed. 2004. *Ramblin' man: The life and times of Woody Guthrie.* New York: W.W. Norton.

Duane, Timothy P. 1999. *Shaping the Sierra: Nature, culture, and conflict in the changing West.* Berkeley: University of California.

Duncan, James S., and David Ley. 1993. *Place/culture/representation.* New York: Routledge.

Ehrlich, Paul R. 1968. *The population bomb.* New York: Ballantine Books.

Few, R. 2001. Containment and counter-containment: Planner/community relations in conservation planning. *Geographical Journal* 167(part 2):111–124.

Freeman, J. 1997. Collaborative governance in the administrative state. *UCLA Law Review* 45(1):1–98.

Fulton, William B., and Paul Shigley. 2005. *Guide to California planning.* 3rd ed. Point Arena, CA: Solano Press Books.

Furuseth, Owen J., and Mark B. Lapping. 1999. *Contested countryside: The rural urban fringe in North America. Perspectives on rural policy and planning.* Brookfield, VT: Ashgate.

George, Henry. 1979. *Progress and poverty: An inquiry into the cause of industrial depressions and of increase of want with increase of wealth . . . the remedy.* New York: Robert Schalkenbach Foundation.

Ghose, R. 2004. Big sky or big sprawl? Rural gentrification and the changing cultural landscape of Missoula, Montana. *Urban Geography* 25(6):528–549.

Gosnell, Hannah, Jeffrey D. Kline, Garrett Chrostek, and James Duncan. 2010. Is Oregon's land use planning program conserving forest and farm land? A review of the evidence. *Land Use Policy* 28(1):185–192.

Harden, Blaine. 2005. Anti-sprawl laws, property rights collide in Oregon. *Washington Post*, February 28, p. A01.

Hardin, Garrett. 1968. The tragedy of the commons. *Science* 162:1243–1248.

Hoch, Charles, Linda C. Dalton, Frank S. So, and ICMA Training Institute. 2000. *The practice of local government planning.* 3rd ed. Municipal management series. Washington, DC: International City/County Management Association.

Hurley, P.T., and A.C. Halfacre. 2009. Dodging alligators, rattlesnakes, and backyard docks: A political ecology of sweetgrass basket-making and conservation in the South Carolina Lowcountry, USA. *GeoJournal*; doi: 10.1007/s10708-009-9276-7, online March 24, 2009.

Hurley, P.T., and P.A. Walker. 2004. Whose vision? Conspiracy theory and land-use planning in Nevada County, California. *Environment and Planning A* 36(9):1529–1547.

Jackson, Kenneth T. 1985. *Crabgrass frontier: The suburbanization of the United States.* New York: Oxford University Press.

Jackson, Philip L., and Robert Kuhlken. 2006. *A rediscovered frontier: Land use and resource issues in the new West.* Lanham, MD: Rowman & Littlefield.

Judd, Richard William, and Christopher S. Beach. 2003. *Natural states: The environmental imagination in Maine, Oregon, and the nation.* Washington, DC: Resources for the Future.

Knaap, Gerrit. 1994. Land use politics in Oregon. In *Planning the Oregon Way*, ed. C. Abbott, D. Howe, and S. Adler. Corvallis, OR: Oregon State University Press.

Knaap, G.J., and Arthur C. Nelson. 1992. *The regulated landscape: Lessons on state land use planning from Oregon.* Cambridge, MA: Lincoln Institute of Land Policy.

Knight, R.L., G.N. Wallace, and W.E. Riebsame. 1995. Ranching the view: Subdivisions versus agriculture. *Conservation Biology* 9(2):459–461.

Kunstler, James Howard. 1993. *The geography of nowhere: The rise and decline of America's man-made landscape.* New York: Simon & Schuster.

Lakoff, George. 2004. *Don't think of an elephant! Know your values and frame the debate: The essential guide for progressives.* White River Junction, VT: Chelsea Green.

Loy, William G., Stuart Allan, Aileen R. Buckley, and James E. Meacham. 2001. *Atlas of Oregon.* Eugene, OR: University of Oregon.

Macpherson, Hector, Jr., with Katharine Macpherson. 2010. *The Macpherson family: Four generations*, ed. Janet Wershow, Eleanor Wershow, and Katharine Rosson. Private collection.

Maestas, J.D., R.L. Knight, and W.C. Gilgert. 2003. Biodiversity across a rural land-use gradient. *Conservation Biology* 17(5):1425–1434.

Mansuri, G., and V. Rao. 2004. Community-based and -driven development: A critical review. *World Bank Research Observer* 19(1):1–39.

Martin, Sheila, Meg Merrick, Erik Rundell, and Katie Shriver. 2007. *What is driving Measure 37 claims in Oregon?* Portland, OR: Institute of Portland Metropolitan Studies, Portland State University.

Mason, Robert J. 2008. *Collaborative land use management: The quieter revolution in place-based planning.* Lanham, MD: Rowman & Littlefield.

McArthur, Lewis A., and Lewis L. McArthur. 2003. *Oregon geographic names.* 7th ed. Portland, OR: Oregon Historical Society Press.

McCall, Thomas L. 1974. The Oregon land use story. Salem: State of Oregon. Online: http://www.orgov.org/Oregon_Land_Use_Story.pdf. Last accessed October 31, 2010.

McGranahan, D. 1999. *Natural amenities drive rural population change.* Agricultural Economic Report No. 781. Washington, DC: USDA Economic Research Service.

McHarg, Ian L. 1969. *Design with nature.* Garden City, NY: American Museum of Natural History/Natural History Press.

Michels, Robert, Eden Paul, and Cedar Paul. 1915. *Political parties; a sociological study of the oligarchical tendencies of modern democracy.* New York: Hearst's International Library Co.

Mitchell, John G. 2001. Urban sprawl. *National Geographic* 200(1):48.

Nash, Roderick. 1982. *Wilderness and the American mind.* 3rd ed. New Haven, CT: Yale University Press.

Nelson, A., and J. Duncan. 1996. *Growth management principles and practices.* Washington, DC: American Planning Association.

Nelson, P.B. 2001. Rural restructuring in the American West: Land use, family and class discourses. *Journal of Rural Studies* 17(4):395–407.

Nelson, Peter B. 2006. Geographic perspective on amenity migration across the USA: National-, regional-, and local-scale analysis. In *The amenity migrants: Seeking and sustaining mountains and their cultures,* ed. L.A.G. Moss. Wallingford, UK: CABI Publishing.

Oregon Biodiversity Project. 1998. *Oregon's living landscape: Strategies and opportunities to conserve biodiversity.* Washington, DC: Defenders of Wildlife.

Ozawa, Connie P. 2008. *Improving land use planning through consensus building techniques: A review of a case in Clackamas County, Oregon.* Portland, OR: National Policy Consensus Center, Portland State University.

Peet, Richard, and Michael Watts. 1996. *Liberation ecologies: Environment, development, social movements.* London: Routledge.

Platt, Rutherford H. 2004. *Land use and society: Geography, law, and public policy.* Rev. ed. Washington, DC: Island Press.

Platteau, J.P. 2004. Monitoring elite capture in community-driven development. *Development and Change* 35(2):223–246.

Plotkin, Sidney. 1987. *Keep out: The struggle for land use control.* Berkeley: University of California Press.

Popper, Frank. 1981. *The politics of land-use reform.* Madison: University of Wisconsin Press.

Randolph, John. 2004. *Environmental land use planning and management.* Washington, DC: Island Press.

Reisner, Marc. 1993. *Cadillac desert: The American West and its disappearing water.* Rev. and updated ed. New York: Penguin Books.

Ribot, Jesse. 1996. Participation without representation: Chiefs, councils, and forestry law in the West African Sahel. *Cultural Survival Quarterly* 30(3):40–44.

Richmond, Henry R., and Timothy G. Houchen. 2007. *Oregon's public investment in conservation, prosperity and fairness: Reduced taxation of farm land and forestry land 1974–2004.* Portland, OR: American Land Institute.

Robbins, William G. 1997. *Landscapes of promise: The Oregon story, 1800–1940.* Seattle: University of Washington Press.

———. 2004. *Landscapes of conflict: The Oregon story, 1940–2000.* Seattle: University of Washington Press.

Rome, Adam Ward. 2001. *The bulldozer in the countryside: Suburban sprawl and the rise of American environmentalism.* Studies in environment and history. Cambridge: Cambridge University Press.

Rusk, David. 1999. *Inside game/outside game: Winning strategies for saving urban America.* Washington, DC: Brookings Institution.

Schmidt, David D. 1989. *Citizen lawmakers: The ballot initiative revolution.* Philadelphia: Temple University Press.

Soja, Edward W. 1996. *Thirdspace: Journeys to Los Angeles and other real-and-imagined places.* Cambridge, MA: Blackwell.

Squires, G., ed. 2002. *Urban sprawl: Causes, consequences, and policy responses.* Baltimore, MD: Urban Institute Press.

Stein, Bruce A., Lynn S. Kutner, and Jonathan S. Adams, eds. 2000. *Precious heritage: The status of biodiversity in the United States.* New York: Oxford University Press.

Terrie, Philip G. 2008. *Contested terrain: A new history of nature and people in the Adirondacks.* Blue Mountain Lake, NY: Adirondack Museum.

Travis, William R. 2007. *New geographies of the American West: Land use and the changing patterns of place.* Orton innovation in place series. Washington, DC: Island Press.

Tuan, Yi-fu. 1977. *Space and place: The perspective of experience.* Minneapolis: University of Minnesota Press.

Vias, Alexander C., and John I. Carruthers. 2005. Regional development and land use change in the Rocky Mountain West, 1982–1997. *Growth and Change* 36(2):244–272.

Walker, Peter A., and Louise P. Fortmann. 2003. Whose landscape? A political ecology of the "exurban" Sierra. *Cultural Geographies* 10(4):469–491.

Walker, Richard. 2007. *The country in the city: The greening of the San Francisco*

Bay Area. Weyerhaeuser environmental books. Seattle: University of Washington Press.

Walth, Brent. 1994. *Fire at Eden's gate: Tom McCall and the Oregon story*. Portland: Oregon Historical Society.

Weitz, Jerry. 2000. *Sprawl busting: State programs to guide growth*. Chicago, IL: American Planning Association.

Williams, Raymond. 1973. *The country and the city*. New York: Oxford University Press.

Wondolleck, Julia Marie, and Steven Lewis Yaffee. 2000. *Making collaboration work: Lessons from innovation in natural resource management*. Washington, DC: Island Press.

Index

1000 Friends of Oregon 9, 69–71, 78, 93, 114, 130, 169, 214, 218

Acknowledgment of comprehensive plans 23, 30
Adams, Sam 160, 161
Administrative review 23
Amenity migration 181
American Planning Association 26
Areas of Critical State Concern 56, 181, 199, 200, 245
Armstrong, Ward 72–73, 116
Ask Damascus organization 172
Association of Oregon Counties 81
Atiyeh, Victor 63, 64, 140

Ballot initiatives process 133–137
Bateman, Allen 68–69
Beach Bill (1967) 41, 102, 241
Bear Creek Valley 19
Bear Creek Valley Regional Problem Solving planning process 205, 214–216, 247
Bend (OR) *Bulletin* newspaper 85, 196
Benner, Richard 108, 213
Big Look (Oregon Task Force on Land Use Planning) 119, 120, 121, 123, 140–154, 202
Big Look, narrowing of vision 147
Big Look, public anger toward 147, 151
Bipartisanship. *See* nonpartisanship
Bonneville Power Administration 6

Bosselman and Callies's *Quiet Revolution in Land Use Control* (1972) 25, 47
Bottle Bill (1971) 7, 59, 102, 241
Burdick, Ginny 196
Bureaucratization 20, 126–132, 154
Burton, Mike 22, 167
Bush, George W. 82, 99

California migrants 65, 165, 209, 211–212
Californication 64–67
Calthorpe, Peter 165, 169
Cavallaro, Michael 135, 211, 220, 222, 225, 228
Central Oregon 19, 40, 84
Central Oregon Landwatch 193
Chandler, Jon 156, 230
Change, resistance to 242
Charbonneau 45, 50
Cogan, Arnold 68, 177, 247
Complexity in land use policy 127, 216
Consultants, private 246
Copycat ballot measures 10
Courtney, Peter 97, 141

Daggett, Walt 62
Damascus, OR "debacle" 173
Damascus, OR 18, 163–173
Damascus, OR as a "blank slate" 169
Damascus, OR cityhood campaign 168–170

Day, L.B. 50, 55–56, 72, 74, 152
Democratic Party 11, 64, 66
Department of Land Conservation and Development (DLCD) 47, 68, 106, 131, 139, 140, 142, 184, 213, 226
Destination resorts 181, 185
Dust Bowl 4

Eastern Oregon 40
Echeverria, John 22, 230
Eco-resorts 191, 252
Ecotopia 8, 49
English, Dorothy 76–79, 83, 87, 103, 105, 106, 113, 114, 124, 198, 235
Environmental values 20, 236
Environmentalism 49, 57–62, 233
Expand-and-pray 177, 178
Exurban growth 23

Fadeley, Nancie 56–58, 132, 137
Fairness in planning policy 18, 106, 109, 120–125, 202, 233, 237, 243, 251
Farmers, pressure on 43, 44, 50, 117, 238
Flexibility in planning policy 18, 102, 127, 130, 205, 213, 216, 226, 229, 233
Forest products industry 72–73, 115
Forestry Practices Act 72
Framing planning policy 248
Fregonese Associates 142, 144, 145

George, Larry 82
Goal 5, 29
Goldschmidt, Neil 164
Grange, The 51
Guthrie, Woody 4

Hallock, Ted 55–56, 62, 159
Halprin, Lawrence 54
Hansell, Stafford 131

Hatfield, Mark 63, 81, 223
High-tech industry 73, 116
High-value farmland 46, 105, 167, 187, 217–218
Hobby farms 117, 122
Holmes, Greg 218, 221, 227
Home builders 70, 74, 115
House on the rimrock 85–86
Housing bubble 118–120, 238
Hunnicutt, Dave 99, 103, 107, 109, 110, 112, 119

Infill 39, 40, 146, 156, 159, 160, 166, 218, 224
Infrastructure 115, 166, 177
In-migration 6, 138
Iron law of oligarchy 126, 246

Jackson, Kate 216, 224, 227
Johnson, Betsy 193, 195, 197
Johnson, Jim 97
Just compensation 86, 110, 112

Kitzhaber, John 212
Kool-Aid (ideological dogmatism) 161
Kulongoski, Ted 78, 88, 98, 101, 141, 197, 198

LaLande, Jeff 209, 210
Land Conservation and Development Commission (LCDC) 37, 47, 66–68, 71, 75, 95, 126, 167, 168
Land Use Board of Appeals (LUBA) 38, 75, 167, 187, 189, 194
Leadership 53–57
League of Oregon Cities 83
League of Women Voters 57, 81, 217
Liberty, Robert 131, 169, 211, 245
Local control 170, 213, 216, 225
Logan, Bob 48, 59
Lundgren, Shane 191

Macpherson action group 48

Macpherson, Greg 95, 103

Macpherson, Hector Jr. 14, 25, 42, 53, 54, 60, 63, 67, 92, 95, 137, 152, 159, 176, 233

Mail Tribune (Medford, OR) newspaper 219, 220

Management style in land use agencies 129

Martin, Sheila 88

McCall, Audrey 83

McCall, Tom x, 7, 8, 9, 14, 41, 44, 47, 48, 49, 54, 57, 58, 61–64, 67, 69, 73, 77, 79, 80, 94, 95, 125, 151, 177, 183, 199, 202, 223, 233, 234, 246, 252

McHarg, Ian *Design with Nature* (1969) 46

Measure 10 (Ballot Measure 10, 1976 and 1978) 80

Measure 11 (Ballot Measure 11, 1970) 44, 80

Measure 37 (2004 Ballot Measure 37) 9, 10, 11, 17, 18, 37, 77, 79, 84–94, 96, 104, 112, 153, 203, 211, 231, 235

Measure 37 "clock" 98, 104

Measure 37 "express lane" 101, 105

Measure 37 development impact 106

Measure 37 maps of impacts 97

Measure 37 neighbors, impacts on 90–92

Measure 37 public opinion polling 93, 94

Measure 37 transferability of rights 89, 98, 99, 205

Measure 49 (2007 Ballot Measure 49) 10, 17, 51, 79, 95–110, 159, 211, 231, 234, 248

Measure 49 appraisals 108

Measure 49 effects on future regulation 86, 107–110, 154, 235

Measure 7 (2000 Ballot Measure 7) 9,

11, 17, 18, 78, 81–84, 87, 92, 111, 112, 153, 231, 235

Meehan, Brian 3

Merkley, Jeff 98

Metolian destination resort 191

Metolius Basin 19, 185, 193–201

Metolius Basin as a special place 194, 201

Model Land Development Code of the American Land Institute 47, 67, 176

Moshovsky, Bill 138

Myers, Linda 225

New West 19, 181

Niche-market agriculture 117

NIMBY (not in my back yard) effect 74, 195

Nims, Frank 139

Nonpartisanship 14, 62–64, 66, 70

Non-regulatory approaches to land use planning 124, 239

Obama, Barack 3, 12, 48

One-size-fits all argument 127

Oregon Department of Agriculture 167

Oregon Farm Bureau 14, 51, 71, 167

Oregon Forest Industries Council 73, 116

Oregon Land Conservation and Development Actl. *See* Senate Bill 100

Oregon statewide planning Goal 1 (citizen involvement) 30, 140

Oregon statewide planning Goal 10 (housing) 34, 75, 115

Oregon statewide planning Goal 11 (public facilities) 34

Oregon statewide planning Goal 14 (urbanization) 34, 237

Oregon statewide planning Goal 2 (land use planning) 30

Oregon statewide planning Goal 3 (agricultural lands) 29, 31

Oregon statewide planning Goal 4
(forest lands) 29, 32
Oregon statewide planning Goal 5
(natural resources, scenic and open
areas) 33
Oregon statewide planning Goal 8 (recreational needs) 33, 186, 190
Oregon statewide planning goals 28, 29
Oregon Student Public Interest Research Group (OSPIRG) 69
Oregonian (Portland) newspaper 82,
87, 94, 101, 109, 131, 173, 199
Oregonians in Action 9, 82, 99, 107,
112, 119, 131, 136, 139, 213

Packwood, Bob 63
Palin, Grover and Edith 85
Paradise, Oregon viewed as 4, 6, 12,
15, 254
Pearl District (Portland) 157
Periodic review 37, 38
Phegley, Dan 172
Planning 22–38
Planning, culture of 245
Plum Creek Timber Company 88, 116
Polarization of politics 100
Political alliance for land use planning
70–75, 114–118
Political mood 137–140
Ponderosa destination resort 191
Population growth 6, 167, 182, 208,
209, 236
Populist conservatism 177, 209
Portland Metro 18, 39, 121
Portland Metro Council 18, 159, 168
Project Foresight 54
Property rights activism 53, 81, 120,
122, 138, 225
Property values 119, 236, 243
Prozanski, Floyd 98, 103, 233
Public engagement in planning 25, 68,
140, 227, 237, 247

Public engagement, containment of 147
Public perceptions of land use planning
130, 238, 239, 240

Reagan, Ronald and conservatism 61,
137, 225
Region 2040 planning process (Port-
land Metro) 165
Regional problem solving 19, 36, 213
Regional problem solving, capture by
local interests 222
Renz, John 121, 129
Republican Party 62, 66, 140
Richmond, Henry 44, 69, 70, 75, 114,
115, 120, 123, 125, 151, 241, 252
Robbins, William 43, 53, 55
Rogue River Valley 40, 205
Rogue Valley Council of Governments
211
Rural exceptions areas 31, 184
Rural reserves 35
Rural subdivision 19
Rurbanistas 173–175

Senate Bill 10 (SB 10, 1969) 44, 67
Senate Bill 100 (SB 100, 1973) 7, 8, 17,
19, 20, 43–48, 52–54, 62, 67, 74,
127, 159, 179, 199, 231
Senate Bill 101 (SB 101, 1973) 51–53
Senate Bill 30 (SB 30, 2009) 196, 197,
199
Sexually related businesses, exemptions
from property rights ballot initiatives
83–84, 87
Shetterly, Lane 96, 98, 122, 127, 140,
148, 239
Sizemore, Bill 134
Smart growth 27
Social change 20, 231
Social inequality 20
Social memory of land use issues 138
Southern California 6, 7, 44, 66–67

Southern Oregon 40
Southern Oregon as "different" 209
Special Joint Committee on Land Use
    Fairness 98, 101
Spotted owl conflict 73, 116, 212
Sprawl 20, 23, 24, 50, 67, 102, 120,
    190, 249
Stacey, Bob 87, 93, 99, 110, 111, 124,
    132, 149, 234, 235, 240
State of Jefferson 211
Statewide planning 23, 26, 27, 28
Stegner, Wallace 21
Sunrise Corridor 164–165
Sustainability 158–159, 252

Tax benefits for rural land owners 125
Taxation of rural land 125
The Country and the City 15
Thorne, Mike 51, 53, 60, 62, 118, 119,
    142, 148

University of Oregon Environmental
    Studies Program 48
Up and not out 160, 161
Urban farming 173–175
Urban growth boundary (UGB) 19, 22,
    27, 36, 115, 118, 157, 160, 161, 236,
    237
Urban reserves 35

Usurpation of state land use laws 196
Utopian visions 126

VanLandingham, John 176, 202
VanNatta, Fred 56, 115
Visioning landscape 152, 153, 165, 220,
    221, 233
Visioning landscape, sclerosis of 175,
    178, 250
Visit but don't stay (Tom McCall inter-
    view) 8, 64, 65
Voters' pamphlet 135

Walth, Brent 17
Weyerhaeuser Corporation 72, 116
Whitman, Richard 109, 139, 142, 175,
    244–245
Wilkeson, Ray 116
Willamette Valley 13, 39, 45, 144
Willamette Valley agriculture 50–53
Willamette Valley farmers 17, 42, 45, 71
Williams, Raymond 15–16, 18, 249
Wind energy 14, 117
Wine industry 117
Wyden, Ron 164

Yap, Anita 173, 175, 241

Zoning 24

About the Authors

Peter Walker is Associate Professor in the Department of Geography and the Environmental Studies Program at the University of Oregon. He received his undergraduate degree in economics and his Ph.D. in geography at the University of California at Berkeley, and his master's in public policy at Harvard University. Walker served as an agricultural extension adviser in the U.S. Peace Corps in Sierra Leone, West Africa. His recent research focuses on human use of the environment in the western United States and southern Africa. This work has focused on the political and social dynamics of land use choices among "exurban" property owners in northern California, and the role of population growth and economic change in shaping land and natural resource use among farmers in Malawi. His current research focuses on the political dimensions of land use planning and sustainability programs in Oregon.

Patrick Hurley is Assistant Professor of Environmental Studies at Ursinus College in Collegeville, PA. He received his undergraduate degrees in German and government from the University of Maryland at College Park. He earned his master's in environmental studies and Ph.D. in environmental science, studies and policy from the University of Oregon. Before moving to Oregon for graduate school, Hurley worked in World Wildlife Fund's Conservation Science Program in Washington D.C. on several conservation planning initiatives. Hurley's research focuses on human-environment interactions in urbanizing areas of the United States, particularly the intersection of land use change, planning, and natural resource-based livelihood practices. Recently, Hurley has begun research in western Turkey that examines these dynamics in areas experiencing rapid amenity migration.